Rethinking Peace

Discourse, Memory, Translation, and Dialogue

Edited by
Alexander Laban Hinton,
Giorgio Shani and Jeremiah Alberg

ROWMAN &
LITTLEFIELD
INTERNATIONAL
London • New York

Published by Rowman & Littlefield International, Ltd.
6 Tinworth Street, London SE11 5AL, United Kingdom
www.rowmaninternational.com

Rowman & Littlefield International, Ltd., is an affiliate of Rowman & Littlefield
4501 Forbes Boulevard, Suite 200, Lanham, Maryland 20706, USA
With additional offices in Boulder, New York, Toronto (Canada), and Plymouth (UK)
www.rowman.com

British Library Cataloguing in Publication Data
A catalogue record for this book is available from the British Library

ISBN: HB 978-1-78661-037-9
       PB 978-1-78661-038-6

Library of Congress Cataloging-in-Publication Data Available

ISBN 978-1-78661-037-9 (cloth : alk. paper)
ISBN 978-1-78661-038-6 (pbk. : alk. paper)
ISBN 978-1-78661-039-3 (electronic)

∞™ The paper used in this publication meets the minimum requirements of
American National Standard for Information Sciences—Permanence of Paper
for Printed Library Materials, ANSI/NISO Z39.48-1992.

Printed in the United States of America

Contents

Acknowledgements

We would like to express our appreciation to the three institutions that partnered for the Rethinking Peace Studies initiative: Japan International Christian University, the Japan ICU Foundation and Rutgers University's Center for the Study of Genocide and Human Rights. A special thanks goes to the Japan ICU Foundation for its financial support for the workshops that led to this volume as well as the editorial team at Rowman & Littlefield, especially Dhara Snowden, Rebecca Anastasi, Christine Fahey, and Bruce Owens. Several other people helped make this volume possible, including Mustapha Kamal Pasha, Nela Navarro, Lorne Alexander Anderson, and Wilhelm Vosse, director of the ICU Social Science Research Institute. Finally, we would like to extend our thanks to Surinder Shani for allowing us to use his image 'Explosion of the Universe' as cover art.

Preface

In 1943, the Nakajima Aircraft Research Facility was constructed on the corporate campus of Fuji Heavy Industries 20 kilometres west of downtown Tokyo. It was in this complex that many of the fighter jets used by the Imperial Japanese Army Air Service were designed and produced. After the war, a group of educators in Japan and in the United States came together to establish a university founded on Christian values and committed to international reconciliation and human rights. In 1949, the charter of International Christian University (ICU) was signed, and soon after, General Douglas MacArthur arranged for the sale of the Nakajima Aircraft Research Facility to ICU for its campus.

One year earlier in New York City, the organization that I now lead, the Japan ICU Foundation, was formed to help raise funds for ICU. In the early years, the Japan ICU Foundation covered almost all of the operating expenses of the university, but as Japan's economy grew, our partnership with ICU has evolved.

In 1953, ICU's first undergraduate classes were held in what had been the Nakajima facility. To this day, ICU continues to utilize the facility as the main classroom building. It serves as a reminder of the war and as an example of ICU's commitment to peace building through education. In the past 65 years, ICU has developed into one of Japan's leading institutions of higher education. It is home to Asia's only Rotary International Center for the Study of Peace and Reconciliation, and many ICU graduates are deeply involved in supporting international development throughout the world.

In October 2012, ICU hosted the Aspen Institute Cultural Diplomacy Forum. The forum brought together more than 100 participants with a multiplicity of professional backgrounds for three days of dialogue around the theme 'the art of peace building and reconciliation'. Topics covered included peace-building education, media and peace building, the arts and peace, religious freedom and tolerance and preventive diplomacy.

Immediately following the forum, I joined a small group of participants for a meeting to share feedback and discuss next steps. One of the participants in this postmortem was the lead editor of this volume, Alex Hinton. While many important topics were discussed at the Aspen Forum, there was consensus amongst us that we had only scratched the surface. Our small group agreed to explore ways in which we might remain engaged with each other. This conversation was the genesis of what became *Rethinking Peace Studies*.

In 2014, the Japan ICU Foundation, ICU and Rutgers University's Center for the Study of Genocide and Human Rights launched Rethinking Peace Studies (RPS). The RPS project consisted of three seminars and a culminating conference. Each seminar brought together 10 to 15 academics and practitioners from a variety of disciplines and professional fields for two days of intensive dialogue. The seminars were each informed by a theme (translation, memory and dialogue), and materials were compiled and distributed to participants that included works from a wide range of disciplines and mediums, including critical theory, peace studies, international relations, translation studies, memory studies, philosophy, anthropology, poetry and film. The participants were asked to review the material and to come prepared to answer two questions: what does it mean to rethink something, and what needs to be rethought in peace studies?

Seminar participants were subsequently invited to join the Rethinking Peace Studies Conference at ICU in June 2016. At the conference, participants presented original papers inspired by their involvement in the seminars. In addition, keynote addresses were presented by Shin Chiba, Johan Galtung and Ashis Nandy. This book is based on a collection of papers presented at the conference and supplemented by solicited chapters from leading authorities in peace and conflict studies.

As the editors write in the introduction, the academic discipline of peace studies is both driven and held back by 'four key and interrelated tendencies: hypostasis, teleology, normativity and enterprise'. Rethinking Peace Studies as a project has been an attempt to probe these tendencies. For example, what happens when we stop seeing peace as a concrete reality? How do we understand the human experience if peace is not a goal? What happens when we question whether peace is desirable or good? What are the intended and unintended consequences of peace-building projects? The contributions to this volume address these types of questions. They are multidirectional and cross disciplinary, and as such we aim to expose the reader to unique viewpoints. It is our hope that this volume inspires continued rethinking.

Paul Hastings
Japan ICU Foundation

Introduction

Rethinking Peace Studies

Alexander Laban Hinton,
Giorgio Shani and Jeremiah Alberg

In June 2016, as civil war raged in Syria and Yemen and a global refugee crisis unfolded on the shores of Europe and North Africa, the final conference of the Rethinking Peace Studies project was held on the campus of International Christian University in Tokyo.[1] The proceedings, involving leading scholars from a variety of fields, were headlined by three invited keynote speakers—Ashis Nandy (India), Shin Chiba (Japan) and Johan Galtung (Norway)—Galtung, as he noted in his keynote, sometimes being referred to as 'the father of Peace Studies'. The three were invited because of their pioneering work not only in establishing peace studies as an academic field of study but also, to varying degrees, in questioning the assumptions upon which this young discipline is based. The same was true of the fourth invited keynote, Judith Butler, who was unable to attend.

At the centre of the project, comprising workshops in three regions (East Asia, North America and South Asia), was a common commitment to *rethink* peace (studies). To this end, scholars from different disciplines and backgrounds—many from outside the field of peace studies—were invited to participate. The discussions began with two questions posed by the conveners that were supposed to be answered based on the scholar's own work and a set of peace-related readings, ranging from the classic to the contemporary, which had been distributed prior to the workshops. The first question was 'what does it mean to rethink something?;' the second was 'what needs to be rethought [in peace studies]?'.

The chapters in this volume are the outcome of this exercise. They don't provide a clear and singular answer. Indeed, towards the end of the June 2016 conference, we discussed whether it might not be better to frame the volume in terms of a series of peace aporias, such as 'The exercise of rethinking peace studies is doomed from the start; this realization is the key to its success'; 'Peace studies has a genealogy. Once you write its beginning, you have already written its end'; 'To find peace is to find war'; and 'The formula for peace is avoiding formulas'.

Such aporias provide one heuristic for rethinking, an endeavour that entails, among other things, subverting dominant paradigms, catalysing new understandings, expanding peace studies far beyond international relations (IR), and refocusing attention towards generative approaches. Indeed, the chapters in this volume, while diverse, are loosely focused around such a generative, open-ended, processual approach to peace.

To this end, the chapters centre on issues such as gaps (translation), power (discourse), conjunctions of past and present (memory and temporality), and plurality and exchange (dialogue). Accordingly, we have grouped the chapters in this volume around these themes, even if they crosscut the categories and involve other ones. The intent of the chapters in this volume, then, is—like the feminist and postcolonial critiques upon which it draws—both to subvert what is taken for granted and naturalized in the study of peace and in IR and, by so doing, to imagine new paths forward for an interdisciplinary field of peace studies.

These strategies range from a focus on silence (Payne) and relationality (Behr) to a consideration of graphic narratives (Curran) and alternative writing and representational styles (Hinton). The chapters also, to a differing extent, highlight and interrogate the normativity and teleology of peace, which can be traced back to certain religious traditions (Alberg and Shani). Since peace is the stated goal of many different faith traditions, some of the chapters argue that religion should be taken into account when rethinking peace. Therefore, the volume also offers a critical perspective on the role of religion in international politics challenging the secular assumptions of peace studies as a subfield of IR.

THE ENDS OF PEACE

This discussion brings us back to Galtung's keynote address. While Galtung himself, as he noted during his keynote, had undertaken broad, interdisciplinary work and attempts to reimagine peace studies, he had also promulgated a series of ideas that had become canonical in the field. He had often expressed his key concepts through charts or diagrams involving key terms and formulas, such as one he presented at the beginning of his keynote (Galtung 2016; see also figure I.1 below).

While serving as useful frames to parse the complexities of peace and convey ideas to a broad audience, formulistic renderings of Galtung's 'truths' by a generation of peace studies scholars illustrate four key and interrelated tendencies: an inclination to employ hypostasis, teleology, normativity and enterprise.

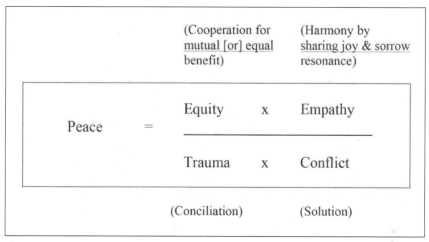

Figure I.1. "Peace" diagram, presented by Johan Galtung (2016) at the June 2016 Rethinking Peace Studies Conference, Tokyo, Japan.

First, peace is often *hypostasized*, or imagined as a substance or concrete reality (e.g., a 'thing' as opposed to dynamic processes). Second, peace is often assumed to have a *teleology*, or end point (as opposed to being open and multidirectional). Third, this *telos* is often intertwined with a set of *normative* goods, ones often linked to a particular genealogy and the Judeo-Christian tradition (as opposed to alternative traditions and beliefs that, if sometimes acknowledged, are largely pushed out of sight). And, finally, these three tendencies conjoin in *enterprise*, undertakings large and small meant to achieve the ends of peace (but ones of a particular sort that accord with a teleology and normative goals).

Even as we sometimes accentuate these tendencies, we note that there is variation in the extent to which they are manifest in peace studies and indeed Galtung's work as well. There is a growing literature in broadly 'critical' approaches to peace studies framed mainly within the context of IR (see, e.g., Autesserre 2015; Behr 2014; Chandler 2017; Mac Ginty 2016; Mac Ginty and Richmond 2013; Pugh et al. 2008; Richmond 2011, 2016). This work also draws on and includes feminist critiques of peace and security studies, which highlight the role that intervention plays in reproducing patriarchy and discourses of masculinity in postconflict societies and explore the creative potential for a gendered approach to peace (see Enloe 2014; Hudson 2016; Porter 2016; Shepherd 2017; Tickner and True 2018; Wibben 2010).

Our critical peace studies approach, while acknowledging the importance of this work, diverges from much of it by approaching peace studies from humanistic and social science perspectives outside of IR (and peace studies itself) and by a focused questioning of the teleological assumptions and normativity of peace studies. There is, indeed, a questioning of the very Enlightenment narratives of emancipation that are at the heart of Marxist-inspired, Frankfurt School of 'Critical Theory'. Furthermore, our preference for processual rather than static understandings of peace shares common ground with John-Paul Lederach's *elicitive* approach to conflict (see Lederach 2014).[2]

These tendencies in peace studies are manifest in what is perhaps Galtung's most famous idea and one that is at the core of much work in the field: the distinction between 'negative' and 'positive peace' (Galtung 2012). Negative peace refers to a state of nonviolence in keeping with the term's primary English sense of 'freedom from, or cessation of war or hostilities', as in 'the state of a nation or community in which it is not at war with another' (*Shorter Oxford English Dictionary* 2007).

A negative peace is, therefore, seen to exist when there is an absence of violent conflict between states. This is the dominant understanding of peace as operationalized through the United Nations. The UN Charter encourages the 'pacific settlement of disputes' (Chapter VII) and gives the Security Council 'primary responsibility for the maintenance of international peace and security' (Chapter V, Article 24). Emphasis is placed on maintaining the preexisting international order, and the responsibility for 'peacekeeping' is shouldered by the UN peacekeeping operations under the control of the Secretariat.

Positive peace, on the other hand, involves not only such freedom from conflict but also the establishment of institutional mechanisms through which to realize social justice and its associated values: equity, cooperation, empathy and harmony. In this respect, 'positive peace' leads to the cessation of not only 'direct violence' but also 'structural violence'. For Galtung, violence can be understood not merely in its physical instantiation but generically as the difference between the potential and the actual, between what *could have been* and what *is*. The main source of this 'structural' understanding of violence is when structures of unequal power do not allow the individual to realize his or her own potential (Galtung 1969).

Contemporary examples of structural violence include gender and racial discrimination, as highlighted in the United States by the '#MeToo' and Black Lives Matter movements, social or economic inequality, poverty, unemployment, illiteracy and lack of educational opportunities. To this, Galtung later added 'cultural violence' as the violence that naturalizes existing modes of domination (Galtung 1990). Insofar as peace-building efforts are often predicated on intervention by the powerful and take place within a given framework of action that naturalizes prevailing power structures, Galtung's concept of 'cultural violence' opens up the possibility of viewing the reified, hypostatized, teleological and normative conception of peace favoured by the 'international community'—the 'Liberal Peace' (Paris 2010)—as potentially a source of violence.

This distinction between negative and positive peace is widespread in peace studies and often naturalized in discourses about peace in IR. Indeed, the notion that 'in the state of nature' people are inherently violent, a condition that requires abatement from a sovereign or forceful intervener, is, in its Hobbesian iteration, the foundation of the dominant realist perspective in IR. In both cases, peace is assumed to be concrete and have a telos associated with certain normative goods. The distinction between negative and positive peace is so central that it is often used as a framing device to parse the field and its genealogy.

Oliver Richmond's (2014) *Peace: A Very Short Introduction* illustrates this point, as he uses the negative/positive peace binary to unpack the field and its genealogy, even as he offers the notion of 'hybrid peace' as a third pillar to Galtung's binary (Richmond 2014, 6; see also Richmond, in this volume). If peace was largely viewed as 'negative' prior to the Enlightenment (what he calls first-generation 'victor's justice'), Richmond argues that peace increasingly began to be seen in 'positive' terms during the Enlightenment, perhaps most famously by Kant's (1983) *Perpetual Peace*.

Kant's tract also illustrates a key Enlightenment dynamic that undergirds positive peace: the design of projects, based on science and reason, which will lead to progress and social transformation towards a better, sometimes utopian state—an idea that again manifests the aforementioned four disciplinary undercurrents of peace studies: *hypostasis, teleology, normativity* and *enterprise*. In their more extreme manifestation, such projects may entail massive projects of social engineering, often legitimated in utopian terms that end in failures large and small (Bauman 1989; Scott 1998).

Peace studies and related fields, such as transitional justice, development studies, human security and democratization, are filled with examples of such enterprises doomed by the hubris of Enlightenment certainty combined with disdain for or ignorance about local complexities (e.g., Autesserre 2015; Escobar 1995; Ferguson 1990; Shani 2014). Indeed, we might speak of a 'peace imaginary' and 'peace facade' that parallel the 'transitional justice imaginary' and 'justice facade' that one of our authors has described in the field of transitional justice (Hinton 2018).

In Richmond's (2014) *Peace* genealogy, positive peace initiatives are increasingly prominent in the post-Enlightenment world—even if hindered at times by the premium on sovereignty enshrined in the Treaty of Westphalia—gaining steam with the antislavery movement, the Red Cross, and other humanitarian impulses in the nineteenth century, including the beginnings of humanitarian law and modern human rights discourse. The twentieth century culminated in liberal peace, projects of positive peace undergirded by an increasingly complex architecture composed of a set of values (democracy, human rights and market exchange), institutions (ranging from the United Nations to the World Trade Organization) and civil society mobilizations for peace (by nongovernmental organizations religious organizations, social movements and so on) (Richmond 2014).

The enterprise of liberal (positive) peace reached its ascendancy after the Cold War as the new possibilities of realizing the original democratization, peace and human rights goals of the UN Charter suddenly seemed possible. An immediate manifestation was Boutros-Ghali's (1992) 'Agenda for Peace' and the sudden proliferation of peacebuilding in places like Cambodia, El Salvador and Mozambique. These trends have continued into the present, even as liberal peace has conjoined with related transitional justice, democratization and human rights initiatives as well as related doctrines, such as security studies (Richmond 2014; see also Donnelly 2013; Hopgood 2013), fields in which many of our contributors have also worked.

Richmond's positive peace genealogy ends with the current moment, a twenty-first century emphasis on 'the local'. In peace studies and related literatures, such as transitional justice, this current reorientation has sometimes been dubbed 'the local turn' (Autesserre 2015; Fetcher and Hindman 2011; Hughes, Öjendal, and Schierenbeck 2015; see also Mac Ginty and Richmond 2013), even as scholars in other fields, such as development studies, have warned of the dangers of reifying and even instrumentalizing 'the local' (Escobar 1995; Ferguson 1990). Richmond (2014, in this volume; see also Richmond and Mitchell 2012) offers the notion of 'hybrid peace' as a conceptual rubric to understand this latest manifestation of positive peace reoriented as a dialogic local–global project to realize aspirational peace goals.

While ranging far beyond 'negative' and 'positive peace' and offering his third, hybrid prong to it, Richmond's (2014) framing strategy in his _Peace_ nevertheless highlights the centrality of this binary and related tendencies (hypostasis, teleology, normativity and enterprise) to the field, including the dominant liberal peace paradigm of the present. His contribution to this volume builds upon his continuing effort to rethink such assumptions, even as they are necessary to foreground in an introduction to the field.

MULTIDIRECTIONAL PEACE

The chapters in this volume are enmeshed in this current paradigm, even as they seek ways to rethink it. They do so to different extents and in different ways. Some rethink the premises of sovereignty in peace studies, others its cultural bias and essentializations. In one way or another, all of them seek ways to move beyond the reductive binaries, formulas, naturalizations and the aforementioned tendencies of peace studies towards hypostasis, teleology, normativity and enterprise. They succeed at times and fall short at other points. But all seek to help push peace studies towards a reformulation, one that might be thought of as akin to the way that Michael Rothberg's (2009) *Multidirectional Memory* helped spur a reconceptualization of memory studies from linear and 'competitive' models of memory towards its more multidirectional and relational dynamics.

This volume similarly seeks to push peace studies in new directions, reorienting it away from hypostasis, teleology, Eurocentric normativity and (utopian) enterprise. While the chapters crosscut categories, we have grouped them loosely around four rubrics that helped propel our rethinking and that speak to the contributors' attempt to reenvision peace studies in ways that move beyond some of its essentializing tendencies: *discourse* (destabilizing the hypostasized and the structures of power often naturalized therein), *translation* (revealing the gaps of normativity and emphasizing plurality), *memory and temporality* (multidirectionality as opposed to linear teleology) and *dialogue* (emphasizing relationality, performativity and a back-and-forth as opposed to the more monologic and even sometimes utopian enterprise). We conclude by discussing each thematic in turn, describing related keynotes and chapters as we proceed.

PART I: DISCOURSE

In his June 2, 2016 conference keynote, included in this volume, Ashis Nandy highlights some of the aims of this volume by drawing attention to the 'black holes' of peace studies. What, he asks, is masked, elided and erased by peace studies, particularly by dominant 'research' drive formulations in IR? The 'underside' of peace studies, he argues, are the subjectivities and 'nonpersons' rendered irrelevant by the discourses of peace studies, including its narratives of progress and related enterprise.

Nandy's insights highlight a recurrent theme in this volume and its goal of rethinking peace studies: destabilizing peace studies hypostases by focusing on gaps and erasures—black holes in Nandy's formulation, an idea visually highlighted as well by the redactions in Hinton's erasure in this volume—in peace studies. Each theme takes up these black holes in different ways.

Part I does so through a focus on discourse, or the often power-laden, hypostasized narratives and epistemologies that undergird peace studies and peace-building enterprises. Such ground has been trodden by others (e.g.,

Escobar 1995; Foucault 1990; Said 1978), including work in related fields, such as postdevelopment studies and anthropology, which has critiqued democratization, human rights, human security, peace building and transitional justice discourse. These critiques have often centred on hypostasizing discourses that, as is often the case with peace studies, essentialize and reduce complex peoples and places to racial or cultural types characterized and stigmatized in particular ways that legitimate related projects and assert power (such as in the depiction of more primitive 'traditions' in need of fixing by the enterprises of 'civilizing' moderns who can bring 'progress', 'development' and, in the context of this volume, 'peace' to 'failed states').

Part I begins with Ashis Nandy's eynote, 'The Inner Battles of Peace Studies: The Limits and Possibilities of Nonviolence'. The black holes of astrophysicists, he states, are sometimes matched by the black holes of political science and IR. These erase an entire range of 'researchables'—from invisible genocides and designer famines to pogroms and contraband memories exiled by history. They do sometimes invite the curiosity of those in peace studies but are often found difficult to locate within the larger theoretical frames of its mother disciplines. This, Nandy suspects, is part of a larger problem. For, as time passes, these black holes also erase traces of everyday events, emotions, values and theories of social transformation and visions of good society and myriad little cultures and their experiences of suffering.

However, while these experiences are exiled from the cosmos of academic social knowledge, they survive in the netherworld of individual and collective memories and wait for an opportune moment to come back to mock our disciplinary cultures and academic canons. This is an attempt to identify the unacknowledged underside of peace studies—the subjectivities and noncultures ignored, exiled or museumized as irrelevant—that sometimes reemerge in public discourse.

In his chapter, 'Sovereignty, Interference and Crisis', Stephen Eric Bronner critiques traditional IR models from a different direction. IR, Bronner contends, has traditionally been constructed using the nation-state as a unit of analysis with regard to both war and peace. Reified in the theory and practice of IR since the Peace of Westphalia, the nation-state is assumed to be the *only* sovereign unit of international life. Sovereignty, here, presupposes monopolization of the means of coercion and the existence of a sovereign who decides the 'exception' (Schmitt [1934] 2006).

Bronner contends that the situation no longer prevails in the Middle East (if it ever existed). The state is viewed as an imperialist import, and not only power but also loyalty have devolved to tribes, ethnic organizations and religious institutions; the state lacks a legitimate monopoly as, simultaneously, internal paramilitaries and external proxies have become ever more powerful;

and balance of power and traditional conflict between states are becoming tainted if not overshadowed by religious battles (Sunni–Shia) and the emergence of transnational organizations, such as al-Qaeda and ISIS. Bronner's chapter deals with each of these issues in turn and offers a different and prescriptive treatment of sovereignty for the future.

Oliver Richmond's chapter, 'Towards a Peace with Global Justice', also inveighs against traditional models of IR and liberal peace building in particular. Drawing on critical, feminist, poststructural and postcolonial thinking in IR, as well as critical movements in other disciplines and, in particular, a combination of the local and spatial 'turns', he states that we now know a lot about an 'emancipatory peace'. This is both in terms of the many major and minor war settlements since Westphalia (in particular, since 1989) and in terms of structural violence and inequality after the Cold War.

Such thinking points to how individuals are bringing a new and hybrid 'international' into sight: they may seek their own peace, emancipation, and social justice. The 'stable' grounds of the states-system and international architecture have become inadequate, though international citizenship, a global commons and 'community of the governed' have become clearer. Clusters of localized interaction, which transcend territoriality, now bypass the formal states-system and international architecture where they are deemed to have materially and normatively failed. Everyday mobility, networked peace and emancipation seem to be a sophisticated response by contrast. This is peace formation writ large, Richmond argues, and points to the need for significant rethinking not only in peace studies but in IR in general. Rethinking peace entails the reconceptualization of IR.

In his chapter, 'Saving Liberal Peace Building? From the "Local Turn" to a Post-Western Peace', Giorgio Shani offers a note of caution. Despite attempts by critical scholars like Richmond to suggest alternative pathways, Shani notes, peace and conflict studies still appears trapped in a Eurocentric gaze. Whereas security studies—in its conventional or critical guises (see Bronner, in this volume)—continues to prioritize the needs of states and not peoples, thus reifying the Westphalian order of territorialized nation-states, attempts to go beyond Westphalia and articulate a liberal peace tend to reproduce a colonial imaginary which places responsibility for the maintenance of global peace and security on the West or its myriad agents, including the United Nations.

On the one hand, emancipatory approaches to peace and security, which aim to empower individuals and communities, feed into this colonial narrative since they fail to engage with 'local' target populations in their own terms and thus build 'legitimate' institutions. On the other hand, attempts to build a 'postliberal' hybrid peace sufficiently sensitized to 'local alterity' (Richmond xxiiIntroduction

2011) appear to reify the 'local' as a space distinct from the 'global' or 'international' and ignore the role that colonialism played in the construction of such spaces.

Shani's chapter outlines a 'postsecular' approach to peace and security that would permit the articulation of multiple claims deriving from different cosmological traditions without prioritizing any one 'tradition' as having a monopoly over defining peace and security. Implicit in such an approach is a recognition that a postsecular approach may be suited to the demands posed by cultural diversity in an increasingly post-Western world.

PART II: MEMORY AND TEMPORALITY

Nandy's keynote also highlights the issue of memory and temporality, which are directly linked to the black holes of discourse. If peace studies has tended towards a teleology directed at a singular 'end', this linear and singular movement is disrupted by the multidirectionality and plurality of subjectivities and narratives that are redacted from these teleological articulations (on this point, see also Hinton 2016, 2018).

To illustrate, Nandy, like the other contributors in this part, focuses on memory and temporality. While there are always attempts to co-opt memory into teleologies linking past, present and future in the progressive peace enterprise (and related hypostasizing discourses) at hand, memory also subverts this teleology through its plurality, including the temporality of the lived experience of the past and present, which diverge from and erode these grand narratives. Nandy's keynote argued for greater attention to these exiled subjectivities and identities, 'skeletons' that suddenly and unexpectedly could come 'tumbling out of a cupboard'. The chapters in this part, which focus on issues like identity, silence, truth and irony, make a similar point about the excesses of memory and temporality that undermine peace teleologies.

The point is made perhaps most explicitly by Natasha Zaretsky's chapter, 'Justice in the Land of Memory: Reflecting on the Temporality of Truth and Survival in Argentina'. Memory has been a central foundation of democracy and civil society in Argentina. Indeed, during years of repressive state violence by the military dictatorship (1976–1983), citizens turned to memory as a space for protest and dissent, which becomes formative for the civil society that would take shape after the dictatorship ended. Democracy brought many important changes, including a landmark truth commission, the CONADEP, which documented systematic patterns of state violence and abuses—but also amnesty laws ensured that impunity reigned, allowing perpetrators of the crimes of the dictatorship to remain free and unpunished. After years of advocacy, the amnesty laws were finally overturned in 2003, allowing human rights trials to begin again in Argentina, forcing perpetrators to be held accountable and bringing justice back to the land of memory.

Despite these advances, Zaretsky states, other forms of impunity remain, revealing the uneven terrain that shapes the contours of justice in Argentina and the continued need for cultural memory and a truth that transcends juridical understandings. Drawing on ethnographic fieldwork in contemporary Argentina on memory and political violence, her chapter examines the complex temporalities of truth and survival there. Zaretsky begins by reviewing the current state of justice, including an analysis of the genocide and human rights trials in contemporary Argentina in relation to ongoing impunity in other important cases of political violence, such as the 1994 AMIA Bombing in Buenos Aires. She then examines the continued salience of memory within this context of justice, exploring its significance as a space of citizenship and healing through national holidays and public sites.

Zaretsky concludes by contemplating the complex temporalities of truth and survival in Argentina, including what they reveal about broader issues pertaining to transitional justice and the continuing importance of truth and memory for genocide prevention. In this way, her chapter rethinks peace studies by exploring the pervasive challenges of repair that inform any process of peace, experience of empathy towards the other and the process that needs to be renewed in and through civil society.

Marita Sturken's chapter, 'Cultural Memory in the Wake of Violence: Exceptionalism, Vulnerability and the Grievable Life', examines the relationship between memorialization and the movement towards peace. The past few decades, she notes, has witnessed a global memory boom, with memorials and memorial museums built in Europe, the United States, Latin America and Africa. Yet this memorialization has largely not contributed to a deeper understanding of the consequences of violence and the peaceful resolution of conflict.

Sturken's chapter looks at the different modes of cultural memory, such as exceptionalism, reparation, the grievable life, human rights, countermemorials and irony, analysing those that can open up a space for a moving past conflict rather than its perpetuation through cycles of revenge and retaliation. Her chapter thus makes an argument for how memorialization processes that engage with human rights discourse and with irony can provide a means to rethink the relationship of memory and peace.

In her chapter, 'Negotiating Difference and Empathy: Cinematic Representations of Passing and Exchanged Identities in the Israeli–Palestinian Conflict', Yael Zerubavel takes up the issue of memory and temporality in a particular context where identity and narratives are often frozen in singular, hypostasizing terms. Traumatic memories involving groups with clashing histories of victimhood, violence, dislocation and loss, Zerubavel notes, create a strong attachment to the past that undermines the ability to engage in a meaningful dialogue in conflict situations. The arts provide an alternative venue for moving beyond the political discourse as it features the impact of war and trauma on individuals and opens up the possibility of experiencing empathy.

Zarubavel's chapter addresses three cinematic representations of identity (ex)changes between Israeli Jews and Palestinians that turns these issues into its explicit focus. These films vary in their portrayals of the motivation and circumstances of the process of identity exchange ranging from a deliberate passing to human error and leading to different outcomes. Yet in spite of these variations, she argues, these works critically examine the dichotomized view of Israeli/Palestinian identities that bolsters the conflict situation and offer alternative perceptions as well as the constraints of assuming the other's perspective, raising questions about the challenge of sustaining human bonds across the national divide in a conflict fraught with prejudice, hostility and violence.

Leigh Payne's chapter, 'Silence and Memory Politics', turns the analytical lens in a different direction, focusing on an underlying tension that exists within peace studies. On the one hand, peace has often hinged on 'moving on', closing the book on the past and instilling silence to avoid new forms of violence. On the other hand, the call for 'Never again!' and to 'remember to not repeat' urges voice—active, iterative expressions of condemnation of past atrocity to avoid its recurrence.

Payne's chapter attempts to find a way in which silence is not at the service of oblivion, as one model in peace studies would advance, but rather an active communicative form that improves on sound and language and can be purposefully engaged to fight against forgetting. Payne's chapter considers the forms that silence takes that contribute to peace, such as powerful unspoken performances or sacred sites of memory. Payne also explores silence as a speech act that more effectively communicates a peace message. The chapter also considers silence as both protection and subversion. Ending with a discussion of silence as power, the chapter attempts to rescue from peace studies two incomplete and contending view of silence. Silence is neither fundamental to suppressing future violence nor incompatible with remembrance. An alternative way to understand silence, Payne's chapter offers, is in its expressive power to advance peace.

PART III: TRANSLATION

If Nandy's keynote highlighted the black holes of peace studies, Shin Chiba's keynote inflected this point through the concept of translation—a notion that undermines normative tendencies in peace studies, which often assert a set of shared values (reconciliation, human rights, democratization and social justice) undergirding 'peace', a concept translated in different ways.

To 'translate' something is to 'bear, convey, or remove from one person, place, time or condition to another' and is etymologically related to the idea of 'transfer' and the Latin *transferre*, 'to bear, carry' (*ferre*) and 'cross' (*trans-*) (*Shorter Oxford English Dictionary* 2007). This 'transfer' always involves a gap and an exile, as there is no return in the crossing, as meaning is situated in the 'bushy undergrowth' of time, place and person (Berman 2012; Hinton 2018). Translation always involves excess and transformation, a point also highlighted by Benjamin's (1996) 'Task of the Translator'.

Chiba's keynote made this point through a discussion of the idea of 'peace' in Japan, which cannot be translated in a simple manner and is intertwined with 'multiple streams of peace', ranging from Buddhism and Confucianism to Kant and feminism. This plurality, linked to complex flows over time and accelerated by contemporary global flows (Appadurai 1996), undermines any sort of singular, universalist conception of peace, a point that, if it sits uneasily within his conceptual framings at times, is also raised in Galtung's work.

In his chapter in this volume, 'The Crisis of Japan's Constitutional Pacifism: The Abe Administration's Belated Counter-Revolution', Shin Chiba builds upon the comments in his keynote address to look at a particular manifestation of peace in Japan: the current 'constitutional politics' in Japan that has played out in the Abe administration's attempt to revise the postwar constitution of Japan. Chiba's contribution focuses on the cardinal aspect of the 'constitutional politics', that is, the vital issue of whether Japan's constitutional pacifism as expressed in the preamble and Article 9 should be revised. The chapter attempts to make sense of the issue in a broader perspective by providing critical analyses of the ideology and policies of the Abe administration that have led to its advocacy for the revision of this constitutional pacifism. It focuses particularly on the so-called 'positive (or proactive) pacifism' (*sekkyokuteki heiwashugi*) advocated by the Abe administration. It is a problematic naming for deterrence-based military expansionism, accompanied with *State-Shinto*-based and narrow-minded *Yasukuni* nationalism.

In doing so, Chiba's chapter sheds light on some positive aspects of postwar Japan's constitutional pacifism by paying attention first to Japan's various historical pacifist heritages ('multiple streams of peace'): Buddhism, Confucianism, Christianity, democratic and peace movements, socialism, literature, journalism, women's peace movements, academia, Kant's and Tolstoy's influences and so forth.

Second, the chapter argues that the postwar constitutional pacifism was meant to be an expression of war apology and responsibility for the Asia-Pacific nations that were victimized by imperial Japan's aggressive acts

during World War II. Third, the chapter points to the significance of this constitutional pacifism for creating and deepening a 'culture of peace'. From it
emerged various postwar social movements promoting and enhancing peace,
democracy, human rights and social welfare and environmental protection.
Thus, the chapter tries to lay down some of the materials for readers to examine critically regarding current Japanese 'constitutional politics' by showing
the arguments of both sides on the issue.

Beverley Curran's chapter, 'A Translational Comics Text and Its Translation: *Maus* in Japanese', builds upon some of the insights about the
translation of peace in the context of Japan, in part by drawing on Waïl S.
Hassan's (2006, 753) description of translational texts as 'performances of
interlinguistic, cross-cultural communication, operating on several levels of
mediation and contestation'. Such texts are sites of interlingual intervention
where knots of social unease can continue to be scrutinized and reconsidered.
A translational comics text such as Art Spiegelman's *Maus* draws attention to
other forms of mediation at work, including the visual and sonic, the verbal
and the unspoken and the friction created among space, time and movement
through the comics form. It is a translational text whose performance is not
only interlinguistic and cross-cultural but also intralingual and intrapersonal
as well as intersemiotic.

Maus is an intralingual translational text that makes visible two different
experiences that have led to the conversations in two different Englishes between Artie's father Vladek, an Auschwitz survivor, and his cartoonist son.
Vladek's English is inflected by Polish, but when *Maus* depicts memories
in which he was speaking Polish, they are rendered in 'standard' American
English. It is an interlingual translational text in its strategic use of different
languages in the story; that is, in addition to the range of Englishes, there is
also the presence of German, Polish, Yiddish and Hebrew. *Maus* uses comics
culture to record traumatic testimony, and the material medium of comics
gives *Maus* the visual capacity to foreground the temporal complexity of the
story in the structural juxtaposition of moments in time that allows different
pasts and presents to coexist in order to register change.

Maus has been translated into more than 30 languages, including Japanese.
According to Spiegelman, the Japanese translation by Ono Kosei did not receive much attention possibly because 'Jews are totally exotic' and because
it did not conform to manga reading conventions. Yet Spiegelman makes an
explicit connection between Hiroshima and the Holocaust—'the twentieth
century's other central cataclysm', Spiegelman notes—and comics and 'the
inexorable art of the witness' in his introduction to a collaborative English
translation of Keiji Nakazawa's 1972–1973 manga *Hadashi no Gen*: the
sustained and selective killing project of the Holocaust and the sudden exter-

mination of the atomic bombing of Hiroshima and Nagasaki are distinct but contiguous. Curran's chapter discusses the translational nature of *Maus* and its translation into Japanese and the comic's engagement within and among multiple modes of personal, historical and traumatic memory.

Jeremiah Alberg's chapter, 'To Arrive Where We Started: Peace Studies and Logos', takes up the issue of translation from a different direction, one that explicitly addresses the interrelationship of translation with the other themes of this volume. He argues that while it is true that we all share a rationality formed by violence (we are children of the logos of violence), there exists another rationality that subverts this violent rationality from within. This other rationality allows us, tenuously, to understand reality in another way. There is another logos. Violence is an anthropological problem, so an adequate understanding of violence presumes an adequate anthropology. He gives an outline of such an anthropology based on the work of René Girard. Alberg believes that this anthropology offers the possibility of translating expulsion of the victim into forgiveness and healing memories of the poison they contained so that we become capable of dialogue for the first time—a point that leads us to the last cluster of readings in this volume.

PART IV: DIALOGUE

Judith Butler's work speaks to several themes in this volume, including the focus of the chapters in this part on 'dialogue'. As a noun, a 'dialogue' refers to 'a conversation between two or more people' that involves 'verbal interchange', including discussing of 'opposing or contrasting views'; as a verb, 'to dialogue' is 'to hold [such] a dialogue or conversation' (*Oxford English Dictionary* 2015). This idea of dialogue stands in contrast to the enterprising tendencies of peace studies, or situations in which peace projects are undertaken in a monologic fashion that hypostasizes complex identities and histories and naturalizes a particular set of norms, including the teleological drive towards a singular end.

Butler's (1990) work has challenged such monologic metanarratives, most famously with her arguments about how gender performativity undermines naturalized (and power-laden) discourses about gender. Like Nandy, Butler (2006) also highlights the plight of those whom such monologic metanarratives place in positions of precarity—being devalued, disempowered, silenced and even harmed. And perhaps on this point, Butler and all our keynotes, despite their differences, may agree. Peace, however defined, is undermined when framed as monologic enterprise that reinforces power, structural violence and the status quo. Like other chapters in this volume, the chapters in this part seek to destabilize monologic peace approaches by highlighting their consequences and suggesting dialogic alternatives, such as a focus on relationality and nonbinary thinking.

Morgan Brigg's chapter, 'From Substantialist to Relational Difference in Peace and Conflict Studies', explicitly argues for such a relational approach. Difference, he contends, is suppressed within peace and conflict scholarship by dominant identitarian and substantialist logics that foreground internally coherent and selfsame entities. When these logics combine with European-derived colonial legacies and efforts to domesticate nature in globalized political relations, difference is either selectively valourised or made to atone and submit to the dominant order, including to dominant liberal peace practice. Difference hereby cannot find its own expression or grounding on its own terms. Brigg argues that the solution arises by conceptualizing difference not as substantialist but as simultaneously essential and relational following the work of feminist scholarship, burgeoning relationality scholarship, Indigenous traditions and foundational thinking in the conflict resolution field. Within this frame, difference—both sexed and cultural—is essential because it arises as central to life itself and to human sociopolitical existence. Because related difference is invariably dynamic, it cannot be conceptualized in substantialist terms. By paying greater attention to the interactions and exchanges that generate differences and relations among differences, Brigg concludes, relational theorizing allows difference to stand on its own terms, to be respected in peace-building theorizing and practice and to be a resource for the development of positive peace.

In his chapter, 'Peace through Dialogue about and across Difference(s): A Phenomenological Approach to Rethinking Peace', Hartmut Behr also argues for a relational, dialogic approach to peace studies. Behr notes that whether we as individuals, citizens, political activists, politicians or, most important, conflict parties act in a peaceful way or less so depends on our relation to our fellow humans. Thus, peace always articulates (as) a relation to the other'. Yet the question of the 'other' that underpins the conceptualization of peace includes another question, namely, that of difference. Consequently, issues around peace are to be thought of as questions of difference.

Whether we act in a peaceful way is therefore a question of how we approach, think and negotiate difference. Along these lines, the first argument developed in Behr's chapter is that nonessentialist ways of thinking and acting upon difference(s) are more conducive to peaceful relations than essentialized versions of difference. His second and subsequent argument holds that in practical terms, a nonessentialist way of dealing with difference surmounts in the maxim of political dialogue, a dialogue that is empathetic for differences and steadily moves to and provokes the edges of its own rationality.

In his chapter, '*Zona Intervenida*: Performance as Memory, Transforming Contested Spaces', Nitin Sawhney notes that traces of war and injustice often disappear from physical sites of conflict, lingering only in the fragmented memories of witnesses and those who have lived through the atrocities committed and indirect violence experienced despite the silence and repression imposed. These contested sites may not readily reveal the traumas and fractures hidden beneath their surface, while witness testimony and archival records of untold events that took place there may remain repressed, inaccessible or intentionally obfuscated. Several questions emerge that inform Sawhney's chapter: Under these conditions, how can the body reactivate and transform suppressed or disputed memories? What role do movement, music and poetry play to viscerally make sense of invisible histories in neglected sites of conflict?

Sawhney's introspective visual explores such questions through a performance-based cinematic inquiry conducted over a three-year period at a contested urban site in Quetzaltenango, Guatemala, with a collective of local and international artists residing there. Decades of civil war, forced disappearances and military repression have induced many Guatemalans into a sense of fear and silence about atrocities committed in the past, while human rights investigations only deepen fissures in a divided society. Approaching such sites challenges the role of mediators (including peace activists, journalists and filmmakers), demanding greater ethical responsibility and sensitivity in the process of engaging diverse voices, intervening in undesignated sites of memory and seeking nonconfrontational, subversive or artistic modes of expression. In this chapter, Sawhney shares his experiences engaging with artists in a creative and participatory site-specific inquiry, captured in part in a documentary film, *Zona Intervenida*.

Rethinking Peace concludes with a creative afterword by Alexander Hinton, 'Look Again—Aleppo: The Last Lesson on Prevention'. As the 2016 U.S. presidential election was nearing a vote, Allepo was under siege by Syrian government forces and different rebel groups that battled in the streets of the city. Allepo was headline news, and images of suffering were rampant. The violence continued nevertheless and despite the outcry. Hinton's erasure, an experimental writing piece, foregrounds a month in time, one that already has been largely forgotten, and thereby raises questions about prevention, memory and forgetting, denial, what we see and don't see, and how we think and write about violence and peace.

Hinton's erasure plays on the imperative of a 'last lecture' on prevention and seeks to provoke critical reflection through juxtaposition, visual images and literary strategies. In doing so, it escapes some of the limitations of traditional expository writing and offers a different model for writing and representation in peace studies.

Along these lines, the erasure uses juxtaposition and language to destabilize (hypostatized) discourse, unsettle teleology and narrative and raise questions about enterprise and the norms that underpin it, including the oftheard injunction 'never again'. Hinton's erasure is also a commentary on 'rethinking peace', underscoring the point that new formulations always risk themselves becoming enfolded within 'the ends of peace' and swept into the four undercurrents of peace studies.

Warning against such dangers, Hinton's erasure is subversive and subverts itself, highlighting aporia and the ultimate 'lesson' of 'rethinking peace'—the need to continually 'look again'. Hinton's erasure begins and concludes with this self-subverting injunction, thereby disrupting narrative and teleology, failing to provide a clear 'conclusion' as it redirects the reader's attention to what has come before, encouraging rereadings and further critique, examining what has been redacted and pushed out of sight and emphasizing that rethinking peace is always incomplete.

NOTES

1. The initiative was a collaboration between the Japan International Christian University Foundation, the Center for Genocide and Human Rights at Rutgers University and International Christian University (see Hastings, in this volume).

2. Lederach prefers conflict transformation to resolution and understands it as envisioning and responding to the ebb and flow of social conflict as life-giving opportunities for creating constructive change processes that reduce violence, increase justice in direct interaction and in social structures and respond to real-life problems in human relationships. Many of the contributors to this volume, however, would question the normativity of Lederach's approach.

BIBLIOGRAPHY

Appadurai, Arjun. 1996. *Modernity at Large: Cultural Dimensions of Globalization.* Minneapolis: University of Minnesota Press.

Autesserre, Séverine. 2015. *Peaceland: Conflict Resolution and the Everyday Politics of International Intervention.* New York: Cambridge University Press.

Bauman, Zygmunt. 1989. *Modernity and the Holocaust.* Cambridge: Polity.

Behr, Hartmut. 2014. *Politics of Difference: A Phenomenological Approach to Peace.* Abingdon: Routledge.

Benjamin, Walter. 1996. 'The Task of the Translator'. In *Walter Benjamin: Selected Writings, Volume 1, 1913–26*, edited by Marcus Bulock and Michael W. Jennings, 253–63. Cambridge, MA: Belknap Press.

Berman, Antoine. 2012. 'Translation and the Trials of the Foreign'. *In The Translation Studies Reader*, 3rd ed., edited by Lawrence Venuti, 240–53. New York: Routledge.

Boutros-Ghali, Boutros. 1992. 'An Agenda for Peace: Preventive Diplomacy, Peacemaking and Peace-Keeping'. United Nations A/47/277-S/24111, 21 January. New York: United Nations.

Butler, Judith. 1990. *Gender Trouble: Feminism and the Subversion of Identity*. New York: Routledge.

———. 2006. *Precarious Life: The Powers of Mourning and Violence*. New York: Verso.

Chandler, David. 2017. *Peacebuilding: The Twenty Years Crisis, 1997–2017*. New York: Palgrave Macmillan.

Donnelly, Jack. 2013. *Universal Human Rights in Theory and Practice*. Ithaca, NY: Cornell University Press.

Enloe, Cynthia. 2014. *Bananas, Beaches and Bases: Making Feminist Sense of International Politics*. Berkeley: University of California Press.

Escobar, Arturo. 1995. *Encountering Development: The Making and Unmaking of the Third World*. Princeton, NJ: Princeton University Press.

Ferguson, James. 1990. *The Anti-Politics Machine: 'Development,' Depoliticization, and Bureaucratic Power in Lesotho*. Minneapolis: University of Minnesota Press.

Fetcher, Anne-Meike, and Heather Hindman, eds. 2011. *Inside the Everyday Lives of Development Workers*. Sterling, VA: Kumarian.

Foucault, Michel. 1990. *A History of Sexuality*. Vol. 1. New York: Vintage.

Galtung, Johan. 1969. 'Violence, Peace and Peace Research'. *Journal of Peace Research* 6, no. 3: 167–91.

———. 1990. 'Cultural Violence'. *Journal of Peace Research*, 27, no. 3: 291–305.

———. 2012. 'Peace, Positive and Negative'. *The Encyclopedia of Peace Psychology*. New York: Wiley.

———. 2016. 'On the Art of Peace'. Paper presented at the 'Rethinking Peace Studies' conference, Japan International Christian University, Tokyo, 4 June.

George, Nicole. 2016. 'Light, Heat and Shadows: Women's Reflections on Peacebuilding in Post-Conflict Bougainville'. *Peacebuilding* 4, no. 2: 166–79.

Hassan, Waïl. 2006. 'Agency and Translational Literature: Ahadaf Soueif's "The Map of Love."' *PMLA* 121, no. 3: 753–68.

Hinton, Alexander Laban. 2016. *Man or Monster? The Trial of a Khmer Rouge Torturer*. Durham, NC: Duke University Press.

———. 2018. *The Justice Facade: Trials of Transition in Cambodia*. New York: Oxford University Press.

Hopgood, Stephen. 2013. *The Endtimes of Human Rights*. Ithaca, NY: Cornell University Press.

Hudson, Heidi. 2016. 'Decolonising Gender and Peacebuilding: Feminist Frontiers and Border Thinking in Africa'. *Peacebuilding* 4, no. 2: 194–209.

Hughes, Caroline, Joakim Öjendal, and Isabell Schierenbeck. 2015. 'The Struggle versus the Song—The Local Turn in Peacebuilding: An Introduction'. *Third World Quarterly* 36, no. 5: 817–24.

Kant, Immanuel. 1983. *Perpetual Peace and Other Essays*. Indianapolis: Hackett.

Lederach, John Paul. 2014. *The Little Book of Conflict Transformation*. New York: Good Books.

Mac Ginty, Roger. 2016. *International Peacebuilding and Local Resistance: Hybrid Forms of Peace*. Basingstoke: Palgrave Macmillan.

Mac Ginty, Roger, and Oliver Richmond. 2013. 'The Local Turn in Peace Building: A Critical Agenda for Peace'. *Third World Quarterly* 34, no. 5: 763–83. https://doi.org/10.1080/01436597.2013.800750.

Oxford English Dictionary. 2015. Oxford: Oxford University Press.

Paris, Roland. 2010. 'Saving Liberal Peacebuilding'. *Review of International Studies* 36, no. 2: 337–65. https://doi.org/10.1017/S0260210510000057.

Porter, Elizabeth. 2016. 'Feminists Building Peace and Reconciliation: Beyond Post-Conflict'. *Peacebuilding* 4, no. 2: 210–25.

Pugh, Michael, Neil Cooper, Mandy Turner, and Stuart Croft, eds. 2008. *Whose Peace?: Critical Perspectives on the Political Economy of Peacebuilding*. Basingstoke: Palgrave Macmillan.

Richmond, Oliver. 2011. *A Post-Liberal Peace*. Abingdon: Routledge.

———. 2014. *Peace: A Very Short Introduction*. Oxford: Oxford University Press.

———. 2016. *Peace Formation and Political Order*. Oxford: Oxford University Press.

Richmond, Oliver P., and Audra Mitchell, eds. 2012. *Hybrid Forms of Peace: From Everyday Agency to Post-Liberalism*. New York: Palgrave.

Rothberg, Michael. 2009. *Multidirectional Memory: Remembering the Holocaust in the Age of Decolonization*. Stanford, CA: Stanford University Press.

Said, Edward W. 1978. *Orientalism*. New York: Vintage Books.

Schmitt, Carl. [1934] 2006. *Political Theology: Four Chapters on the Concept of Sovereignty*. Translated by George Schwab. Chicago: University of Chicago Press.

Scott, James C. 1998. *Seeing Like a State: How Certain Schemes to Improve the Human Condition Have Failed*. New Haven, CT: Yale University Press.

Shani, Giorgio. 2014. *Religion, Identity and Human Security*, London: Routledge.

Shepherd, Laura. 2017. *Gender, UN Peacebuilding, and the Politics of Space: Locating Legitimacy*. Oxford: Oxford University Press.

Shorter Oxford English Dictionary. 2007. Oxford: Oxford University Press.

Tickner, J. Anne, and Jacqui True. 2018. 'A Century of International Relations Feminism: From World War I Women's Peace Pragmatism to the Women, Peace and Security Agenda'. *International Studies Quarterly* 62, no. 2: 221–33.

Wibben, Annick. 2010. *Feminist Security Studies: A Narrative Approach*. Abingdon: Routledge.

Part I

Rethinking Peace

Discourse

Giorgio Shani

The discourse of peace studies was established in the mid-twentieth century as a critique of the hegemonic trends in the theory and practice of international relations (IR). Like its parent discipline, peace studies constructs a world in which violence—whether physical, structural or cultural (Galtung 1969, 1990)—exists at multiple levels: individual, state level and international (Waltz 1959). Whereas the first generation of IR scholars embraced the normativity which peace studies still holds sacrosanct and sought to minimize or prohibit violence at an interstate level, subsequent generations inspired by the trenchant realist critique of E. H. Carr (1940) have sought to construct a discipline based on the analysis of its causes and consequences. In Kenneth Waltz's (1979) *Theory of International Politics*, an attempt was made to build on his classic *Man, the State, and War* (1959) by explaining how states were 'socialized' by the structuring principle of the international system to pursue their own interest defined in terms of maximizing power, thus making conflict inevitable. War was, thus, naturalized and accepted, along with diplomacy, as a key mode of *discours* in IR. As a speech act, declarations of war permitted states to reproduce a realist ontology of IR as an anarchic domain populated by self-interested states. Given the anarchic nature of the system, states were responsible for their own security, which often could be guaranteed only by the possession of weapons of mass destruction. Stability was, therefore, best preserved through a balance of power guaranteed by mutually assured destruction. The Cold War, therefore, became the 'Long Peace' (Gaddis 1987).

However, the threat of impending nuclear catastrophe and the still-vivid memories of the Holocaust and other horrors perpetrated by states on civilians during World War II stimulated a desire to *transform* the world and in so doing revisit the normative impulse behind the founding of its parent

1

discipline. Thus, peace research and, in its disciplinary incarnation, peace studies were born. Its 'founding father' and a keynote speaker at the final conference of Rethinking Peace Studies at International Christian University, Johan Galtung, significantly, came from *outside* IR and brought with him a scientific rigor from his own training as a mathematician. Tensions, however, may be discerned between the normative aspirations of peace research and its 'scientific' methodology. This is exemplified by the flagship journal of the Peace Research Institute based in Oslo which Galtung founded: *Journal of Peace Research (JPR)*.

In the editorial of its inaugural issue, *JPR* defined peace research as 'research into the conditions for moving closer to the state we call GCP [general and complete peace] or at least not drifting closer to GCW [general and complete war]' (*JPR* 1964, 2). Despite its explicitly normative commit-ment to peace, it adopts a mainly positivist methodology which may still be hegemonic in the social sciences but has long been questioned by critical theorists. Consequently, *JPR* is now widely embraced by the mainstream IR community with a five-year impact factor of 4.251, making it one of the four most prestigious journals in IR and in the top ten in political science in 2018. This suggests that peace studies has lost its critical edge or, to put it more dramatically—in terms which Ashis Nandy, our other keynote speaker, uses in the opening chapter in this part—that peace studies has been swallowed back into the 'black hole' of mainstream IR and political science.

The chapters in this part examine whether the discourse of peace studies can be saved. If so, how should it be rethought, and what relationship should it have with its parent discipline: IR? This part starts with Ashis Nandy's key-note, which draws our attention to the black holes of IR through which an en-tire range of 'researchables' disappear. These include the details of 'everyday life, emotions, values and tacit theories of social transformation and visions of desirable society of myriad little cultures, along with their experiences of suffering'. Ignored by the academic discourse of peace studies, these 'dispos-able subjectivities' survive in the 'nether world of individual and collective memories', waiting for an opportune moment to come back 'like skeletons tumbling out of a cupboard'. Rather than abandon IR completely, Nandy sug-gests the possibility for peace research to engage with 'dissenting voices in political science and IR'. Ultimately, however, Nandy argues that the 'libera-tion of peace studies lies in freeing itself from the clutches of the dominant cultures of political science and IR and acquiring the self-confidence to walk a lonelier, more autonomous path'.

Nandy concludes by touching on the 'spectacular violence' of al-Qaeda and Islamic State (IS), which, like vendors of other 'secular' revolutionary ideologies, end up 'devouring their own children' or 'targeting their alleged beneficiaries'. The challenges posed by radical political Islam to IR and the Westphalian model of territorialized nation-states in particular are examined in Steve Bronner's chapter. For Bronner, the main discourses of IR have traditionally been constructed using the nation-state as a unit of analysis. The nation-state is assumed to be a sovereign entity characterized by the monopolization of the use of force by a sovereign who decides the 'exception' (Schmitt (2006). This situation, however, no longer prevails in the Middle East, where the state is increasingly viewed as an imperialist import, creating space for the rise of transnational religious organization, such as al-Qaeda and IS, which reject the 'secular' settlement of the Peace of Westphalia. Bronner's chapter offers a prescriptive conception of sovereignty which would allow peace to be rethought beyond today's shallow conceptions of liberal intervention, which are the subject of the final two chapters in this part by Oliver Richmond and Giorgio Shani.

Drawing on critical, feminist, poststructural and postcolonial thinking in IR, Richmond's chapter attempts to sketch a 'peace with global justice'. This would involve, for Richmond, 'relinquishing the territorialised system of state and international architecture . . . and its translation into a new peace architecture' drawing on the experience of the everyday localized interactions which constitute 'peace formation'. In contrast to the orthodoxies of liberal peace building with its highly interventionary nature, Richmond claims that individuals are bringing a new and hybrid 'international' into sight seeking their own 'peace, emancipation and social justice'. These, Richmond argues, can be understood only in local contexts.

Although Shani, in the concluding chapter in this part, agrees with the need for 'local' understandings of peace formation, he draws attention to the tensions in the 'local turn' which Richmond, among others, have helped to introduce. Peace formation, for Shani, does not offer a viable alternative to liberal peace building, as it reproduces the very 'liberal colonial IR' which it seeks to critique. Liberal peace building is critiqued on *liberal* terms as narrow and exclusionary. Shani argues that the 'local turn' needs to be emancipated from the Enlightenment fallacies of the liberal peace and engage seriously with the religious cosmologies of colonized peoples. However, peace formation can never really be 'local', given the legacy of half a millennia of colonization, but only 'post-Western'.

Following Nandy in the opening chapter in this part, we conclude that we should be looking for alternatives to the 'dominant cultures' of political science and IR. This can be achieved only by rethinking the hegemonic understanding of IR as a secular social science. Rethinking peace, therefore, involves not 'saving' peace studies as a subfield of IR but rather rethinking its parent discipline.

REFERENCES

Carr, Edward Hallett. 1940. *The Twenty Years' Crisis, 1919–1939: An Introduction to the Study of International Relations*. London: Macmillan.

Gaddis, John Lewis. 1987. *The Long Peace: Inquiries into the History of the Cold War*. Oxford: Oxford University Press.

Galtung, Johan. 1969. 'Violence, Peace, and Peace Research'. *Journal of Peace Research* 6: 167–92.

———. 1990. 'Cultural Violence'. *Journal of Peace Research* 27, no. 3: 291–305.

Journal of Peace Research. 1964. 'An Editorial'. *Journal of Peace Research* 1, no. 1: 1–5.

Schmitt, Carl. [1934] 2006. *Political Theology: Four Chapters on the Concept of Sovereignty*. Translated by George Schwab. Chicago: University of Chicago Press.

Waltz, Kenneth N. 1959. *Man, the State, and War: A Theoretical Analysis*. New York: Columbia University Press.

———. 1979. *Theory of International Politics*. Reading, MA: Addison-Wesley.

Chapter One

The Inner Battles of Peace Studies

The Limits and Possibilities[1]

Ashis Nandy

The black holes of astrophysicists are sometimes matched by the 'black holes' of political science and international relations (IR). Through these disappear an entire range of 'researchables'—from invisible genocides and designer famines to contraband memories of erased pogroms and cultures casually pushed towards extinction. They do sometimes invite curiosity of the students of peace studies but are often found extremely difficult to accommodate within the major theoretical frames of the mother disciplines of political science and IR.

This I suspect is part of a larger problem. For, as time passes, through these black holes also disappear details of everyday life, emotions, values and tacit theories of social transformation and visions of desirable society of myriad little cultures, along with their experiences of suffering. These subjectivities are seen as so much of noise or as stuff fit for dustbins of history and shelves of museums. They do not match the official expectations from a proper sub-discipline spawned by political science and IR.

However, while these experiences are exiled from the world of academic social knowledge, they survive in the netherworld of individual and collective memories and wait for an opportune moment to come back to mock our disciplinary cultures and academic canons. This brief chapter is an attempt to acknowledge that underside of peace studies—the disposable subjectivities and noncultures ignored, exiled or museumized as irrelevant, which then sometimes reemerge in public discourse like skeletons tumbling out of a cupboard. They then—and only then—threaten to discredit many respectable intellectual initiatives and to demuseumize otherwise undervalued, marginalized, mnemonic or memory-dependent traditions. I have come to suspect that this politics of knowledge constitutes the unacknowledged underworld of the disciplines of political science and IR and limits the possibilities of both.

To give two random examples, the desperate attempts by successive Turkish regimes have not erased the memories of the Armenian genocide despite the passage of time. They have only managed to stoke the interest of scattered activist-scholars all over the world in the subject and kept the issue alive. If the Turkish officialdom were less enthusiastic about dissuading scholars from foraging the memories of that half-forgotten massacre, perhaps Turkey might have been less haunted by the Armenian question (as has indeed happened in the case with the genocide of the Hereros and Namaquas during the German colonial rule in Africa in the first decade of the twentieth century after the German government publicly apologized for the killings).[2] Likewise, as the respected anthropologist of Indonesia Clifford Geertz might have found towards fag end of his life, what he had casually dismissed in his writings as some unimportant 'skirmishes' was nothing less than a full-fledged, organized genocide stoked and supported by the American establishment—thanks not so much to scholarly work, such as those of Robert Cribb, as to Joshua Oppenheimer's disturbing documentary *An Act of Killing*.[3] So much for the famed 'thick description' of Geertz.

In both cases, an invisible genocide suddenly became visible: in one case to return to invisibility, in the other to acquire temporary visibility that may or may not become permanent.

Are there inner dissonances in the cultural and psychological baggage that peace studies carry to be a viable subdiscipline in political science and IR? Does the Enlightenment vision, which frames the culture of knowledge into which many of the social sciences were born, have a place for only negotiated and enforced peace and not for the idea of nonviolence? When later on, armed with the mythos of the French Revolution as the basic design of all radical social interventions, did the Enlightenment values open up some possibilities while closing others? Do we have to go back as far as St. Francis of Assisi (1182–1226) and the Christianity of the first four centuries to reach Europe's disowned traditions of nonviolence? Once again, just because I am raising these questions does not mean that I have the answers.[4]

However, even a preliminary response to these questions has to admit that one part of the story was beautifully captured by Maximilien Robespierre (1758–1794) when the French Revolution was dutifully consuming its children as a regular public spectacle. Without terror, Robespierre claimed, virtue was helpless—a claim that is now only an inescapable part of the mythos of all subsequent revolutions but also of almost all attempts to radically reorder human society, attempts to correct the faulty international order, perhaps also all millennial movements trying to actualize their utopias or visions here and now.

Experience may have shown repeatedly that this piece of inherited wisdom can leave entire sphere of polities caught in a cycle of just wars and attempts to correct historical wrongs on behalf of one's ancestors or of that mythic entity called one's nation. In many instances in many societies, terror becomes an end in itself and might even come close to being institutionalized as almost a way of life, Cambodia being a good example, with Syria giving it tough competition at the moment. Sometimes, even when the system collapses, the brutalization of the society shows, and the idea of terror remains a tacit option in everyday life and even in family relations.[5]

Sometimes those who try to radically alter a way of life through massive violence end up no better after their efforts and leave their children and grandchildren haunted by the question whether all the bloodshed, mass deportations, man-made famines, institutionalized cruelties and attacks on the moral universe of society have left them culturally poorer, ethically impoverished and politically self-destructive. Many actualized utopias, the twentieth century has shown us, have been fraudulent exercises trying to pass themselves off as a new civilization through surveillance, censorship and thought policing.

Russia, the land of Fyodor Dostoyevsky and Leo Tolstoy, should have been one of the first countries in our times to try to answer these questions but has not as yet shown any sign of doing so. If it does, the answers will probably come not from Russia's political class but from its intellectuals—writers, painters, film directors and thinkers. Understandably. An ideological state built around the idea of the infallibility of its ideology, even after its death, leaves behind a state apparatus that is organized around the fear of anarchy and dissolution. It has to fall back upon its coercive might to paper over its democratic failures. Even if the successor state is a nonideological one, it cannot dump its statism and its fear of decentralization, anarchy and free media. Putin's Russia today is blessed with a more primitive and less humane version capitalism than Victorian England.

Robespierre's formulation acquired a sharper edge in the twentieth century when the imperial power structure set up by colonialism began to dissolve. The idea of just war was always there as part of the repertoire of states; it began to get secularized and scientized towards the middle of the nineteenth century. The religious passions that underlay the idea earlier were displaced onto new ideological frames, and progress itself became a rallying call and a self-justification. This allowed more latitude to nation-states and in the hands of unscrupulous regimes became almost infinitely flexible. George W. Bush was only a more clumsy retailer of phoney just wars.

Second, sensing the growing antiwar sentiments in less manageable sections of the people—such as the youth (particularly students), women and

parts of the religious establishment—there has been systematic efforts to de-
limit the scope and the possibilities of 'militant nonviolence'.[6] It can succeed,
it is said, only under a benign, liberal regime, not under fascists and despots.
In some texts, Gandhi's successes—or, for that matter, those of Martin Luther
King, Nelson Mandela and the Dalai Lama—are traced not to politics, world-
view or ethics but to the political sagacity and liberal ethics of the colonial
powers and other despotic regimes. Even though Gandhian nonviolence was
born under a ruthlessly authoritarian, openly racist, colonial regime in South
Africa and tasted its early successes there, it was tried against the Nazi regime
only once. And that effort, too, had succeeded (Stoltzfus 1996).

Such attempts to 'normalize' the radical messages of peace activists have
begun to pay some political dividends, too. In Gandhi's India—more so in his
birthplace, Gujarat—Gandhi is increasingly a nonperson and a ritual presence
in the ruling culture of politics. Nonetheless, despite the attempts to margin-
alize peace research by the mainstream cultures of political science and IR,
peace research has now an expanding, visible culture that is in alliance with
dissenting voices within political science and IR. In the case of IR, peace
studies have also benefitted from the tensions between, on the one hand, the
conventional political wisdom vended by strategic and defence studies and,
on the other, the personal ethics and emotional ties that shape everyday life
and perhaps even what one might identify as our basic humanity acquired
through our developmental experience and socialization.[7]

The issue is also complicated by the diversity in the culture of everyday life
that is being brought into peace research by its practitioners. This has, however,
not been an unmixed blessing. The way peace research is presently conceptualized, the diverse cultural backgrounds peace researchers bring to their discipline do not seem to bring their scholarly vision and the theoretical grids into
a common, more daring, cross-cultural theoretical pool. The diversity seems
to mainly help multiply conventional area studies or satisfies the conventional
demand for geographical coverage masquerading as cross-cultural depth.

Third, the practice of IR, the conventions of diplomacy and warfare have
behind them the sanctions of international institutions, in turn backed by
a 'consensus' that is seen as global and relatively independent of cultural
differences and disparities in military and economic might. The deviations
from this consensus are seen as unfortunate by-products of the birth pangs
of a new, more humane international order. There is little awareness that
this world image clashes directly with the experiences, memories, fears and
desperation in many parts of the world that see the present order as a planned
edifice perched upon the hidden demands of a terribly unequal, quasi-colonial
international order and upon the cultivated forgetfulness associated with the
self-abnegation and ethnocide in the Southern Hemisphere.

Fourth, while both are equally important, but the former is better known than the latter, perhaps because many Southern scholars are reluctant to take a position on Afro-Asian or Latin American despotism when it comes packaged in, what Herb Feith used to call, developmental authoritarianism. Earlier, the handy excuse was nation building and state formation; now it usually is progress or development. Peace researchers, too, have sometimes chosen to be diffident, silent spectators of such self-destruction in the name of protecting the sovereignty of regimes exuding the right kind of radical chic and mouthing politically correct slogans.

Fifth, peace studies have consistently focused on nation-states as the major actors in the global scene and mostly ignored the way nonstate actors have gate-crashed into the global arena to embrace and pursue new causes and sometimes adopt new forms of resistance, using new technologies of violence and nonviolence. The thrust of twentieth-century violence was to make wars more technocratic, 'cleaner' and psychologically distant from us. Such sanitized wars have made wars more palatable not merely to some sections of the citizens but also to the soldiers mobilized to fight the war. Even in India, hardened by its own versions of violence and cruelty, when seeing television coverage of bombing raids during the Gulf War, many complained that it looked too much like a video game and a grand spectacle. (Such sanitization of violence is, of course, part of a larger problem that has to do with the new role of mass media, the changing nature of electoral politics and the scope and limits of individualism in a democracy in the age of virtual reality.) Not merely hard-eyed politicians and other policymakers but also ordinary citizens, even children, are getting brutalized and learning to live with massive, pointless cruelty around them.

Finally, while intellectual work in which disciplines such as psychology, anthropology and biographical studies intersecting political science and IR have declined in salience, one of the few formulations on which a consensus has survived is that, when for some reasons political institutions are wobbly and the nature of politics is fluid, the role of individuals as leaders, ideologues or even assassins matter more, and in-depth studies of such individuals become crucial. This is by now a part of global common sense. Without Gorbachev, it is doubtful if the Soviet Union would have wound up shop so gracefully and peaceably. Without Richard Nixon, Henry Kissinger and Deng Xiaoping, it is doubtful if the post-Vietnam detente between the United States and China would have become such a consequential event.

In some democracies, this salience of individual actors has now been potentiated by the growing power and salience of media. The change is most visible in countries that use the Westminster model of competitive democracy, but the electoral process and campaigning style has become decisively presidential. People's representatives in a newly elected legislature do not choose a prime minister; the electorate are encouraged by the contestants, the media and pundits to choose amongst prime minister–designates. After elections, the winning party might formally elect the prime minister, but that is increasingly a ritual. Examples are countries like Australia, Germany, Bangladesh, India, Pakistan, Sri Lanka and the country that hosts the mother of all parliaments, Britain.

I foresee more studies on the different styles of handling foreign affairs in countries where books like those by James Barber and Fred Greenstein have not been seen till now as particularly relevant.[8] Perhaps the role of human subjectivity itself has been underestimated in international studies. And though some of those working in the area have concentrated on the linear growth of this role, it is implicit in the data that they themselves produce that this role expands and shrinks with the personality of those who are voted into power. Indian democracy, for instance, has developed a love–hate relationship with the activism and decisiveness of incumbent power holders—more so after the institutions of democracy and the constitutional framework have stabilized and the scope of radical interventions in the political system has diminished dramatically. Every regime seems to negotiate with political issues, particularly when it comes to foreign affairs, from within a very narrow range of options. Yet when a power holder looks inactive or indecisive, there is much screaming and lamentation; he or she is accused of incompetence and passivity. When a prime minister or a foreign minister seems overly active in foreign affairs, that invites criticisms for being overly adventurous and imperiling the security of the country.

Perhaps at the moment, one of the most dangerous trends is the attempt to correct historical stereotypes of being passive, demasculinized victims of oppression that haunt a sizeable section of the Indian middle class. In world's largest democracy, large sections of the majority community, comprising four-fifths of India's population, have begun to talk and act like a minority community. Many in the ruling party are fearful that the Hindus will be reduced to a minority and speak of redressing the history of Muslim rule in India that ended nearly 300 years ago. They are not alone in this lament. Some years ago, Johan Galtung told me about his experiences with Palestinian and Kashmiri political activists. Galtung told both groups that his studies showed that both in Palestine and in Kashmir, a nonviolent struggle on Gandhian lines would succeed; the time was ripe for that. And both the Palestinian and the Kashmiri activists told Galtung that he was trying to 'feminize' them.

Let me here also tell you the experience of the late Nirmala Deshpande, a Gandhian freedom fighter, Member of the Indian Parliament and a human rights activist. She once went to meet General Krishna Rao, a former commander in chief of the Indian army and later a governor of Jammu and Kashmir, where a violent secessionist movement has been going on for the past 25 years. Deshpande wanted to know from the general how affective would her efforts be to turn the movement into a nonviolent one. The general kept quiet for quite a few seconds and then said, 'If you are a true nationalist, you should not do what you are planning to do. For then our guns will not work'.

I believe that the liberation of peace studies lies in freeing itself from the clutches of the dominant cultures of political science and IR and acquiring the self-confidence to walk a lonelier, more autonomous path. I wait for the day when peace studies will not remain an unwanted fellow traveller or appendage of political science and IR and will not have to carry the baggage of these two disciplines. And I also hope that an autonomous culture of peace studies will someday inform all the social sciences and perhaps even parts of natural sciences as a discipline that affirms life and is in better touch with reality of its interconnection with other forms of life and will not be seen as an esoteric preoccupation of softheaded, romantic visionaries out of touch with reality.

Al-Qaeda and the Islamic State have been gleefully trying to prove that all millennialism, especially when riding piggyback on political ideologies, must end up targeting their alleged beneficiaries. Like other revolutionaries, vendors of radical Islam, too, live with constant fear of being betrayed by fellow travellers and followers who retain their scepticism and critical faculties or are naïve enough to believe that they can opt out of their mission. Do not be taken in by their spectacular violence and blood-chilling anti-*kafir* rhetoric; a huge majority of their victims till now has been Muslims.[9] You always tend to end up turning against those to whose cause you have seemingly dedicated your life; they are the ones you identify with, and the more you identify with them, the more you suspect them to be contaminated. The seductive power of the enemy that you sense within yourself—and the self-doubts you secretly nurture—dooms your associates and followers. Your temptations become their secret sins.

NOTES

1. Revised draft of a keynote lecture delivered at the Conference on Peace Studies at the International Christian University, Tokyo, 2–4 June 2016.
2. See, for example, Drechsler (1980) and Gewald (2004).
3. For instance, Cribb (1990, 2001); see also Chandra (2017).
4. The dominant idea of peace in peace studies is very different from the principle of nonviolence in Hindu-Jaina and Buddhist traditions of nonviolence and that of their most prominent spokesperson in our times, Mohandas Gandhi. Gandhi, too, had a principle of unavoidable violence built into his theory of nonviolence. He did

say that the Polish army's battle with Nazi war machine was 'almost nonviolent', presumably because not to offer such resistance would have been cowardice, and Gandhi associated valour with nonviolence, not martial prowess. Incidentally, I do not mean to suggest that Gandhi's nonviolence belongs exclusively to some traditions and not to others. As it happens, though Gandhi worked out the principles of militant nonviolence in South Africa, he did so as part of an initiative taken by a triumvirate. The other two involved were Abdul Ghani, the first person to proclaim the principles publicly at Johannesburg in South Africa, and the other was Haji Habib, who first published the declaration. Both were Muslims.

5. A UN functionary visiting Cambodia told me about a Cambodian woman whose husband, a shopkeeper in the local market, had fallen in love with another woman. The angry wife purchased a discarded but live grenade in the black market and threw it at her husband while he was at his shop, killing him and half a dozen others and injuring many others. The visitor was shocked by the casual attitude towards human life.

6. This is Erik Erikson's term for Gandhi's method in place of the term that the British colonial administration used: 'passive resistance' (Erikson 1969).

7. A rather obvious example is Lieutenant Colonel Dave Grossman (1995), which seems to subvert one of the core axioms of mainstream international relations. For another approach through the continuity between international relations on the one hand and everyday life, cultural experiences and ethics on the other, see Darby (2006, 2016).

8. See Barber (1972) and Greenstein (2009); see also Darby (2016).

9. Roughly, 88 percent of the victims of al-Qaida are Muslims (Musharbash 2018). For the Islamic State, the figure ranges between 72 and 97 percent (Obeidallah 2018).

REFERENCES

Barber, James D. 1972. *The Presidential Character: Predicting Performance in the White House.* Englewood Cliffs, NJ: Prentice Hall.

Chandra, Siddharth. 2017. 'New Findings on the Indonesian Killings of 1965–66'. *Journal of Asian Studies* 76, no. 4: 1059–84.

Cribb, Robert, ed. 1990. *The Indonesian Killings of 1965–1966: Studies from Java and Bali.* Clayton: Monash University Centre of Southeast Asian Studies.

———. 2001. 'Genocide in Indonesia, 1965–1966'. *Journal of Genocide Research* 3, no. 2: 219–39.

Darby, Phillip, ed. 2006. *Postcolonizing the International: Working to Change the Way We Are.* Honolulu: University of Hawai'i Press.

———, ed. 2016. *From International Relations to Relations International: Postcolonial Essays.* Oxford: Routledge.

Drechsler, Horst. 1980. *Let Us Die Fighting: The Struggle of the Herero and Nama against German Imperialism (1884–1915).* Translated by Bernd Zöllner. London: Zed Press.

Erikson, Erik. 1969. *Gandhi's Truth: On the Origins of Militant Nonviolence*. New York: Norton.

Gewald, J. B. 2004. 'The Herero and Nama Genocides, 1904–1908'. In *Encyclopedia of Genocide and Crimes against Humanity*. New York: Macmillan.

Greenstein, Fred. 2009. *The Presidential Difference: Leadership Style from FDR to Barack Obama*. Princeton, NJ: Princeton University Press.

Grossman, Dave. 1995. *On Killing: The Psychological Cost of Learning to Kill in War and Society*. New York: Little, Brown.

Musharbash, Yassin. 2018. 'Al-Qaida Kills Eight Times More Muslims Than Non-Muslims'. *Spiegel Online*. http://www.Spiegel.de. Accessed 4 July 2018.

Obeidallah, Dean. 2018. 'No One Wants to See ISIS Defeated More Than Muslims'. https://www.arabamerica.com/no-one-wants-see-isis-defeated-muslims. Accessed 4 July 2018.

Stoltzfus, Nathan. 1996. *Resistance of the Heart: Intermarriage and the Rosenstrasse Protest in Nazi Germany*. New York: Norton.

Chapter Two

Sovereignty, Interference and Crisis

Stephen Eric Bronner

International relations (IR) have traditionally been constructed using the nation-state as a unit of analysis with regard to both war and peace. Even when it comes to 'fragile' states, the legacy of the Treaty of Westphalia is presupposed, namely, the existence of a sovereign who monopolizes the means of coercion and decides the 'exception', as Carl Schmitt put the matter, as well as how it should be handled. That situation no longer prevails in the Middle East. The state is increasingly viewed as an imperialist import, and not only power but also loyalty have devolved to tribes, ethnic organizations and religious institutions. The state lacks a legitimate monopoly, as, simultaneously, internal paramilitary and external proxy have become ever more powerful. Balance of power and traditional conflict between states are becoming tainted, if not overshadowed, by religious battles (Sunni–Shia) and the emergence of transnational organizations, such as al-Qaeda and Islamic State of Iraq and Syria (ISIS). This chapter deals with each of these issues in turn and offers a somewhat new and prescriptive treatment of sovereignty that speaks to rethinking peace not only for today but also for the future.

UNDERSTANDING SOVEREIGNTY

Sovereignty is a crucial concept for making sense of recent events in the Middle East. Emerging as a result of the Treaty of Westphalia and articulated by Enlightenment thinkers beginning with Thomas Hobbes, sovereignty justified the institutional response of the modern state to the premodern 'empire' and its grounding in a loose association of (free and unfree) city-states. Admittedly, all political formulations require some legitimation of authority and all experience crises. In premodern formations such as empires, however, the

15

sovereign is imbued with otherworldly legitimation, as in the case of Egypt, whose pharaoh was also considered a god; in Rome, where legitimation (as empire and republic) derived from the gods and traditions supposedly reaching back to Romulus and Remus; or in the period of absolutism where authority was justified through divine right of kings. Crisis was generated by conflict surrounding succession rather than the existence of the state other than when divinely anointed authorities were confronted with overwhelming military force. Sovereignty is, by contrast, a secular concept threatened primarily by forces and leaders whose authority derives from the divine or integral organic traditions of the community, such as tribe or family.

The crisis of sovereignty became evident in virtually all the states affected by the Arab Spring: Egypt, Iraq, Lebanon, Libya, Mali, Syria, Tunisia and Yemen. Bereft of the ideological authority offered by the mosque and the organizational discipline of the military, incapable of creating strong coalitions and political parties, this transnational democratic revolution produced what Jürgen Habermas once termed a 'legitimation crisis' in which conflict among competing religious/secular, ethnic or tribal constituencies dominated the political landscape. This development strengthened the prejudices of many in the West who assume that Islam is inherently antidemocratic—though, of course, the uprisings were both mass based and republican in intent. Indeed, little that took place is unique to the Middle East. Europe had its own 'Arab Spring' in 1848 when, rebelling against the 'restoration' of reactionary authority and norms in the aftermath of the Napoleonic Wars, a spate of spontaneous transnational revolts called for reintroducing republican institutions (often with socialist programs) in what became known as 'the springtime of the peoples'. The same logic of power appeared as in the uprisings. With their flailing attempts at democracy, wracked by internal conflicts, they ultimately produced power vacuums that were filled by authoritarian governments like those of Napoleon III and Bismarck. Indeed, the dynamics whereby the counterrevolution suppressed the revolution is what Marx described in his classic *18th Brumaire*.

Even worse were the civil wars that had arisen earlier and that generated the modern state. Ongoing conflicts between France and England during what was known as the Hundred Years' War (1337–1453) led to slaughter on a massive scale, while the Thirty Years' War (1618–1648) cost Germany and Central Europe nearly one-third of its population. Of course, these primarily religious wars are mostly forgotten (especially by bigots). Memory is usually jogged only by thoughts of the famous soliloquy from Shakespeare's *Henry V* celebrating the English victory at Agincourt in 1415 or through watching Schiller's *Wallenstein*. Catholics and Protestants butchered one another over the proper road to salvation until the resulting Treaty of Osnabruck and the

Peace of Westphalia (1648) ushered in the primacy of the secular nation-state with the right to determine the appropriate religion within its own confines and, thus, the controversial concept of sovereignty. The English Civil War (1642–1651) reflected this larger European conflict, and in that context, Thomas Hobbes wrote his *Leviathan* (1651)—the first great work that highlighted the centrality of both for modern politics.

Sovereignty is predicated on the legitimacy of the state to represent the (always elusive) national interest. To prove more than merely symbolic, in the first instance, this calls for the state to lift itself above the particular needs of economic actors as well as the political primacy traditionally given to private associations like the church. It is true that states are susceptible to manipulation by markets (and vice versa) and that private interests usually affect public action. But, still, the distinction between public and private interests remains as surely as that between church and state. Only by separating itself from these interests can the state offer security to its citizens that, in the modern context, translates into delivering basic public services while preventing terrorism and civil war. The kind of state is a secondary concern. Sovereignty is indeterminate with respect to the institutions capable of implementing its imperatives: it can be an authoritarian state built upon the 'cult of the personality', a theocracy, a republic or some mixture of the three. To speak of sovereignty, then, is to speak of a state considered legitimate by its citizens and other regimes—and a *sovereignty deficit* is the opposite.

Following the fall of Colonel Muammar Gaddafi, in 2011, for example, a government of national unity was proposed in 2015 to combat the growing influence of ISIS and end the internecine fighting between city-states, tribes, and private militias. Six months later, however, the nominal national government was asking the Arab League to intervene, ISIS had scored remarkable gains, squabbling among factions continued, and, by 2016, there was talk about reintroducing the monarchy that went into exile following Gaddafi's coup in 1969. Similar events have occurred throughout the Middle East, ranging from Syria, in which civil war has cost the lives of 250,000 citizens; to Egypt, where General Sisi displaced the fledgling parliament led by the Muslim Brotherhood; and to Yemen, which is effectively without a government. Public services have collapsed in concert with growing insecurity, thus undermining sovereignty in Lebanon through 'garbage protests' and in Iraq, where shutdowns in electricity and water occurred during the boiling summer of 2015.

Subversion of the sovereign and the devolution of authority at the expense of the citizenry have become regional trends. But, still, the lessons of intervention and 'nation building' or 'regime change' have seemed to fall on deaf ears. Even after Afghanistan, Iraq and Syria, the United States still allowed itself to be pulled into a conflict in Libya, where the opposition is confused and internally at odds, where there are no unifying organizations or symbols with which to foster unity and where the agent of intervention is still identified with the imperialist of times past. There should be no misunderstanding: qualitative differences exist between a ruling coalition in which none of the partners is able to wield power alone but in which each recognizes the legitimacy of the other parties involved and a political framework in which none can either rule by itself or accept the legitimacy of any rivals. *Recognition of subservience* to the sovereign by all organizations and institutions competing for power is essential since each can express only private interests. Indeed, for just this reason, Max Weber insisted that only the state can have a monopoly over all sources of coercion: the proliferation of paramilitary organizations in fragile states only confirms his insight.

The issue is not simply whether some monopoly over the means of violence exists but whether their citizens recognize the legitimacy of employing these means in defining what Carl Schmitt termed 'the exception' or the emergency situation. Such circumstances appear in the state of siege, the imposition of martial law or, more generally, events that require reliance on *raison d'etat*. The emergency situation is the exception precisely because the future of the state hangs in the balance. That was why Schmitt insisted in his classic *Political Theology* ([1934] 2006) that 'sovereign is he who decides on the exception'. What he meant was not the everyday problems and momentary crises that grip public opinion and that would make the exception the norm but rather the crisis whose defusing might be likened to the 'miracle' in feudal times and through which it becomes possible to determine where power ultimately resides in the normal workings of government. Or, put another way, the sovereign must have the power to both sanction public policies and determine when the state appears threatened and its ability to function is endangered. To conflate the two or view the exception as the rule and the emergency as an ongoing state of affairs in the manner of Giorgio Agamben's *State of Exception* (2005) buys into the logic of dictators like Bashar al-Assad of Syria, where emergency laws have been operative for nearly 40 years but ignores genuine challenges to the legitimacy of the dictatorship as well as the need for exercising sovereignty to prevent the collapse of fragile states and confront the problems of security and citizenship now facing millions of immigrants in the Middle East. Only by understanding the exception is it possible to determine how power is employed in the nonexceptional circumstances of everyday life.

ALIENATED SOVEREIGNTY

Sovereignty was originally an Occidental construct and, since decolonization, the difficulties of translating it into an Oriental context have become ever more transparent. An organic process took shape in the West whereby the sovereign state bolstered an emergent capitalism and thereby helped generate the growth of bureaucracy and expertise, democracy and diversity, science and secularism. That process never really took hold outside the West, or at least not in the same way, if only because the nation-state was artificially imposed by imperialist powers and not only by what were known as the 'great powers' but by smaller and militarily weaker nations like Belgium, Holland, Portugal and Spain. In each case, the imperialist powers ran its colonies indirectly through a *comprador bourgeoisie* that had been educated in the West and (without undue concern about solidarity) did the colonizer's bidding at home. This *ersatz* class stood in the forefront of struggles for national self-determination, which was naturally in its interest but was never able to generate the kind of loyalty that the sovereign demands. At best, the *comprador bourgeoisie* later became buttressed by elites in the imperial country, multinational firms, and (in the Middle East) an oil industry that served the interests primarily of familial monarchies, as in Saudi Arabia and the Emirates. The new sovereign was thus lacking legitimacy yet condemned to walk the tightrope between past and present in exercising authority over the nation.

Modernizing elites among the colonized often accepted the Western model of the sovereign nation-state in good faith. They wished to break the stranglehold of the sheiks and tribes that ruled the region and condemned it to economic underdevelopment. The conclusion of World War I, along with the breakup of the Ottoman Empire, seemed to provide them with an opportunity. As colonial protectorates were constructed and national boundaries were arbitrarily drawn, the ideal of national self-determination seemed to project a new sovereign and a new anti-imperialist rallying cry. Nationalism might successfully contest the hegemony of Islam and facilitate the integration of diverse tribal and religious constituencies, such as Christians and the Druze. Modernizing colonial elites also understood that sovereign states were required to nationalize the huge regional oil reserves and maximize the benefits of still-unexplored natural resources. Nevertheless, the supposedly sovereign state could easily be seen as an alien import and an imperialist ploy for dividing and conquering the region.

Postcolonialism exhibits similarities with the past but with different actors. Where imperialist nations once bribed and coerced the *comprador bourgeoisie* and where multinationals and oil companies built on that foundation, the imperilled sovereign today attempts to form coalitions with a host of private religious, tribal or ethnic interests. That was clearly the case with Hosni Mubarak in Egypt, Saddam Hussein in Iraq, Hamid Karzai in Afghanistan, Bashar al-Assad in Syria and other monarchs and dictators. Crucial is that the coalition is almost always instrumental and that ideological glue to forge national unity and a clear understanding of sovereignty is needed. Instead, the state, with its bureaucracy, turns into a means for sanctioning various forms of patrimony or the exchange of favours. That (uneven) economic development often occurred as a by-product arguably made the situation worse rather than better. Investment and consumer goods turned the city and the countryside against one another, class conflict made itself felt and secularism threatened religious ideology and institutions.

Occurring within a context of omnipresent corruption and authoritarian repression, these developments further intensified an already alienated understanding of sovereignty. Little wonder that the authoritarian sovereigns in power prior to the Arab Spring (and in its aftermath) were usually held in contempt or that the old transnational caliphate or religious community (*umma*), with its insistence on Sharia law, should have appeared increasingly attractive to those seeking a spiritual regeneration of society. By way of contrast, urban intellectuals, white-collar and state employees and an incipient bourgeoisie were all caught in the web of modernity and thus seeking new forms of legitimation. It soon became clear that only an alienated sovereignty could result from some purely mechanical combination of interests. Tensions between urban and secular as against agrarian and religious forces exist in Tunisia as well as in Iran, where the Islamic Republic rests on the power of the revolutionary guards. In Iraq, paramilitary organizations of Sunnis and Shia fighting for power engage in running battles, and bombings occur daily. Turf wars between rival tribes, in concert with Islamic fundamentalist forces, rip apart Afghanistan, Libya and Yemen, while organized gangs enter the mix in Somalia. Tightly knit Islamic extremist vanguards, like al-Qaeda or Islamic Jihad in the Egyptian Sinai and elsewhere, refuse to recognize any more encompassing sovereign power. The more absolute the claims of what were once private interests, the greater the likelihood of violence and the exercise of arbitrary power—and the less viable and legitimate the claims of any potential sovereign.

Especially among nonurban sectors bound to premodern religious ideologies and excluded from the political and economic benefits of modernity, there is an obvious appeal provided by Islamic State (IS) and the dream of a caliphate dominating the Levant. Sovereignty would take transnational form as centralized institutions coordinate something like a decentralized confederation held together by religious principles and a version of Sharia law. Although its advocates skirt questions concerning who decides the exception and determines the emergency situation, they have still drawn the logical conclusion stemming from the crisis of an alienated sovereignty, namely, introduce a premodern political formation that will bolster a precapitalist understanding of social life and an alternative to the modern (liberal) rule of law in a theological legal order. Thus, IS and other radical Islamic fundamentalist organizations offer an encompassing political and antibureaucratic, socioeconomic and moral-legal alternative to the Western view of modernity, in which the claim to sovereignty and the right to political primacy has rested on little more than the 'will to power'.

Authoritarian institutions and religious organizations, it is worth noting, are not alone in employing paramilitary forces to that end. Ethnic groups, tribes, political parties and even large and extended families can use them as well. Also worth noting is that these paramilitary vanguards can spawn competitors. So, for example, al-Qaeda gave rise to IS and the al-Nusra Front, which almost immediately became its rivals in securing the loyalty of mostly nonurban and premodern constituencies. These organizational communal loyalties, rather than those identified with purely formal organizations, like a parliament, often sanction the mores of everyday life, and to this extent, paramilitary associations evince what Trotsky called 'dual power'. Of course, this only further clouds the requisite legitimacy of the sovereign and the potential policies connected with defining the exception or the emergency situation. Like the religious institution, the tribe or the ethnic organization, the paramilitary organization is always representative of a private interest.

Modernizing military rulers may first find themselves in coalition with traditionalists opposing (or supporting) democracy or even mass movements opposing (or supporting) traditionalism. It is also possible that secular democrats and religious traditionalists will join together in opposing the military or, as in Egypt following the fall of the hated Mubarak regime, that the military will make a bid for sovereignty against both. Especially in the aftermath of the Arab Spring, traditional ideological alignments often broke down, resulting less in compromise than in confusion. Institutional preconditions are still lacking that might enable new democratic constituencies to make good on their ideals while traditionalists remain sceptical about the implications of modern politics. It is becoming ever more difficult for the sovereign state to reconcile the interests of forces looking forward to a democratic future as against backwards to an enchanted past. Even the seemingly most homogeneous society has been rent apart by conflicting *institutional* interests.

The state has rarely provided a source of identity, and it has proven incapable of contesting the traditional feelings of belonging offered by the tribe, ethnicity or religion. Instability is thereby built into even the most authoritarian states of the Middle East. Or, to put it another way, the state has been sovereign only in alienated form. Whether that will remain the case is an open question whose answer will determine the viability of the liberal rule of law.

SOVEREIGNTY BY PROXY

Sovereignty may be an artificial construct, but it has real impact. And it cannot simply be implemented or exercised at will. There are preconditions for its imposition, and in the first instance, external states should not labour under the misapprehension that they can simply bypass its indigenous organic formation. Experiences of imperialism left many still unhealed wounds. It renders suspect the best intentions of the 'great powers', which today means those who sit on the UN Security Council, and leads the Middle East and citizens of the Global South to identify intervening external forces less with human rights and national construction or reconstruction than with contractors and mercenaries hired by multinational corporations. There is simply no reason to assume that once-colonized peoples will be happy about foreign soldiers on their soil, entering their homes, desecrating their mosques, ruining their economy and killing their friends. Little wonder that while the intervening power may strengthen its domestic ally in the short-run battle for sovereignty, a legitimacy deficit for the state will usually arise over the long haul. Intervention tends to weaken sovereignty almost by definition. Organizations accepting foreign support are usually condemned as puppets or traitors by their domestic enemies. Hospitals, housing, food and other forms of humanitarian aid by Western nations would go a long way towards building trust, goodwill and bridges. Nevertheless, self-styled realists are sceptical of 'soft' power, though the use of 'hard' power has rarely enabled the intervening nation to impose a legitimate sovereign.

Tough realists engaged in foreign affairs like to identify with the tough-minded Hobbes. They draw from his work the implication that since the war-like state of nature exists where there is no sovereign (such as the international arena), foreign intervention is necessary and ethical constraints on political action are superfluous. As important as they see the sovereign where it does not exist, just as unimportant do they consider the sovereign where it does exist. For all the tough talk, however, these realists ignore Hobbes's *most basic lesson*, namely, that only chaos and bloodshed can come from dislodging a sovereign without having a legitimate substitute waiting in the wings. That has certainly been the story of American involvement in Afghanistan, Iraq, Syria and Libya. The same strategy and the same cavalier attitude towards sovereignty were employed even though the foreign policy establishment expected that outcomes would differ. Indeed, Albert Einstein once likened this attitude with insanity.

Identifying its moral disdain for the Taliban, which bred assumptions concerning its lack of legitimacy as sovereign in Afghanistan, the United States fought against the Islamic fundamentalist regime while bolstering the utterly corrupt 'presidency' of Hamid Karzai, whose family remains a key player in the opium trade, and thereby wound up fighting the civil war that its puppet was supposed to fight. The United States was thereby left with the choice between negotiating in the name of Karzai with an unacceptable victorious partner, withdrawing and leaving the situation worse than before or patrolling Afghanistan (shouldering the costs in lives and materiel) endlessly without an exit strategy. With Iraq, similar assumptions about Saddam Hussein prevailed among American policymakers, while Ahmed Chalabi (an Iraqi businessman in exile) convinced influential friends in the Bush administration that the Iraqi people supported him and that they would welcome American troops with open arms were an invasion undertaken. Unfortunately, when elections were held, Chalabi received about 2 percent of the vote, while the invading army was not exactly greeted with exclamations of joy. When a puppet regime dominated by Shia was finally installed following the fall of Saddam, its ensuing lack of legitimacy left Iraq without sovereignty and the American military under attack not only by protesting Sunni paramilitary organizations opposed to the existing Iraqi regime but also by disgusted Shia militia. In Libya, meanwhile, the overthrow of Muammar Gaddafi led to a disintegration of sovereignty, brutal conflict between tribes and lingering resentment against the United States that exploded in the assault on its embassy by al-Qaeda–affiliated elements. The dissolution of sovereignty in any number of Middle Eastern states helps explain why Islamic extremist groups with a traditional theocratic outlook and seeking a caliphate alternative to the nation-state should have so dramatically capitalized on these conflicts.

External attempts to introduce a new sovereign have all intensified the chaos that they had intended to eliminate. Syria offers perhaps the most complicated case in point. Restoring sovereignty is an unlikely outcome even if the United States is successful in unifying the opposition to President Bashar al-Assad's regime, which is highly unlikely, and focuses solely on a military alliance against ISIS with Saudi Arabia or Iran. Either way, the United States would become even more closely identified with the intensely hated Saudi regime or with Assad (and his Shia supporters in Iraq and Iran), whose sovereignty is steadily eroding even in his own rump state, let alone among the Sunni opposition. Further engagement would leave the United States caught between Shia, Sunni and Islamic extremist states and movements. Internecine squabbling has fractured the anti-Assad rebels, who are lacking a nationally recognized leadership, are falling under the sway of Islamic extremists in the al-Nusra Front and are unclear about the type of regime that would prove a substitute for the dictatorship of Assad. Thousands of foreign fighters from throughout the region have also joined the war. The Syrian conflict has already destabilized Lebanon and divided the Islamic world. Hezbollah and Iran support the government of President Assad, which retains a Shia and Alawite base, while Saudi Arabia and Qatar have already spent more than $3 billion to advance Sunni interests. Caught between rival forces in a civil war, which has now cost more than 250,000 lives, neither the Syrian opposition nor its establishment has a national constituency. With its sovereignty rapidly devolving and the United States targeted in different ways by all parties to the conflict, ISIS and al-Qaeda will remain players. Even if 'vanquished' they can go underground, reassemble and then reappear.

Intervention has become what David Bromwich called a 'rationalized addiction' for the United States. Justifications for intruding upon the sovereignty of other states are usually based on preventing chaos, protecting human rights or serving the national interest. But they are hollow. American intervention in Afghanistan and then Iraq resulted in thousands of civilians killed, nearly 1.5 million wounded and roughly double that number in exiles, wrecked economies, unimaginable environmental devastation and ongoing civil strife. That all of this somehow furthers human rights (even in the long run) is an easy claim to make when others pay the price. The American-supported overthrow of Gaddafi facilitated the flow of arms and troops across its border as well as a new wave of African immigration. It is also difficult to argue that the American national interest has been served when roughly 7,000 American soldiers have been killed, 50,000 wounded and trillions of dollars spent for seemingly no purpose. Use of torture, mercenaries and rendition have also undermined the moral standing of the United States and, by subverting the sovereignty of other nations, generated feelings and memories of national humiliation that will take a very long time to disappear.

SUBTERRANEAN SOVEREIGNS

Sovereignty has become more of an ideal than a reality in the Middle East. Western academics who suggest that it is an outworn concept or that the emergency situation is simply the norm ignore the exceptional gravity of the current crisis. Such a stance relativizes the idea of crisis and, in the process, undermines the attempt to confront its reality. Millions of refugees have been created since the invasion of Iraq—and their concern is for the kind of stability and security associated with the obligations of a sovereign. Whether the sovereign is ultimately a resurrected nation-state or a transnational organization, such as the European Union or the Arab League, is a secondary matter.

Their longing for the benefits of sovereignty in general and for democratic sovereignty in particular is what counts. Attempts to translate desires of this sort into appropriate political institutions will undoubtedly define the subterranean history of the region in the decades following 9/11.

Making sense of this history in the West initially calls for looking in the mirror. It was not the religious hatred between Sunni and Shia that sparked the bloody political conflicts plaguing the Middle East as the twenty-first century unfolds; it was rather the other way around. These two branches of Islam, along with various religious and ethnic minorities, had lived more or less peacefully for generations in any number of states. That changed dramatically in the aftermath of the Iran–Iraq War (1980–1988), which resulted in the death of more than 1 million people, and the later invasion of Iraq by the United States in 2003 that completely reshaped the region. A chain reaction of events eroded sovereignty in Afghanistan, Iraq, Lebanon, Libya, Syria and Yemen well before the Arab Spring of 2011. Millions more were killed, wounded or driven into exile; environmental damage was unimaginable; and hatred of the West blended with a dramatic sovereignty deficit in the region that produced offshoots of al-Qaeda and new rivals, such as the al-Nusra Front and IS. What first appeared as national conflicts evincing geopolitical ambitions soon turned into transnational forms of civil war fuelled by absolutist religious as well as ethnic and tribal claims on the loyalty of citizens in the region. Paramilitary organizations flourished that, in turn, created incentives for intervention and the extension of military support. National wars became transnational wars between external proxies with regional clients. Conspiracies and collective phobias multiplied as national sovereignty degenerated in favour of ethnic and tribal loyalties and the emergence of religious extremism with radical political ambitions.

The Arab Spring was the counterpoint to all of this. National rebellions became linked with one another through a transnational chain reaction that expressed cosmopolitan sentiments. This was the case even with respect to the seemingly entrenched Occidental–Oriental divide. What Samuel Huntington (1993) and Bernard Lewis (1990) termed the 'clash of civilizations', essentially implying that the Middle East was bereft of democratic aspirations, now appeared as what it always was—little more than an ideological prop for bigotry. The Arab Spring highlighted what had been repressed beliefs in the political ideals usually associated with Western Enlightenment: the liberal rule of law, civil liberties, republicanism and the accountability of institutions to the public. Rebels in one country learned from those in another through a form of democratic pedagogy. The 'Green Revolt' in Iran, which targeted the religious authoritarianism instituted by Khomeini's Islamic revolution of 1979, spread to Lebanon in 2005 and then to Tunisia, Syria, Egypt, Yemen and Libya before circling back to Lebanon and the 'You Stink' revolts of 2015. In short, what had long been a subterranean understanding of *popular sovereignty* burst into the open.

Grounded in the cities, the Arab Spring was supported primarily by intellectuals, young people without job prospects, unemployed technocrats, nascent bourgeois and workers. In short, the mass base for the Arab Spring was the cluster of urban classes and strata whose identities and material hopes entangled with globalization and modernity. Counterrevolutionaries correctly intuited that the rebels with their liberal notions of sovereignty had little use for the traditional preeminence accorded to the military and the rigid customs and beliefs of agrarian society and village life. Little wonder that the military and the mosque mistrusted the Arab Spring. Military dictators like Assad, Saddam and Gaddafi may have viewed themselves as secular modernizers and critics of Islam (at least until their hold on power began to tremble), but they never advocated liberal political principles. As for Islam, moreover, it had a certain radical character. It confronted the religious beliefs of Western imperialists, and just as with the Catholic Church in Eastern Europe under the communists, Islam often defended rebellion and served as a refuge even for secular rebels. In most of the Middle East, however, Islamic muftis were employees of the state. Appointed and with their fatwas approved by dictators, their interests often contradicted the state even as their words gave religious energy to secular institutions and agendas. The Arab Spring threatened both the military and the mosque, and thus, unsurprisingly, the enemy of the enemy often became a friend—at least as long as circumstances dictated.

New liberal republics in economically disadvantaged circumstances had to navigate a swirl of conflicting economic interests and illiberal institutional claims. Soon enough, storms were darkening the Arab Spring. Revolutions in Tunisia, Jordan, Egypt and elsewhere fell into disarray as activists attempted to translate democratic ideals into institutional reality. Established monarchies trembled in Bahrain and even Saudi Arabia—and for good reason: their authoritarian state structures were marked by arbitrary exercises of power, labyrinthine forms of hierarchy, corruption and rank cronyism. Lack of civil liberties, fairness, transparency and institutional accountability were—along with lack of economic opportunity— perhaps the primary sources of revolt for partisans of the Arab Spring. They all crystallized in the idea of a liberal republic. But that goal was sometimes implicit and other times explicit. Most movements vacillated between reform and revolution. Their inability to decide, determine the exception or make good on the emergency situation was connected with their inability to act as sovereign. Indeed, the mirror reflection of such vacillation by partisans of the Arab Spring has plagued American foreign policy in the Middle East, namely, 'mission creep'. Here too an inability to recognize the demands of sovereignty has been interconnected with an inability to decide whether the intervention is meant to bolster a particular domestic actor, change the regime or engage in 'nation building'.

The Arab Spring was marked by spontaneous revolts, lack of charismatic leaders, youthful exuberance and disdain for more traditional forms of organizational discipline and political focus. The Green Rebels in Iran could not decide whether they were opposing electoral corruption, calling for a new electoral arrangement, seeking to introduce regime change or rejecting the entire legacy of the Islamic revolution of 1979. Its leaders were culled mostly from the establishmentarian reformists, and there was little talk of alternative institutions. The situation was similar elsewhere. Speaking truth to power proved insufficient. The Arab Spring floundered in its inability to deal with internal weakness and conflicts, disorganization and sectarianism. Its participants were what Machiavelli would have termed 'unarmed prophets', and in the long run, its movements did not have a chance. All came under attack and, to a greater or lesser extent, suffered defeat. But the current despair also obscures the successes: the legitimation of parliament, the pressure exerted on regimes like Jordan and Tunisia, the new popularity of new social movements and—perhaps most important—the ideological force of human rights. The Arab Spring overthrew dictators, and its legacy still hovers over those authoritarian regimes that remain. Indeed, the liberal values and demands animating these subterranean sovereigns will undoubtedly continue to fester: they continue to offer the only meaningful alternative to religious intolerance, authoritarian politics, and an atavistic cultural vision that is currently either in power or threatening to seize it in so much of our world.

Overestimation of the modern nation-state as the point of reference made it more difficult to counter pressing transnational and often premodern threats. Little wonder, then, that combating al-Qaeda and its offshoots has been undertaken in state-centric terms. Bush's misguided invasion and occupation of Iraq to Obama's funding of inchoate rival anti-Assad forces in the beleaguered Syrian Civil War created the preconditions for IS's rise. Lacking in each instance was an appreciation for the role that sovereignty plays in an increasingly complex globalizing world. Reinterpreting sovereignty from a standpoint that is less anachronistic and Eurocentric is part of the political challenge facing the West. It will, it is hoped, provide the kind of analysis that will allow peace to be rethought beyond today's shallow conceptions of liberal intervention (see Shani, in this volume, and Richmond, in volume) as an end unto itself when facing sovereign crises.

BIBLIOGRAPHY

Agamben, Giorgio. 2005. *State of Exception*. Translated by Kevin Attell. Chicago: University of Chicago Press.

Hobbes, Thomas. 1968. *Leviathan*. Edited by C. B. MacPherson. New York: Pelican.

Huntington, Samuel P. 1993. 'The Clash of Civilizations?' *Foreign Affairs* 72, no. 3 (Summer): 22–49.

Lewis, Bernard. 1990. 'The Roots of Muslim Rage'. *The Atlantic Monthly* (September).

Schmitt, Carl. [1934] 2006. *Political Theology: Four Chapters on the Concept of Sovereignty*. Translated by George Schwab. Chicago: University of Chicago Press.

Chapter Three

Towards a Peace with Global Justice

Oliver Richmond

> Prefer what is positive and multiple, difference over uniformity, flows over unities, mobile arrangements over systems. Believe what is productive is not sedentary but nomadic.
>
> —Foucault, cited in Dean and Villadsen (2016, 92)

Drawing on critical, feminist, poststructural, and postcolonial thinking in international relations (IR) as well as on critical movements in other disciplines and, in particular, a combination of the local and spatial 'turns' (Ferguson and Gupta 2002, 981; Mac Ginty and Richmond 2013; Tickner 1992), we now know a lot more about an emancipatory peace. This is in terms of the many both major and minor war settlements since Westphalia and, in particular, since 1989 but also in terms of structural violence and inequality after the Cold War (Boulding 1978, 2000). The shift to the subaltern perspective as a mode of critique of hegemony and the locality of scalar and temporal networks underline crucial but normally ignored political claims and agency, which, as Shani notes in his chapter in this volume, are effectively 'post-Western'.

A number of gaps have thus emerged, significantly relating to global justice issues: to power relations, rights and equality and identity across time and space, but the solutions that were devised (according to models of positive, liberal and neoliberal forms of peace and order) have created new dynamics of violence. Critical solutions from the recent past to war and violence themselves have proven to have limitations in dealing with the new. Dialogue between different versions of order and their constituencies, past, present and future, are in danger of breaking down due to the loss of authority of democracy and rights as well as the exposure of the capitalist global governance model under the weight of questions about distributive justice (Sassen 2008).

It is no accident that in recent times, mainstream IR theory is becoming interested in practice and appears to be shifting, superficially at least, towards the critical and Foucauldian engagements with the everyday and micropolitics (drawing on developments in other disciplines and perhaps 30 years later than those other disciplines) (Bueger and Gadinger 2015; Pouliot 2013). This is a domestication of previously radical and critical, feminist or poststructural contributions, including the still-prevalent Foucauldian approach to critical IR (Selby 2007). It has tended to moderate their radical implications. Theories that have resisted critical influences or failed to engage with interdisciplinary debates continue to refute the implications of this accumulation of peace knowledge, which partly explains the emerging middle ground of constructivism in its critical and more mainstream guises which has succeeded though co-opting critical literatures. Often this position is deemed preferable to a closer engagement with Marx or with the implications of historical materialism or core–periphery thinking (Tickner 2013).

Through practices, the everyday—not in the sense suggested by de Certeau (1984) but instead a banal and resilient sense (Chandler 2013)—and micropolitics (Solomon and Steele 2016) have entered the mainstream discourse of IR. However, they rarely engage with the evolution of peace or rights in modern IR beyond the liberal canon. This is a common feminist, post- (and anti)colonial and environmentalist critique (Sjoberg 2009) of such quasi-critical work (Paris 2010), which often posits that the state and international architecture is conceptually and materially fixed by historic patterns of political, military, economic or bureaucratic forms of power. Instead, they point to resilience and the engine of subaltern agency by way of facilitating or supplanting debates about rights and justice. Often government is avoided in any material sense (Chandler 2015), which is reflected in how peace building and state building focus on rights and security rather than an everyday ethics of peace (Richmond 2011a, 2011b). This has stripped out the essence of peace, echoing neocolonial counterinsurgency thinking (Mitchell 2002) as well as undermining the legitimate authority of the emerging interventionary/international system and its broad range of architecture. These have been designed to both extend rights and maintain order (though mainly in the interests of the Global North) (Darby 2000; Hobson 2007). Its contradictions are rife, not least between economic and social rights, and capital or environmental sustainability as well as across temporal and distributive dimensions of justice (Richmond 2018). Most outcomes of peace building and peace settlements around the world since 1990 veer between authoritarianism and external intervention. One could draw a historical analogy here connecting the emergence and marginalization of the Non-Aligned Movement with the failed revolutions of the Arab Spring—a hollow victory for those who refused to engage with the Non-Aligned Movement over the past 60 years (Devetak, Dunne, and Nurhayati 2016; Mishra 2012).

By contrast, revisiting the critical legacy of liberal progressivism and Marxist thought, as well as including feminist, postcolonial, poststructural and environmental thought, aimed at the limitations of the colonial, postwar and post–Cold War settlements, we should be able to begin to build a picture of the requirements for peace in the twenty-first century. This needs to incorporate the political, social and economic organization fit for the twenty-first century at local, state, regional and international levels as well as being relevant to the increasingly transnational and transscalar, mobile and networked nature of IR (i.e., an emerging framework of digital IR) (Taylor 2016). It draws a lineage from revolutionary, human rights, mobilization narratives, connecting to human security, global civil society, democratization, peace building, welfarist and development and other frameworks (Arendt 1951). Peace formation is as significant as state formation or the strengthening of the international architecture and should shape both the state and the international (Richmond 2016). Are the older elements of peace—a stable and territorially sovereign state, an international conference system and international institutions, collective security, minimalist goals of self-defence and the prevention of aggression and rights of varying sorts—fit for the purpose of providing the foundations for peace treaties and peaceful polities today?

NEW CRITICAL CURRENTS

The answer is partially negative. Rights and material claims have expanded beyond the potential of the modern state and the related international architecture, especially in view of the circulation of agency, materiel, capital and technology in the modern world. Rights claims lead to further, upwards-cascading rights claims, and top-down representative frameworks of legitimate authority must respond institutionally, legally and materially. This is also true of the shift from a neoliberal understanding of a null relationship between politics and the physical environment (with implications for both war and peace) towards critical Anthropocenic engagements (Lövbrand et al. 2015). One hopes that this critical linkage in the scientific literature, which is increasingly being shifted into international law, will not suffer the same fate as previous UN and international conventions covering matters from decolonization, indigenous rights and independence struggles to the global economic order, which risk becoming dead letters if renewed nationalism ever overtakes multilateralism.

All of this means that the underlying normative framework for peace is now much more complicated, no longer legitimately based upon a single version of a citizen, single model of state, scaled up to a liberal international architecture. Intervention (broadly defined as emanating from the full scope of the current international architecture), government and governance associated with peace and order need to be significantly rethought. What makes this imminent are the escalating rights claims relating to peace formation's dynamics, cascading upwards—rather than downwards as envisioned by Western liberal and constructivist theorists (Finnemore and Sikkink 1998)—with an increasingly material nature and connected with long-standing issues of historical and distributive injustice, such as in the Middle East, the states of the MENA region, and many others, often in the Global South. Subaltern rights claims inevitably cascade upwards, testing the legitimacy of existing structures and frameworks. An 'interventionary order' has emerged to respond to such tests on the legitimacy of international order, but it has so far failed to engage with the expanded rights claims that are now connected with peace in critical and popular debates. Instead, it still often prefers the liberal grounds of the 1990s despite their late postcolonial and Eurocentric leanings (Richmond 2016).

As a consequence of peace formation and of new technological possibilities, new and more mobile, transnationally and transversally networked scalar forms of political agency and rights claims are emerging to challenge the older notions of territorial states, fixed architecture and static citizenship grounded in natural rights, human rights and various forms of law (Scholte 2005). Mobility across networks reflects new spatial and scalar possibilities despite neoliberal governmentality appearing to limit the possibility of expanded rights and their materialization in more concrete forms (Gupta and Ferguson 1992, 8).

BLOCKAGES, CHECKS AND BALANCES

IR theory generally has worked with nineteenth- and twentieth-century liberal conceptions of peace, order and rights, determined mainly by power or structure and a fixity in the relationship between states, institutions and citizens. This both provides rights and security but may also act as a blockage. It presents an ontological narrowness of praxis, which limits peace and order to territorialism (the nation-state), centralized authority (hegemony) and a hierarchy of states arranged through this framework. The overlay of liberal international peace architecture, as in the United Nations, is a modest historical checking-and-balancing framework, also carrying forward some progressive ideals drawn from historic civil society campaigns. As other chapters in this volume attest, there are many more dimensions of peace to consider (see the introduction) which stem directly from a combination of normative, interdisciplinary and multidimensional thinking. However, critical and interdisciplinary contributions have pushed much further, first identifying gaps and then moving into new normative and conceptual terrains, particularly during the course of the past 25 years. These have built upon existing layers, which are often in tension. We know from orthodox forms of realism rooted in the nineteenth century that military security and law and order are required (Morgenthau 1975). From the twentieth century's evidence and that of the post–Cold War era, we know that a state and institutions, along with law, rights and public services, are necessary, normally in some varied configuration of liberalism (Doyle 1983a, 1983b). From Marxist approaches, we know that material equality and global solidarity are strong demands (Wallerstein 1974). From feminism, poststructuralism and postcolonialism, we know that broader forms of equality, empathy for everyday conditions, historical justice and sustainable development are needed (Fanon 1967; George 1994; Said 1978; Sylvester 2002). Later variants of political liberalism gave us new understandings about the nature of the state and society, the relationship between inequality and rights and the normative and institutional expansion of the 'international community' (Frost 1994).

As cosmopolitan thinking developed with the contributions of the likes of Held, Habermas, Giddens and many others (Beck 2006), balancing these approaches into a new universal framework of understanding and international order became imperative. This tried to balance what we know about a recognition of identity and materiality, along with complex constitutional and regional architectures, all lessons of the twentieth century and more recently. It posited that a compromise and a global agreement on norms and international organization is also necessary to approximate global justice. But reactions, misapplications and abuses of this system of thinking, especially in view of postcolonial perspectives, raised the problem of socially legitimate resistance. Finally, we learned that practices, culture, micropolitics, local agency and the everyday are very important—and often in unexpected ways. We also now understand the limitations of political liberalism, liberal internationalism and liberal institutionalism and of neoliberal approaches to capital and development, territorialism, the problem of the arms economy and the limits of technology in achieving peace or order in the light of global justice claims, which themselves emanate from subaltern positionalities.

FROM BLOCKAGES TO CRITICAL
AGENCY AND PEACE FORMATION

Over the period since the end of World War II and since the end of the Cold War, it has become apparent, however, that the academy tends to take either a power-oriented or a liberal-oriented perspective of IR and the production of order, replicated by the character of international policy (without much clarity on which leads to which). This line repeats itself through the evolution of 'new' theory, leading to blockages: the rise of critique, the return of the 'ancien regime', the beheading of the king and the return of critique and its co-optation into revised forms of hegemony and so on. However, the rise of transnational epistemological networks engaged with questions of peace and order, past and present, means, given the ease of access to detailed information about conflict, perhaps for the first time, that subaltern and conflict-affected citizens are unlikely to reflect on scholars', policymakers' or the international community's performance very positively. This leaves them little option but to exercise agency in the greyer areas of IR (i.e., outside of the liberal and balance-of-power order and even beyond the transnational system which has more recently emerged, as Foucault and before him Marx foresaw) (Goulder 2015, 16).[1] This is a direct challenge to the political theory of the state and its centrality to order, good or bad, as well as to liberal political theory's interest in a liberal international order, rights and justice and related interventionary praxis (as can be seen with the many problems which have faced the doctrine of 'Responsibility to Protect'). Where the state, the global economy and the liberal international order have failed to deal with conflict or expand rights, conflict-affected citizens must look to other tactics while exploiting the space which liberal order provides. They are bringing into being a new world as a consequence, one which modern liberal subjects also recognize but also often reject because of its otherness (Chandler and Richmond 2015).

Peace formation reflects these dynamics, complete with opportunities for expanded rights claims and limitations in confronting entrenched power from a subaltern positionality. It stems from local-scale agency, networks and forms of mobilization for legitimate and progressive forms of peace. It makes use of everyday, localized understandings of positionality vis-à-vis politics, justice and reconciliation and is scaled up—at least theoretically—towards the state and international order (Richmond 2016) through networks, scale jumping and a broader engagement with digital developments. It often draws upon liberal international norms but makes further claims upon governance. It is central to generating legitimate authority within the state and to embed a sustainable level of peace, but the growth of political entanglement and relationality indicate that a more complex form of polity (and therefore order and peace) is now emerging (Qin 2016). Its varied dynamics are hinted at in formal peace-building or peace processes, from Bosnia, Kosovo, Cyprus and Colombia to various revolts against unjust authority, like the recent ones in the MENA region (Hinnebusch 2015, 335–57).

A MOBILE PEACE: MOBILITY, AGENCY, HYBRIDITY AND ARBITRAGE

Thus, it is clear that the entwined, relational, networked and often agonistic, contradictory mobility of people, knowledge, capital and arms is now very important. On the other hand, the state and international architectures are incredibly static and welded to territory and status to the point of moribundity. By contrast, everyday agency is clever, hidden, committed and ingenious (Scott 2009). Increasingly, it is transnational, transscalar and transversal. It is often resistance based, perhaps revolutionary, but normally more subtle and disguised for reasons of safety and effectiveness, as Scott has famously argued. It cannot defeat direct or structural forms of power, but it has an impact on legitimate and effective governance as well as being able to produce parallel state and international systems (as, say, in Kosovo, with the parallel state and regional diaspora or the so-called fourth United Nations) (Weiss, Carayannis, and Jolly 2009). Perhaps it is becoming true to say that if an emancipatory peace is to overcome the contradictions caused in the liberal international system by highly mobile capital and arms, then everyday agency must also be mobile, networked and agile. Peace formation, meaning peaceful, political self-making, which is never complete and always constrained by structure, emerges from related peace formation actors rather than state formation (which represents power sharing over military, territorial and economic resources at best) (Richmond 2016). Multilateralism can rarely reach these everyday agencies consensually, though they are relational and networked, often informally and subtly: a new system of multiverticalism is required to connect multilateralism to informal, transscalar peace formation actors and networks. These agencies need to help iron out three dimensions of conflict and inequality—historical, economic and social—leading to historical and distributive, global forms of justice. This potential could perhaps be seen in UNHCR and UNICEF's 'Blue Dot Hub' system, which supported people fleeing the Syrian war across Europe and was designed to engage with questions of need and rights under mobile as opposed to state-centric circumstances (UNHCR and UNICEF 2016).[2]

The capacity of everyday agency also helps us understand the limits of the current state and international architecture and theories which are torn between mobility and fluidity along with the networked relationality of any social order, as most critical theories claim, or the fixity of an institutional and territorial order or international system. Reconciling order—inequalities relating to history, identity, materiality, gender and mobility—is a major task, which we can actually assume to shape the essence of IR in orthodox theory (Tickner 1992). Forget interests, forget balancing between states, forget the mutual constitution of identity and institutions (Bleiker 1997), meaning that the foundations of the current international order are now an obstacle to peace. Even more crucially, everyday agency and peace formation also help us understand the limitations of social actors in dealing with war and conflict through the strategies and tactics they have available to them. It helps us understand the path dependencies, interests, hierarchies and inertias in current systems and discourse of peace and development and points towards ways forward. The limits of peace formation and its local-to-global networks, combined with the limits of state and international peace architecture, provide a map for future development.

Peace settlements, responses to structural violence, inequality, poverty and environmental degradation operate in a core–periphery environment of IR and impose limits. These limits—the failure of the state to domesticate its power, the failure of the international community to prevent or stop wars (as in Syria) and the limits of everyday agency in the face of state and international power—often mean that the most emancipatory step that an individual can take is to migrate away from violence, in the absence of state or international assistance. Yet the power of states and warlords is often based upon the control of populations and territory. To regain legitimacy and authority, international architecture has to respond to this dynamic of mobility, which is a 'right' in some aspects of international and domestic law (asylum seekers, refugees, and so on). This has now been the case since at least the nineteenth century. The liberal state and the liberal international architecture, along with nonliberal states, are often obstacles to this sort of agential, mobile and networked, informed and technologically enabled, emancipatory form of 'peace' through political-geographic arbitrage. The international system defends structure and privileges, and its legitimacy has been weakened as a result. After the warlords, the dictators and the nationalists, the modernizers, the conservative state and twentieth-century architecture (including regional organizations such as the European Union to some extent) now ultimately block such mobility even where it is urgently needed (as today in Syria). Globalization, rights and democracy require mobility; otherwise, they degrade into domination, trusteeship types of authority, and Northern-centrism or Eurocentrism.

Thus, contemporary peace cannot be found in land, blood or glory or in fixed settlements and inflexible institutions in the twenty-first century, which have all created their own violence or inertia. Critical theoretical contributions have pointed us in the direction of identity, resource distribution, gender and historical power relations and have generally agreed on the fluidity, networked and mobile nature of critical agency in dealing with such matters (Richmond 2011). Capturing the essence of such critical intent across different methodologies and epistemologies (from quantitative and qualitative,

North and South) has remained theoretically difficult (though possible, as Shani's chapter in this volume illustrates). As with institutional development, intellectual development confronts the difficult task of reconciling the irreconcilable, hence the very awkward nature of constructivism's relationship with the state, power, identity and expanded rights claims; poststructuralism's rejection of any political project, fixed claims or unified system; and cosmopolitanism's attempt to shoehorn difference into global solidarity in an enormously unequal, postcolonial world.

CONCLUSION

Peace may well be emerging, ironically, through the agential and critical and subaltern subject, armed with twenty-first-century technology, information and potential, following the global political economy towards the world's centres of relative stability and prosperity and away from violence or structural violence. The peace of Westphalia, the UN peace and even the liberal peace now look as antiquated and anachronistic layers of the international peace architecture and even an obstacle to peace networks and positionality arbitrage. Mobility across multiscalar networks is perhaps emerging as a new right claimed by modern subalterns as they build their claims for expanded rights. Global inequality and untreated direct and structural violence causes a significant 'peace arbitrage' within IR, where the failure of local politics and economics, the state or the regional and international organization leads not to voice but to exit. The UN Human Development Index (along with the Gini Index, the Failed States Index, the Peace Index and Freedom House's rankings and others), which ranks states according to their development, rights and stability, provides an excellent road map for subjects claiming these new rights according to their new capacities. The dexterity of local agency has made mobility through global networks— formal, informal and shadow connections—the new emancipation and the new social justice. It is disaggregated, sometimes divisive and individualistic, not to mention of ambiguous relational and ethical quality, lacking the firmament of institutional creations like the state and international architecture, but also offering the possibility of new rights claims and progress.

It points to how individuals are bringing a new and hybrid 'international' into sight: they may seek their own peace, emancipation and social justice through migration, trading failed states for shadowland journeys, in order to reestablish themselves in a better environment, even if they sacrifice possessions, status, identity and rank along the way. The 'stable' grounds of the states-system and international architecture have become inadequate, though international citizenship, a global commons and 'community of the governed' have become clearer (Foucault, cited in Goulder 2015). Clusters of localized interaction, which transcend territoriality, now bypass the formal states-system and international architecture, where they are deemed to have materially and normatively failed (Gupta and Ferguson 1992, 8). Hybridity, temporality and mobility do not necessary belong anyway and are not fixed to institutions, norms, law or standards. Universal rights are also not necessarily the goal, though there is a strong sense that peace and order are based upon the right to claim rights as part of an ongoing self- and institutional formation. They relate peace to critical agency as much as to existing institutions, law or expert knowledge. This should be no surprise, as it is a dynamic that has existed in every phase of international order throughout history. However, 'governmentalities'—geopolitical, economic, bureaucratic, legal, and digital, amongst others—have always arisen, appended to direct and structural forms of power, to temper emancipatory claims.[3]

Critical agency and peace formation is a consequence of the material inequality that currently undermines the legal equality of states, differences in national rights frameworks, the failure to address historical and distributive matters of justice (a painful example being the Palestinians and the failure of the Middle East Peace Process), failure to reform the UN system and the unsuitability of the modern states system in addressing the contemporary dynamics of IR and its problems in a progressive, equitable and fair manner. In the twenty-first century, relative emancipation and justice for the individual is found through mobility, relationality and networking by any plausible means over the bare life of remaining in geopolitical and territorial situ and remaining subject to war, multiple forms of violence, underdevelopment and failed development, peace building and state building. This is only a limited indictment of the liberal international order designed to bring peace and prosperity, the capacity of politicians and policymakers to respond to modernity and the ethics of our relations with others. Everyday mobility, networked and relational peace, contributes empathetically to a wider emancipation. This is peace formation writ large and points to the need for significant rethinking in IR and to the importance of international reform.

A grander interrogation of peace than has historically been possible now points in the direction that relates peace building, a peace agreement or document and any related practice not merely to the state or a form of liberal constitution, to basic rights or to a regional and international organization but rather to global forms of justice. This has postcolonial, historical and environmental as well as political, social and economic dimensions. This would involve relinquishing the territorialized system of state and international architecture and its memorialization across countless forms and its translation into a new peace architecture with a far more complex understanding of the actual and current dynamics of conflict—and suitable responses. Nevertheless, a dilemma would arise in the interaction of such translation and a dialogue laden with historical and institutional baggage to achieve it: how to mediate between different layers of historical conflict and their settlements (e.g., the nineteenth-century realist balance of power, postwar liberal interventionism and the UN system, recent neoliberal global governance and contemporary digital IR), keeping their peacemaking forms intact while also bringing in the new. If this problem is not addressed, the twenty-first-century layer of peace—perhaps increasingly operating in a digital framework (Taylor 2015)—will emerge as a form of governmentality and hence as a recolonization rather than an expansion of rights in a postcolonial epistemic context: meaning peace with or without global justice.

NOTES

1. Here I am drawing on Ben Golder, who is writing about Judith Butler's interpretation of Foucault (Golder 2015, 72).
2. Thanks to a confidential source at UNICEF for this example (New York, 2015).
3. See, for example, the experience of the G77 and NEIO in the 1960s and 1970 (Devetak et al. 2016).

REFERENCES

Arendt, Hannah. 1951. *The Origins of Totalitarianism*. New York: Harcourt Brace.
Beck, Ulrich. 2006. *The Cosmopolitan Vision*. Cambridge: Polity Press.
Bleiker, Roland. 1997. 'Forget IR Theory'. *Alternatives: Global, Local, Political* 22, no. 1: 57–85.
Boulding, E. 2000. *Cultures of Peace: The Hidden Side of History*. Syracuse, NY: Syracuse University Press.
Boulding, Kenneth. 1978. 'Future Directions in Conflict and Peace Studies'. *Journal of Conflict Resolution* 22, no. 2: 342–54.
Bueger, C., and F. Gadinger. 2015. 'The Play of International Practice'. *International Studies Quarterly* 59, no. 3: 449–60.
Chandler, David. 2013. 'Resilience Ethics: Responsibility and the Globally Embedded Subject'. *Ethics and Global Politics* 6, no. 3: 175–94.
———. 2015. *Resilience, the Governing of Complexity*. London: Routledge.
Chandler, David, and Oliver Richmond. 2015. 'Contesting Postliberalism: Governmentality or Emancipation?' *Journal of International Relations and Development* 18, no. 1: 1–24.

Darby, Philip. 2000. 'Postcolonialism'. In *At the Edge of International Relations: Postcolonialism, Gender and Dependency*, edited by Philip Darby, 12–32. London: Continuum.

de Certeau, Michel. 1984. *The Practice of Everyday Life*. Berkeley: University of California Press.

Dean, Mitchell, and K. Villadsen. 2016. *State Phobia and Civil Society: The Political Legacy of Michel Foucault*. Stanford, CA: Stanford University Press.

Devetak, Richard, Tim Dunne, and R. Nurhayati. 2016. 'Bandung 60 Years On: Revolt and Resilience in International Society'. *Australian Journal of International Affairs* 70, no. 4: 358–73.

Doyle, Michael. 1983a. 'Kant, Liberal Legacies, and Foreign Affairs'. *Philosophy and Public Affairs* 12, no. 3: 205–35.

———. 'Kant, Liberal Legacies, and Foreign Affairs, Part 2'. *Philosophy and Public Affairs* 12, no. 4: 323–53.

Fanon, Frantz. 1967. *Black Skin, White Masks*. New York: Grove Press.

Ferguson, James, and Akhil Gupta. 2002. 'Spatialising States: An Ethnography of Neoliberal Governmentality'. *American Ethnologist* 29, no. 4: 981–1002.

Finnemore, Martha, and Kathryn Sikkink. 1998. 'International Norm Dynamics and Political Change.' *International Organization* 52, no. 4 (Autumn): 887–917.

Frost, Mervin. 1994. 'The Role of Normative Theory in IR'. *Millennium—Journal of International Studies* 23, no. 1: 109–18.

George, Jim. 1994. *Discourses of Global Politics: A Critical Introduction to International Relations*. Boulder, CO: Lynne Rienner Publishers.

Goulder, Ben. 2015. *Foucault and the Politics of Rights*. Stanford, CA: Stanford University Press.

Gupta, Akhil, and James Ferguson. 1992. 'Beyond "Culture": Space, Identity, and the Politics of Difference'. *Cultural Anthropology* 7, no. 1: 6–23.

Hinnebusch, Raymond. 2015. 'Globalization, Democratization, and the Arab Uprising: The International Factor in MENA's Failed Democratization'. *Democratization* 22, no. 2: 335–57.

Hobson, John. 2007. 'Is Critical Theory Always for the White West and for Western Imperialism? Beyond Westphalian towards a Post-Racist Critical IR'. *Review of International Studies* 33, no. 1: 91–116.

Lövbrand, Eva, et al., 2015. 'Who Speaks for the Future of Earth? How Critical Social Science Can Extend the Conversation on the Anthropocene'. *Global Environmental Change* 32: 211–18.

Mac Ginty, Roger, and Oliver Richmond. 2013. 'The Local Turn in Peace Building: A Critical Agenda for Peace'. *Third World Quarterly* 34, no. 5: 763–83.

Mishra, Pankaj. 2012. *From the Ruins of Empire*. London: Penguin.

Mitchell, Timothy. 2002. *Rule of Experts: Egypt, Techno-Politics, Modernity*. Berkeley: University of California Press.

Paris, Roland. 2010. 'Saving Liberal Peacebuilding'. *Review of International Studies* 36, no. 2: 337–65.

Pouliot, Vincent. 2013. 'The Logic of Practicality: A Theory of Practice of Security Communities'. *International Organization* 62, no. 2: 257–88.

Qin, Yaqing. 2016. 'A Relational Theory of World Politics'. *International Studies Review* 18, no. 1 (March): 33–47.

Richmond, Oliver. 2011a. 'Critical Agency, Resistance and Post-Colonial Civil Society'. *Conflict and Cooperation* 46, no. 4: 419–40.

———. 2011b. *A Post-Liberal Peace*. London: Routledge.

———. 2016. *Peace Formation and Political Order*. Oxford: Oxford University Press.

———. 2018. 'Peace in Analogue/ Digital IR'. Unpublished paper.

Said, Edward W. 1978. *Orientalism*. New York: Random House.

Sassen, Saskia. 2008. *Territory, Authority, Rights*. Princeton, NJ: Princeton University Press.

Scholte, Jan. 2005. *Globalization: A Critical Introduction*. Houndmills: Palgrave Macmillan.

Scott, James. 2009. *The Art of Not Being Governed: An Anarchist History of Upland Southeast Asia*. New Haven, CT: Yale University Press.

Selby, Jan. 2007. 'Engaging Foucault: Discourse, Liberal Governance and the Limits of Foucauldian IR'. *International Relations* 21, no. 3: 324–45.

Sjoberg, Laura. 2009. 'Introduction to Security Studies: Feminist Contributions'. *Security Studies* 18, no. 2: 183–213.

Solomon, Ty, and Brent Steele. 2016. Micro-Moves in International Relations Theory. *European Journal of International Relations* 23, no. 2: 267–91.

Sylvester, Christine. 2002. *Feminist International Relations: An Unfinished Journey*. Cambridge: Cambridge University Press.

Taylor, Owen. 2015. *Disruptive Power: The Crisis of the State in the Digital Age*. Oxford: Oxford University Press.

Tickner, J. Anne. 1992. *Gender in International Relations: Feminist Perspectives on Achieving Global Security*. New York: Columbia University Press.

———. 2013. 'Core, Periphery and (Neo)Imperialist International Relations'. *European Journal of International Relations* 19, no. 3: 627–46.

UNHCR and UNICEF. 2016. 'UNHCR, UNICEF Launch Blue Dot Hubs to Boost Protection for Children and Families on the Move across Europe'. UN High Commission for Refugees. http://www.unhcr.org/news/press/2016/2/56d011e79/unhcr-unicef-launch-blue-dot-hubs-boost-protection-children-families-move.html.

Wallerstein, Immanuel. 1974. *The Modern World System: Capitalist Agriculture and the Origins of the European World Economy in the Sixteenth Century*. New York: Academic Press.

Weiss, Thomas, Tatiana Carayannis, and Richard Jolly. 2009. 'The "Third" United Nations'. *Global Governance* 15, no. 1: 123–42.

Chapter Four

Saving Liberal Peace Building?

From the 'Local Turn' to a Post-Western Peace[1]

Giorgio Shani

Despite attempts to resuscitate it in the early years of this century (Paris 2010), liberal peace building is dead (at least for now). As the president of still the world's most powerful state put it while announcing his 'new' strategy for Afghanistan and South Asia, the overriding objective is to 'kill terrorists', not 'use American military might to construct democracies in faraway lands or try to rebuild other countries in our own image' (National Public Radio 2017). In truth, the 'principled' realism[2] the president favours has long guided U.S. decision making in the postcolonial world, but, shorn of the façade of a commitment to building liberal democratic institutions, the 'civilizing mission' of the post–Cold War period has lost much of its lustre. Now entrusted to middle powers, such as Canada, Australia, the United Kingdom and, within the constraints of its own postwar constitution, Japan; regional organizations, such as the European Union and NATO; and, above all, the various agencies of the United Nations, especially the UN Peacekeeping Operations, the agents of the liberal peace have turned to the 'local'. In part, this reflects the greater representation afforded to the interests of the Global South—the majority of mankind—in the UN system (Mac Ginty and Richmond 2013). The 'local' here is tantamount to the interests of the postcolonial state, which continues to define and shape the 'nation' it is attempting to build and protect. In part, this reflects the limits of not only Western power but also the very commitment to reshape the world in its own image which has its roots in the legacies and contradictions of (neo)colonial governmentality (Chatterjee 1993; Shani 2014).

For Foucault, governmentality referred to (1) 'the ensemble formed by institutions, procedures, analyses and reflections . . . which has as its target population, political economy as its principal form of knowledge, and apparatuses of security as its essential technical instrument'; (2) 'the tendency . . . that for a long time and throughout the West, has constantly led towards

43

the pre-eminence of over all other types of power—sovereignty, discipline and so on—of the type of power that we call 'government', resulting, on the one hand, in the formation of a series of specific governmental apparatuses (*appareils*) on the one hand, [and on the other] to the development of a series of knowledges (*savoirs*)'; and (3) finally, 'the process, or rather the result of the process, through which the state of justice of the Middle Ages, became the administrative state in the fifteenth and sixteenth centuries' (Foucault 2007, 108–9). However, as Partha Chatterjee has pointed out, there were significant differences between governmentality as it developed in Europe and the governmentality which emerged in the colonies. While 'governmentality' in Britain treated the 'population' as a homogeneous, undifferentiated mass of individuals, 'colonial governmentality' recognized and built upon seemingly 'primordial' categories of 'race' and 'religion' through the introduction of censuses, separate electorates and employment opportunities for ethnoreligious 'communities' (Chatterjee 1993). At the same time, it attempted to construct 'liberal' subjects (at least at the elite level), through education and public policy, unencumbered by the very primordial attachments it helped reify. After decolonization, colonial governmentality became the basis for the development of a 'liberal-colonial international relations [IR]' (Richmond 2016b; see also Richmond, in this volume) which sought to erase culturally defined difference in the name of peace, security and development. The principal agent for the transformation of postcolonial societies was, of course, the state. This is not to deny that the temporal break afforded by decolonization did not impact upon the international order (Jabri 2013) or to dismiss anticolonial struggles for self-determination but rather to highlight that these struggles were articulated in a liberal idiom which was intelligible to the colonial powers. Ultimately, the 'revolt against the West' (Bull and Watson 1984), as epitomized by the 'Bandung impulse' (Phạm and Shilliam 2016), did not succeed in bringing about an alternative international order but rather reproduced the Westphalian architecture of the international system. In liberal-colonial IR, the racialized, postcolonial 'other' is simultaneously assimilated to the 'self' through the projection of the values of Westphalian international society, articulated in a language of rights, territory and authority, onto the colonized; or its difference is translated as inferiority (as articulated through conventional narratives of development) and pathologized as a danger (as articulated through failed states).

The rise to regional and, perhaps in the future, global hegemony of the People's Republic of China and, to a lesser extent, India has, however, recently challenged the central tenets of liberal-colonial IR and opened up the possibility of a reconceptualization of IR and peace studies along 'post-Western' lines (Shani 2008). This chapter seeks to critically interrogate the 'local' turn in peace building (Mac Ginty 2016; Mac Ginty and Richmond 2013; Richmond 2016a) through a broadly post-Western perspective. By post-Western, I refer to any approach which seeks to 'provincialize' Western IR (Chakrabarty 2000) by engaging with the ontologies, epistemologies and histories of non-Western peoples. The extent to which this is possible given the colonial legacy marks a point of contention and possible point of departure with postcolonial[3] approaches to IR (Seth 2013), which share the same assumptions about the Eurocentric nature of IR theory (see Hobson 2012; Hobson and Sajed 2017). A post-Western approach would also avoid the romanticism of much of decolonial IR, which appears to suggest that the recovery of indigenous voices and interconnected histories unmediated by Western imperialism is possible while sharing its normative premises and analytical critique of coloniality.[4]

The post-Western critique of the 'local turn' mirrors and draws upon critical feminist approaches to peace building. Feminists have argued that the inclusion of gender-related issues into the liberal peace-building agenda has tended to essentialize women as victims depriving them of agency. This reproduces global patterns of patriarchy which form the condition of possibility of armed violence in the first place. For postcolonial feminists, patriarchy intersects with coloniality to construct the bodies of non-Western women as sites of intervention for peace-building actors. To borrow Spivak's (1999) words, saving 'brown women from brown men' thus becomes central to discourses of liberal peace building. The focus upon the local, however, also participates in the reproduction of patriarchal and neocolonial power relationships (Rigual 2018). By labelling spaces as 'local', it constructs the 'international' as a self-contained and reified space from which interventionary practices emanate and entrusts local peace-building initiatives often to 'local' male elders, the 'brown men' from which liberal peace building was supposed to emancipate 'brown women'.

THE LOCAL TURN: SAVING LIBERAL PEACE BUILDING?

Liberal peace building refers to the dominant model employed by the 'international community' following the collapse of the Soviet Union and the proliferation of civil wars at the end of the Cold War. Drawing both upon Boutros Boutros-Ghali's (1992) 'An Agenda for Peace' and the neoliberal ideas underpinning the newly emerging 'Washington Consensus', it consists of four main components: security sector reform, economic and political liberalization and transnational justice (Jackson 2017, 2). First, security sector reform, which includes disarmament, demobilization and reintegration programmes, are expected to be implemented by the state with the assistance of the international community. Second, economic liberalization and market reforms designed to facilitate a free flow of goods and services are instituted, often coercively through International Monetary Fund/World Bank structural adjustment policies. Third, and most important, liberal peace building entails an explicit commitment to political liberalization in the form of liberal-democratic institutions, constitutionally guaranteed rights and competitive multiparty elections. Finally, attempts are made at reconciling warring parties or perpetrators and victims through truth and reconciliation committees or transitional justice mechanisms in some but not all postconflict societies.

Critics of the liberal peace building have pointed out that the *ideological* focus on liberal democratic reforms, neoliberal economic reform and state building has failed to prevent postconflict violence and mitigate the root causes of conflict. The emphasis on 'capacity building' has greatly strengthened the role of the state in postconflict society, particularly its coercive apparatuses, making intervention to protect its interests more likely. This undermines the 'liberal project' of creating vibrant civil societies consisting of reflexive, autonomous, rights-bearing individuals. Neoliberal reforms, on the other hand, have considerably weakened the state's legitimacy in the eyes of its citizens by undermining its capacity to intervene in the market to boost employment, guarantee social and economic rights or prevent capital flight. Furthermore, the importance of holding elections so soon after conflict has ended in many cases inflames already volatile situations, leading to widespread violence, fraud or voter apathy. This can be seen periodically in Afghanistan and Iraq since their occupation as part of the U.S.-led 'war on terror'. In the case of the Democratic People's Republic of the Congo, peace-building efforts have arguably contributed not only to domestic instability but also to fanning the flames of a regional war in the Great Lakes region (Prunier 2005).

Its empirical record moreover suggests that liberal peace building is conceptually flawed. As previously pointed out, the role of the state is central to the maintenance of a 'liberal' peace. This is, to return to Galtung oft-repeated dichotomy (see the introduction), a fundamentally 'negative' rather than 'positive' vision of peace. It is rooted in a realist, Hobbesian perspective which sees the state as *leviathan* guaranteeing security from internal and external threats to societal cohesion, peace and stability. However, in many cases, the state itself is the main source of *insecurity* as a result of its actions or by virtue of its monopolization of the use of force within societies where its legitimacy is contested (Shani 2014). This has led some to argue that the liberal peace building should more accurately be conceived of as a *state-building* project (Jackson 2017, 2). Certainly, liberal approaches to peace building have emphasized 'statebuilding or state reform as their main methodology' in common with 'orthodox approaches' to state building which accept 'the parameters or structures within which the conflict occurs . . . without challenging the meta-structures that support the conflict' (Mac Ginty 2008,146).

However, the most persistent criticism is that, given its centralized, top-down and hierarchical nature, liberal peace building does not take *local* needs and perspectives into account. For Mac Ginty (2008), 'The liberal peace is operationalized in highly standardized formats that leave little space for alternative approaches' (144). Local participation and ownership of the peace-building process is needed if peace building is to be successful. But what is meant by the 'local'? For Mac Ginty and Richmond, the 'local' refers to the range of locally based agencies present within a conflict and postconflict environment, some of which are aimed at identifying and creating the necessary processes for peace, perhaps with or without international help, and framed in a way in which legitimacy in local and international terms converge. The peace which results from an engagement with the local is 'an everyday and emancipatory type, in which authority, rights, redistribution and legitimacy are slowly rethought, and are reflected in institutional and international architecture' (Mac Ginty and Richmond 2013, 769).

Although the engagement with the 'local' focusing on the micropolitics of the 'everyday' (de Certeau 1984) constitutes a welcome departure from the Eurocentric grand narratives of liberal peace building, emancipatory approaches which aim to empower individuals and communities through a reification of local 'agency' fail to go beyond liberal peace building. Instead, they reproduce its central tenets while simultaneously constructing a space outside of its interventionary practices—the 'local'—which does not exist in reality. On the one hand, emancipatory approaches to peace feed into neocolonial narratives of liberal peace building since they fail to engage with 'local' target populations on *their own terms* and thus build 'legitimate' institutions. On the other, attempts to build a 'postliberal' hybrid peace sufficiently sensitized to 'local alterity' (Mac Ginty 2016; Mac Ginty and Richmond 2013; Richmond 2011) appear to reify the 'local' as a space distinct from the 'global' or 'international' and ignores the role which colonialism played in the construction of such spaces. The result is that liberal peace building is critiqued in liberal terms as 'narrow' and 'exclusionary' (Randazzo 2016); it is insufficiently 'liberal' enough to account for the diversity of local, hybrid identities that were themselves by-products of the contradictions of a (neo) colonial governmentality which veered between the construction of liberal subjects and the 'rule of colonial difference' (Chatterjee 1993). This can be seen in the preference for 'peace formation' over 'peace building'. Peace formation, as Richmond (2016a) points out, 'highlights the structural violence inherent in modernization, liberalizing peace, neoliberalizing the state' and is critiqued on the grounds that it partially contradicts 'liberal norms, rights and self-determination' (189). Consequently, the critique reproduces the linear, normative assumptions of liberal peace building which seeks to emancipate the individual from the constraints upon its agency imposed by seemingly 'primordial' attachments to 'local' culture in a *thick* sense (i.e., kinship, ethnicity and religion).

This gives rise to the view that 'there is no realistic alternative to some form of liberal peacebuilding strategy' (Paris 2010, 340). Nor, for defenders of the liberal peace, should there be. As Paris asserts, peace-building missions have done 'more good than harm', and abandoning them 'would be tantamount to abandoning tens of millions of people to lawlessness, predation, disease and fear' (338). Saving liberal peace building, for Paris, thus involves both (1) 'continuing to press forward with efforts to dissect and understand the paradoxes and pathologies of peacebuilding' and (2) 'ensuring that this critical enterprise is well-founded and justified' (339). Without specifying the criteria he employs to come to his conclusion, Paris asserts that 'nothing in critical theory or critical scholarship per se implies that liberal peacebuilding, broadly defined, should be rejected' (339). He appears to have a point when examining the critical credentials of the 'local turn'.

Localization, from a critical, emancipatory perspective, entails the *translation* of liberal, normative values into the *vernacular*. Peace formation 'constructs emancipatory projects in contextual scales, reconciling demands for self-determination and autonomy. It does so in local languages, through *translation*, while respecting identity' (Richmond 2016, 177, emphasis added). This appears to be at odds with the 'bottom-up' approach advocated by proponents of local ownership and is consistent not only with late twentieth-century liberal peace building but also with the 'civilizing mission' of the late nineteenth-century imperialism, both of which sought to actively impose a '*cultural conversion of non-Western states to a Western civilizational standard*' (Hobson 2012, 27, emphasis in the original). The agents of the contemporary 'civilizing mission', however, are no longer European empires, private companies such as the East India Company or missionaries but rather an 'international community' centred on the UN system dominated by powerful Western states (most of which were colonial empires) working in tandem with multinational corporations and selected international nongovernmental organizations to institutionalize liberal peace building in 'fragile' postcolonial states. They continue to speak to, for, and on behalf of the 'subaltern', who are reduced to silence even when they engage with the 'local'.

DESECULARIZING THE LOCAL

However, the focus on 'local-scale agency' opens up the possibility that the liberal 'international' also may act as a constraint upon the agency of individuals to shape their environment in ways which maintain the 'biographic continuity' (Giddens 1991) of the communities in which they inhabit. As Richmond (2016a) correctly notes, in order to 'understand the local agents of peace formation and their role, we have to comprehend *subaltern* power' (178, emphasis added). The subaltern is not silent, as Spivak (in)famously notes, but their myriad voices are articulated in a register which cannot be captured by the prosaic language of liberal peace building. For the 'song' sung by the subaltern (cf. Hughes, Öjendal, and Schierenbeck 2015) is frequently a spiritual, or gospel, in comparison with the technocratic religiously, tone deaf rhythms of liberal peace building (and social science) with which we are familiar.

Liberal peace building, by adopting a secular straitjacket, thus places constraints on vernacular articulations of subaltern power and local-scale agency. In contrast, a 'postsecular' approach would focus on subaltern cosmologies articulated in 'religious' terms. A cosmology seeks to explain the origins of the cosmos in which we find ourselves and shares many similarities with ontology which, at its most basic, is a set of metaphysical assumptions about being. For Jürgen Habermas, the term 'postsecular' refers to societies where the continued existence of religious communities in an increasingly secularized environment necessitates on the one hand the inclusion of religious-based worldviews into the public sphere and on the other the *translation* of religious-based claims into secular terms in order to guarantee the neutrality of the public sphere. Since the constitutional state is able to guarantee its citizens equal freedom only on the basis of mutual recognition as members of a single political community, all norms that can be legally implemented must be formulated and publicly justified in a language that all the citizens understand. Religious claims should, according to Habermas, be permissible in the public sphere but barred entry into the 'institutionalized decision-making process' in order to guarantee the principle of neutrality of the state towards competing worldviews. Political decisions, therefore, need to be formulated and be justifiable in a language intelligible to all citizens (Habermas 2008, 134).

However, the translation of faith-based claims into secular terms requires that they be not only 'privatized' but also rendered intelligible to a *specific* 'religious' tradition. As Talal Asad has persuasively argued, there can be no *transhistorical* understanding of religion.[5] Asad sees the emergence of 'religion' as inextricably linked to developments within Christianity and particularly its relationship with political power. Its genealogy in the Judaeo-Christian tradition poses problems for the entry of *other* religious and/or cultural traditions into the public sphere, blurring the distinction between 'religious' and 'secular' claims. Secularism, as Asad (2003) and José Casanova (2011), among others, have pointed out, can be understood only with reference to 'religion'. The 'secular' at one time was 'part of a theological discourse (*saeculum*)', denoting the transition from a monastic life to the life of canons. After the Reformation, it signified the 'privatization' of Church property, that is, its transfer to laypersons and entry into market circulation. Finally, in the 'discourse of modernity, the 'secular' presents itself as the ground from which theological discourse was generated . . . and from which it gradually emancipated itself' (Asad 2003, 192). Consequently, the secularization of religious claims may require their insertion into an ontotheological framework which may be alien to the adherents of a particular 'faith'.

It is suggested here that, instead of *translating* faith-based claims into a secular language, an attempt should be made to understand these claims in their *own* terms. Sensitized to cultural difference, a postsecular understanding of peace should permit the articulation of multiple claims deriving from different religiocultural traditions without prioritizing any one 'tradition' as having a monopoly over peace and security (Shani 2014). This stands in opposition to the totalizing tendencies of secular, liberal peace building, which, in adopting a 'one-size-fits-all' approach, may be considered an 'imperial peace' (Behr 2014) in that it fails to adequately deal with cultural difference, thus reproducing colonial hierarchies. If the task of postliberal peace building is to conceptualize difference in a nonhierarchical way, then an engagement with different cosmological traditions can help but not if they are inserted within the hegemonic framework of liberal peace building and subordinated to the imperatives of 'problem-solving' theory (Cox 1981).

CONSTRUCTING THE LOCAL

In this section, a brief attempt is made to engage with a cosmological tradition, *Sikhi*, which was transformed by the colonial encounter into *Sikhism*. *Sikhi* is a monotheistic (or, strictly speaking, *panentheistic*) cosmological tradition which originated in the Punjab area of North India, open to all those who are prepared to accept its doctrines and practices. Central to *Sikhi* is the concept of *Vahiguru*, the omnipotent and omnipresent transcendent creator and sovereign of the universe who lies beyond human understanding, time and space and does not take human form. The *Vahiguru*'s intentions were revealed to Guru Nanak (1469–1539), who saw the divine to reside in all.

Since we are all part of the One (*Ik*), Nanak believed that humanity cannot be reduced to any name, history or people. This is encapsulated in the symbol *Ik Ōankār*, which literally means 'One, whose expression emerges as Word'. Consequently, there could no 'no Muslim, no Sikh'. *Sikhi*, therefore, defies categorization and promotes a radical equality inclusive of caste, creed, ethnicity or gender.

Although a Sikh cosmological tradition predates the annexation of the Punjab by the British, it was transformed by the colonial encounter. In short, it is not possible to speak of *Sikhism* (as opposed to *Sikhi*) as predating colonialism. The colonial state facilitated the imagination of collective indigenous identities through the introduction of modern scientific techniques of classification and enumeration that altered the political landscape of South Asia. The introduction of the Censuses in particular transformed previously 'fuzzy' into 'enumerated' communities (Kaviraj 2010). As Bernard Cohn (1996) points out, 'What was entailed in the construction of census operations was the creation of social categories by which India was ordered for administrative purposes' (8). In contrast to the ideals of *Sikhi*, which posited a formless and timeless universalism inclusive of otherness, Sikhs found themselves inserted into colonial narratives of 'religion' and 'nation' (Shani 2008, 2017; Singh and Shani, in press). However, these categories were empty signifiers and did not command the loyalties of adherents to these traditions in themselves. Rather, it was the centralization of all political power in the colonial state and the construction of a public sphere which stimulated competitive mobilization by the three major 'religious' communities of the Punjab: Hindus, Muslims and Sikhs. Taking advantage of the introduction of what Benedict Anderson (1991) has termed 'print-capitalism', reform movements sought to redefine their own traditions in terms intelligible to colonial authorities in order to secure advantages for their community in terms of allocation of jobs in the civil service which was awarded on communal lines. Responding to attempts by the *Arya Samaj*, a Hindu reform movement, to reclaim *Sikhi* as part of an overarching Hindu religious tradition, Sikhs organized themselves in *Sabha* (assemblies) and articulated, through books, periodicals, newspapers, pamphlets and even novels, a distinct identity, one based on the 'myths and memories' (Smith 1999) of the establishment of the *Khalsa* by the tenth and last guru, Gobind Singh.

Harjot Oberoi has persuasively argued that a cohesive Sikh religious identity arose in the late nineteenth century as a result of the activities of the *Singh Sabha* movement and their articulation of a *Tat Khalsa* discourse which became hegemonic in the early years of the twentieth century. From an 'amorphous entity', Oberoi (1994) claims that the Sikh reformers rapidly turned the Sikhs into a 'homogeneous community' by purging their faith of religious diversity (421). Such a view, however, overstates the role which the new Sikh elites played in redefining their tradition, which was based on the teachings of Guru Nanak and the ten successive gurus. The role of the tenth and final guru, Gobind Singh (1666–1708), in establishing the *Khalsa* was central for the development of a Sikh *political* as well as religious tradition. Literally meaning 'community of the pure', the *Khalsa* gave the Sikhs a co-hesive identity as embodied in the five external symbols of Sikh, commonly known as the Five Ks.[6] Sikhs were required to maintain these symbols in order to differentiate themselves from other communities in the Punjab. In so doing, they constituted a *sovereign* body as encapsulated in the salutation '*Raj Karega Khalsa*' (the *Khalsa* shall rule and be sovereign). After Guru Gobind, there would be no further human gurus with their spiritual authority (*miri*) invested in the Holy Book, the *Guru Granth Sahib*, and their temporal authority invested in the *Khalsa*.

The main point I am attempting to make here is twofold. First, to categorize a cosmology such as *Sikhi* as 'local' is to *particularize* it. Although Sikhism arose in the Punjab, where the majority of its adherents live, *Sikhi* articulates a formless and timeless universality and, embodied in the *Khalsa*, is not con-fined to a particular region, territory or ethnicity. If *Sikhi* can be regarded as a 'local' tradition with its *thick* commitment to universality,[7] then surely so must liberal peace building with its much thinner conception of universality! The second point is that there remains no authentic *Sikh* religious or political tradition which has not been impacted by the process of colonization. Even the translation of *Sikhi* into secular terms in order to render it intelligible for an academic audience entails assimilating it into a preexisting ontotheological framework originating in the West (Mandair 2010; Shani 2017).

CONCLUSION

In his contribution to this volume, Ashis Nandy sought to liberate peace studies from the 'clutches of the dominant cultures' of political science and IR which Oliver Richmond in his chapter termed a 'liberal-colonial IR' (see also Richmond 2016b). In a similar vein, I argue that the 'local turn' needs to be emancipated (for want of a better term) from the Enlightenment fallacies of the liberal peace which reproduce the institutional architecture of the very liberal colonial IR, which it seeks to critique. Saving liberal peace building should not be the task of peace studies. Rather, we should be looking for al-ternatives to it. For, as Nandy notes in his chapter, conventional approaches to peace studies have, like IR, 'consistently focused on nation-states as the major actors in the global scene and mostly ignored the way non-state actors have gate-crashed into the global arena to embrace and pursue new causes and sometimes adopt new forms of resistance, using new technologies of violence and nonviolence'. Many of these nonstate actors have been guided by different cosmologies from that underpinning the liberal peace, ones in which the boundaries between the 'sacred' and 'profane' and 'self' and 'other' are difficult to draw with firm conviction. However, these cosmologies are *not* 'local'; rather, they articulate a universality—one which in the case of *Sikhi* is timeless and formless—which can be applied to different regions of the world. The 'local turn' should not entail the *vernacularization* of the key tenets of liberal peace building; that is the translation of security sector reform, structural adjustment policies, human rights and transitional justice mechanisms into local dialects and ethical frameworks. It should instead start from the premise that the very tenets of the liberal peace are themselves 'local', that is, internal to a particular cosmology arising in Enlightenment Europe. These tenets have, however, been globalized by successive waves of imperialism and the establishment of a Westphalian international order based on the nation-state. Attaining the 'self-confidence to walk a lonelier, more autonomous path' (Nandy, in this volume) may mean rejecting the nation-state and its monopoly of the use of violence within a particular territory as the *only* legitimate actor in global politics.

This is not to suggest that 'local' cosmologies are in any way authentic or self-contained. Colonization *rearticulated* local cosmological identities into 'global' narratives of 'religion' and 'nation' which became resources upon which postcolonial peoples could draw in their search for peace and security. The insecurity felt by many postcolonial subjects results from this *misrecognition* with these Eurocentric categories causing a split in the 'self'. This is best illustrated in Frantz Fanon's ([1952] 1991) *Black Skins, White Masks*, where he accounts for the fragmentation experienced by racialized, colonial subjects forced to put on 'white masks' in order to integrate into a world not of their making. The promise of acceptance into white, colonial society elicits a desire to assimilate, but assimilation is continually deferred. The racialized postcolonial subject is, as Homi Babha puts it, 'almost the same but not quite' (Bhabha 1994, 85). However, in many parts of the postcolonial world, this fragmentation of the 'self' is not necessarily expressed in terms of inferiority but, rather, in terms of *difference* from the West. For inferiority to be felt, as Ayşe Zarakol points out, one must have first accepted and internalized the normative standards that the other is using for evaluation (Zarakol 2011). In the case of many colonized peoples, the standard of civilization used by the West for classification was never internalized. Indeed, the colonizers were not interested in what their 'native subjects' thought. Consequently, many postcolonial people *never* felt inferiority before the West.

This opens up the possibility of multiple understandings of peace and security coexisting at the same time and, frequently, in the same place. The everyday negotiation of these narratives is undertaken by 'local' actors who inhabit these multiple cosmologically framed temporalities, but to assume that they can do so at will is to impose one *conception of rationality* upon local actors who may operate according to different understandings of rationality intelligible only to their own particular cosmological constellations. However, as Jabri (2013, 6), among others, has pointed out,[8] the West continues to profoundly influence the psychic structures of postcolonial rationality even when it appears absent, representing an idealized 'mirror' through which postcolonial subjectivity is (mistakenly) constituted. Thus, peace formation can never be 'local' but can be only *post-Western*.

NOTES

1. Based on a paper presented at the annual conference of the International Association of Peace and Conflict Studies, University of Manchester, 11 September 2017. My thanks to Jeremiah Alberg, Hartmut Behr, Hinata Imai, Roger Mac Ginty, Sandra Pogodda, and Oliver Richmond for their comments. At times, it draws on Shani (2017) but has been substantially revised for this volume.

2. It is not clear what President Trump meant by 'principled' realism, but the prioritization of U.S. geopolitical interests—a sacred tenet of the realist perspective of IR—has long guided U.S. foreign policy despite statements to the contrary.

3. By postcolonial, I refer to any approach which places emphasis on the formative impact of colonialism in the constitution of the present. For an introduction to postcolonialism, see Seth, Gandhi, and Dutton (1998).

4. See the various contributions to Mignolo and Escobar (2010).

5. Furthermore, Asad (1993) asserts that there can be no 'universal definition of religion, not because its constituent elements and relationships are historically specific, but that definition itself is the product of discursive processes' (29).

6. The Five Ks are as follows: *kes* (long hair, usually but not necessarily kept in a turban), *kanga* (a comb used for the hair), *kachh* (knee-length breeches), *kara* (a bangle) and, finally, a ceremonial sword (*kirpan*).

7. For Andrew Linklater (1998), a 'thick' conception of universality was characterised by a 'single universalisable conception of the good life'. A 'thin' conception of universality had 'no fixed and final vision of the future' (48–49).

8. Jabri (2013) argues that 'while a colonial rationality would view the juridical-political boundaries of the postcolonial state as irrelevant in its calculations and formulations of schemes of government, a postcolonial rationality would take the politics of the postcolonial condition very seriously; including the political contestations that generate conflict and contention about those very boundaries' (6).

REFERENCES

Anderson, Benedict. 1991. *Imagined Communities: Reflections on the Origin and Spread of Nationalism.* 2nd ed. London: Verso.

Asad, Talal. 1993. *Genealogies of Religion: Discipline and Reason of Power in Christianity and Islam.* Baltimore: Johns Hopkins University Press.

———. 2003. *Formations of the Secular: Christianity, Islam, Modernity.* Stanford, CA: Stanford University Press.

Behr, Hartmut. 2014. *Politics of Difference: Epistemologies of Peace.* Abingdon: Routledge.

Bhabha, Homi K. 1994. *The Location of Culture.* London: Routledge.

Boutros-Ghali, Boutros. 1992. 'An Agenda for Peace: Preventive Diplomacy, Peace-making and Peace-Keeping'. United Nations A/47/277-S/24111, 21 January. New York: United Nations.

Bull, Hedley, and Adam Watson, eds. 1984. *The Expansion of International Society.* Oxford: Blackwell.

Casanova, José. 2011. 'The Secular, Secularizations, Secularism'. In *Rethinking Secularism,* edited by Craig Calhoun, Mark Jurgensmeyer, and Jonathan VanAntwerpen, 54–75. New York: Oxford University Press.

Chakrabarty, Dipesh. 2000. *Provincializing Europe: Postcolonial Thought and Historical Difference.* Princeton, NJ: Princeton University Press.

Chatterjee, Partha. 1993. *The Nation and Its Fragments: Colonial and Postcolonial Histories.* Princeton, NJ: Princeton University Press.

Cohn, Bernard. 1996. *Colonialism and Its Forms of Knowledge.* Princeton, NJ: Princeton University Press.

Cox, Robert W. 1981. 'Social Forces, States and World Orders: Beyond International Relations Theory'. *Millennium: Journal of International Studies* 10, no. 2: 126–55.

de Certeau, Michel. 1984. *The Practice of Everyday Life.* Berkeley: University of California Press.

Fanon, Frantz. [1952] 1991. *Black Skin, White Masks.* London: Pluto.

Foucault, Michel. 2007. *Security, Territory, Population: Lectures at the College de France, 1977–78.* Translated by Graham Burchell. Houndmills: Palgrave.

Giddens, Anthony. 1991. *Modernity and Self-Identity: Self and Society in the Late Modern Age.* Cambridge: Polity Press.

Habermas, Jürgen. 2008. *Between Naturalism and Religion.* Cambridge: Polity Press.

Hobson, John M. 2012. *The Eurocentric Conception of World Politics: Western International Theory 1760–2010.* Cambridge: Cambridge University Press.

Hobson, John M., and Alina Sajed. 2017. 'Navigating beyond the Eurofetishist Frontier of Critical IR Theory: Exploring the Complex Landscapes of Non-Western Agency'. *International Studies Review* 17, no. 4: 547–72. https://doi.org/10.1093/isr/vix013.

Hughes, Caroline, Joakim Öjendal, and Isabell Schierenbeck. 2015. 'The Struggle versus the Song—The Local Turn in Peacebuilding: An Introduction'. *Third World Quarterly* 36, no. 5: 817–24. https://doi.org/ 10.1080/01436597.2015.1029907.

Jabri, Vivienne. 2013. 'Peacebuilding, the Local and the International: A Colonial or a Postcolonial Rationality?' *Peacebuilding* 1, no. 1: 3–16. https://doi.org/10.1080/21647259.2013.756253.

Jackson, Richard. 2017. 'Post-Liberal Peacebuilding and the Pacifist State'. *Peacebuilding* 6, no. 1: 1–16. https://doi.org/ 10.1080/21647259.2017.1303871.

Kaviraj, Sudipta. 2010. *The Imaginary Institution of India: Politics and Ideas*. New York: Columbia University Press.

Linklater, Andrew. 1998. *The Transformation of Political Community*. Cambridge: Polity Press.

Mac Ginty, Roger. 2008. 'Indigenous Peace-Making versus the Liberal Peace'. *Cooperation and Conflict* 43, no. 2, 139–63. https://doi.org/10.1177/0010836708089080.

———. 2016. *International Peacebuilding and Local Resistance: Hybrid Forms of Peace*. Basingstoke: Palgrave Macmillan.

Mac Ginty, Roger, and Oliver Richmond. 2013. 'The Local Turn in Peace Building: A Critical Agenda for Peace'. *Third World Quarterly* 34, no. 5: 763–83. https://doi.org/ 10.1080/01436597.2013.800750.

Mandair, Arvind Singh. 2010. *Religion and the Specter of the West: Sikhism, India, Postcoloniality, and the Politics of Translation*. New York: Columbia University Press.

Mignolo, Walter, and Arturo Escobar, eds. 2010. *Globalization and the Decolonial Option*. Abingdon: Routledge.

National Public Radio. 2017. 'Full Text and Analysis: Trump's Address on Afghanistan, Plans for U.S. Engagement'. 21 August. http://www.npr.org/2017/08/21/545038935/watch-live-trump-s-address-on-afghanistan-next-steps-for-u-s-engagement.

Oberoi, Harjot S. 1994. *The Construction of Religious Boundaries: Culture, Identity and Diversity in the Sikh Tradition*. New Delhi: Oxford University Press.

Paris, Roland. 2010. 'Saving Liberal Peacebuilding'. *Review of International Studies* 36, no. 2: 337–65. https://doi.org/10.1017/S0260210510000057.

Phạm, Quỳnh N., and Robbie Shilliam, eds. 2016. *Meanings of Bandung: Postcolonial Orders and Decolonial Visions*. London: Rowman & Littlefield International.

Prunier, Gerard. 2005. *From Genocide to Continental War: The 'Congolese' Conflict and the Crisis of Contemporary Africa*. London: Hurst & Company.

Randazzo, Elisa. 2016. 'The Paradoxes of the "Everyday": Scrutinising the Local Turn in Peacebuilding'. *Third World Quarterly* 37, no. 8: 1351–70. https://doi.org/10.1080/01436597.2015.1120154.

Richmond, Oliver. 2011. *A Post-Liberal Peace*. Abingdon: Routledge.

———. 2016a. *Peace Formation and Political Order*. Oxford: Oxford University Press.

———. 2016b. 'Escape from a Liberal-Colonial International Relations (IR): Hints of a 21st Century Peace'. *E-International Relations*, 4 November. https://www.e-ir.info/2016/11/04/escape-from-a-liberal-colonial-ir-hints-of-a-21st-century-peace.

Rigual, Christelle. 2018. 'Rethinking the Ontology of Peacebuilding: Gender, Spaces and the Limits of the Local Turn'. *Peacebuilding* 6, no. 2: 144–69. https://doi.org/10.1080/21647259.2018.1453640.

Seth, Sanjay, ed. 2013. *Postcolonial Theory and International Relations*. Abingdon: Routledge.

Seth, Sanjay, Leela Gandhi, and Michael Dutton. 1998. 'Postcolonial Studies: A Beginning'. *Postcolonial Studies* 1, no. 1: 7–11.

Shani, Giorgio. 2008. 'Toward a Post-Western IR: The Umma, the Khalsa Panth and Critical International Relations Theory'. *International Studies Review* 10, no. 4: 722–34. https://doi.org/10.1111/j.1468-2486.2008.00828.x.

———. 2014. *Religion, Identity and Human Security*. London; Routledge.

———. 2017. 'Human Security as Ontological Security: A Post-Colonial Approach'. *Postcolonial Studies* 20, no. 3: 275–93. https://doi.org/10.1080/13688790.2017.1 378062.

Singh, Gurharpal, and Giorgio Shani. In press. *Sikh Nationalism*. Cambridge: Cambridge University Press.

Smith, Anthony D. 1999. *Myths and Memories of the Nation*. Oxford: Oxford University Press.

Spivak, Gayatri Chakravorty. 1999. *A Critique of Postcolonial Reason: Toward a History of the Vanishing Present*. Cambridge, MA: Harvard University Press.

Zarakol, Ayşe. 2011. *After Defeat: How the East Learned to Live with the West*. Cambridge: Cambridge University Press.

Part II

Rethinking Peace

Memory and Temporality

Jeremiah Alberg

During a sabbatical year (2015) spent in the small Bavarian town of Eichstätt, an ongoing project with the name 'Stolperstein' (literally, "stumbling stone" and so reminiscent of 'stumbling block' or 'scandal') came to us and was thus in the local news. Around the same time, I also read about it in *The New Yorker*. This project began in 1992 when Gunter Demnig placed the first of these Stolpersteins in front of the Cologne City Hall. It bore the text of Himmler's order of deportations of the Roma, 'gypsie persons'. Demnig then exhibited 250 Stolpersteins for the murdered Roma. These were then put in different locations throughout the city. Gradually, the idea arose of putting out one of these stones for each of the victims of the Nazi regime, locating it at the last place of residence or work of the person prior to deportation. Most Stolpersteins begin with the words '*Hier wohnte*' (Here lived), emphasizing that it was at this concrete location from which that person had been uprooted, deported and murdered. According the website, 'In April 2017, there were over 61,000 STOLPERSTEINE in about 1200 places in Europe'.[1]

As I walked around the town, I began to 'stumble across' these Stolpersteins—simple brass plates, level with the street or the sidewalk and bearing the name of one or perhaps two people who had lived in the building and had been taken away to a concentration camp. I remembered something I never knew, or I was given a new memory about someone who before had been not only nameless but also without a place. Demnig calls it 'a trace against forgetting'. Time, too, altered slightly. The past became present. I was aware that I was standing in a place that had witnessed something awful, something that people at the time probably hoped no one would notice and no one would remember. But someone had remembered.

The chapters in this part explore ways of remembering and forgetting as they are connected with thinking about how we can encourage peace in the face of conflict and violence. As the world has moved out of its bipolar, superpower structure to a looser, more diffuse configuration, many factors have entered to complicate the way we think about peace: nonstate actors, religious commitments, gender issues and environmental problems are now all a part of peace studies. So also is memory and the way we memorialize. In this way, artistic endeavour finds its theoretical or conceptual home within peace studies.

When this project started, each of editors had his or her own dreams and visions of what it might lead to. Doubtless, none of these has been perfectly fulfilled, but for me, it was important that the arts and the humanities find 'a place at the table' in peace studies. Instinctively, we know that art has a role to play in this area. We also know that art can be used to serve the ends of violence. There have been representations, movies, novels and paintings that have encouraged various forms of violence. We have grown more sensitive to some of these. But we are still struggling to understand the ways in which the arts can encourage a turning of the heart towards peace.

Memory can be a means towards peace or towards further conflict. Not only the painful memories of injustices endured, but unaddressed, repressed, even forgotten memories still wield a great influence. Each of these chapters suggests ways in which memories can be taken into account—can be rendered an account—so that they are properly honoured and lead towards peace. The authors do not back away from the hard work that needs to be done, but they also lace their contributions with moments of beauty and hope so that the reader is encouraged in following the course of their reflections.

Perhaps the most important sentence in this part was penned by Marita Sturken when she wrote, 'Forms of cultural memory activate discourses of morality'. In many ways, I think this encapsulates what all of the authors are writing about. The various forms of cultural memory—memorialisations, dance, film, protests, silence—all of these are ways in which discourses of morality get pushed or pulled into existence. Often, the memories are painful. They are connected with defeat or injustice, with things that make us rethink the reality we thought we knew. The pain of the suffering breaks our hearts so that they open up to new ways of conceiving things.

There is truth, as Payne points out in her chapter, that sometimes silence is the only adequate response. 'There are no words'. The point is that the silence is a *response*. It is a way of expressing the inexpressible and responding to that which is somehow beyond us.

Zaretsky traces one of the recurring arcs of history, from situations of oppression or at least indifference in which memorials keep the memory alive in the face of justice denied to those situations in which the trials themselves become memorials.

Zerubavel explores how exchanging one's identity is not only a way that one might deal with traumatic memories but also a way that artists represent possibilities so that we might imaginatively explore experiences that will remain in the realm of the possible. This kind of imaginative exploration opens one to empathy for the Other.

The chapters in this part share in and help us to understand such things as the Stolperstein project. We understand more deeply the need for various forms of cultural memory that act against our forgetting.

NOTE

1. http://www.stolpersteine.eu/en/technical-aspects (accessed 3 July 2018).

Tokyo → many 9/11 memorials

* exception on diem

No 'freedom center', ie

museum of historical analysis
v.
just memorializing killed, etc.

Q. What makes a grievable life?
Q. Can we mourn a stranger?

COUNTER MONUMENTS
* in Buchenwald
→ one stone heated to 18.6°
* Harburg → a memorial underground (invisible)
* Berlin

memorials – often connected to ward therefor memorial one side

v. peace memorialization

Chapter Five

Cultural Memory in the Wake of Violence

Exceptionalism, Vulnerability and the Grievable Life

Marita Sturken

An embrace of cultural memory as a social force began to emerge around the world starting in the 1980s. These past few decades has witnessed an extraordinary number of memory projects, including memorials, memory museums, countermonuments, countermemorials and artistic projects on memory, primarily though not exclusively in the United States, Europe, Latin America and Africa. In many ways, this preoccupation with memory, often referred to as the 'memory boom', has involved a reckoning of some kind with twentieth- and twenty-first-century violent events, from World War II and the Holocaust to state terrorism throughout Latin America to genocide in Rwanda to 9/11 and global terrorism.

Memory and memorialization was not a dominant cultural mode prior to this time. The violent events of World War II, which defined in many ways the twentieth century, produced in their immediate aftermath narratives not of memory but of triumph and defeat. Engagements with the memory of the Holocaust and the destruction of World War II emerged several decades (effectively a generation) afterward and then only in certain parts of the world. For instance, the national engagement with the memory of World War II, German fascism and the Holocaust has been deep in Germany and also in France and Great Britain, but the Pacific war has received comparatively less memorialization in Japan or China, with its histories still highly contested 70 years later.

In the United States, it was the divisive effects of the Vietnam War, largely understood as a war of defeat, that prompted a turn towards memorialization. The opening of the Vietnam Veterans Memorial in Washington, D.C., in 1982 and the broad public embrace of the memorial as a site for the expression of loss and mourning opened up an affective space for cultural memory in a nation that had mythologized its participation in World War II as one of triumph and victory. A memorial culture has followed in the wake of the Vietnam memorial, with the construction of numerous memorials on the National Mall and several memorial museums. This enabled the sense that all traumatic events need memorials—as a consequence, discussion of memorialization of September 11 began within days, when the event itself was ongoing and the number of the dead was yet to be known.

Latin America's engagement with memory has derived quite differently out of the work of human rights and protest movements (in Argentina, Chile and Uruguay), truth and reconciliation commissions (in Peru, Chile and elsewhere) and ongoing conflict (Colombia) and has, after several decades, produced a broad range of responses to the U.S.-sponsored regimes of state terrorism. These projects began in the 1990s and 2000s, after a period in which erasure and amnesty were often the dominant norms and thus benefitted from a temporal distance. In Argentina, for instance, this memory culture is steeped within debates about human rights in the present. Yet Argentina is also the site of continued trials of the perpetrators of state terrorism, which functions at times to generate and reproduce cultural memory (Zaretsky, in this volume).

Why has memory emerged as such a powerful global cultural force in these past few decades when it had not been prior? Is this, as many have argued, an embrace of victim culture, a postmodern rejection of history, a response to the disappointments of modernity? Is it an indication of changing concepts of time? Andreas Huyssen (2003) writes that in certain ways, 'our contemporary obsessions with memory in the present may well be an indication that our ways of thinking and living temporality itself are undergoing a significant shift' (4). Perhaps it is simply that once loss was expressed in these cultural forms, it opened up long-repressed needs to give form to pain and grief. The process proliferated once it began because discourses of memory tend to produce competitive frames of affective power. Memorialization is inherently about inclusion and exclusion. Memorials tend to proliferate when their modes of naming and representation leave certain groups feeling left out. So, for instance, the Vietnam Veterans Memorial and the statue that was constructed next to it of three soldiers (itself a compromise because of a debate over aesthetics) made not only the women veterans but also the Korean War veterans feel excluded. The memorial's presence on the mall ultimately produced the imperative that all wars have individual memorials, ultimately resulting in the creation of the World War II Memorial in 2004, nearly 60 years after the conflict was over. Michael Rothberg has written about the ways that collective memory is often viewed within a framework of scarcity, with the memory of one particular traumatic event literally crowding out other potentially equally important memories of trauma. He asks, does memory have to work like 'real estate development' in this way? He proposes,

> Against the framework that considers collective memory as *competitive memory*—as a zero-sum struggle over scarce resources—I suggest that we consider memory as multidirectional: as subject to ongoing negotiation, cross-referencing, and borrowing; as productive and not privative. (Rothberg 2009, 3)

Rothberg's entreaty is also about rethinking the importance of memory itself as a cultural force. In other words, understanding how cultural memory functions to crowd out and erase certain memories as it affirms others allows us to see the detrimental political effects of the overdetermination of memory, whether intentional or not. This raises the broader question of whether forgetting is preferable—or even possible in some contexts—if memory can be less determined, more mutable, less a politically charged entity. David Rieff (2016) has argued that memory itself can be an incitement to violence but that forgetting may open avenues to peace. In her chapter in this volume, Leigh Payne discusses the uses of silence as a form of repression and enforced forgetting and also as a means to avoid the demands of retribution and revenge that come from remembering. Must all violent conflict be remembered?

The assertion of cultural memory, through processes of memorialization, museumization, memory tourism and testimony, is inherently political. How we remember traumatic events is crucial to how we move forward as societies, how we resolve conflict; how we remember wars is enormously influential in how future wars are waged. This leads us to the question, how does memorialization relate to the possibility of peace? Do memorials help move cultures towards peaceful resolutions? Sadly, the memory boom of the past 30 years has largely not contributed to a deeper understanding of the consequences of violence and the peaceful resolution of conflict. Yet certain modes of memorialization can open up a space for a moving past conflict rather than its perpetuation through cycles of revenge and retaliation. By examining these different modes of cultural memory, we can begin to see this relationship between modes of cultural memory and the social aims of peace.

THE EXCEPTIONALISM OF MEMORY

One of the key ways that we can understand the dynamics of the memory of violence and conflict is within the framework of exceptionalism. When traumatic events are seen as exceptional, they have the power to crowd out other traumas, as Rothberg notes; as such, they can be used to justify conflicts in their wake, providing a kind of moral cushion that disallows counternarratives. In other words, exceptionalism is counter to any movement towards peace.

The primary example of a traumatic event that is defined by exceptional discourses is, of course, the Holocaust. While it was not understood in these terms for several decades, by the 1960s, the Holocaust had been defined in many realms—political, historical and scholarly—as an event with no equal in history, an event that effectively redefined the terms of humanity. This narrative has been the subject of significant debate and contestation, yet it has remained powerful nevertheless. As Rothberg notes, the belief that the Holocaust transcended history became widespread by the latter half of the twentieth century and then prompted many challenges in relation to other histories of genocide and extreme violence. He writes, 'The dangers of the uniqueness discourse are that it potentially creates a hierarchy of suffering (which is morally offensive) and removes that suffering from the field of historical agency (which is both morally and intellectually suspect)' (Rothberg 2009, 9). Exceptionalist discourses such as this function not only to create moral hierarchies but also to produce heightened forms of reparation and compensation. In the case of the Holocaust, for instance, this has resulted in the Holocaust serving as justification for the policies of the state of Israel towards Palestine and for the brutal and violent repression of Palestinians in the name of the moral right to a Jewish homeland.

The dominance of the Holocaust as a historical event has a parallel in the field of memory studies, in which there has been a debate about the way the Holocaust looms over the field in general. A preoccupation with Holocaust memory can be seen as distorting understandings of World War II and casting a veneer of sacredness on memory that in turn has produced a policing of the aesthetics of memory. The narrative that the Holocaust was unrepresentable in its horror and the influence of Theodor Adorno's famous statement that 'after the Holocaust, the writing of poetry has become barbaric' had the effect of defining any aesthetic engagement with it as a violation of its exceptional status in history. When the memory of particular historical events becomes overdetermined in this way, it is easily deployed as justification for further conflict in ways that negate any peaceful resolution of conflict.

In more recent history, competitive memory is a key force in the narratives that shape an understanding of 9/11 as a defining event of this century. The events of 9/11 were subject to exceptionalist discourses from the very beginning—of U.S. exceptionalism (one with a long history of defining the United States as an exemplary nation) and of 9/11 exceptionalism that defines the events of September 11 as a unique event of global terrorism, one in which the United States is an innocent and resilient player (attacked out of the blue). 9/11 exceptionalism has had deep political consequences since it effectively justified the changing of legal norms and moral stances that followed in its wake.

The memorialization of 9/11 has been deeply implicated within to this exceptionalist discourse. The construction of a museum and memorial at Ground Zero in New York was shaped by the idea that this event has no parallels in history. The space of destruction at Ground Zero was defined as sacred, a site where reference to other historical contexts was considered to be sacrilege (an early proposal for an International Freedom Center that would address issues of violence and freedom throughout the world was hotly debated and roundly rejected for its aim to see 9/11 in context). The belief of the uniqueness of 9/11 is thus effectively embedded into the scale of the memorial and museum at Ground Zero, with its oversized memorial pools of the two enormous footprints of the original twin towers and a huge underground museum. While the museum's exhibition is quite effective in telling the story of survival of 9/11—with deeply moving stories of those who died and survived that day, of strangers helping each other, of compassion and tragedy—it is deeply flawed in addressing the political and historical meaning of 9/11.

At one end, the museum has on display a large memory gallery with life stories of those who were killed that day and, at the other end, a historical exhibit with an elaborate time line that barely mentions the wars that took place in its aftermath. Memorialization often functions to define events within a particular time frame, with political consequences, and at the museum, the event of 9/11 is defined mainly as one day of terror and death. The exhibition thus fails largely at the task of situating that day in relation to the political context before that day and to make sense of what happened in its wake (Sturken 2015). For instance, the museum has one image of Guantánamo, one poster about a protest against the war in Iraq, one picture of Afghanistan and one mention of the Patriot Act. That the events of 9/11 drove this nation, with enormous public support, to enter two disastrous and costly wars that resulted in hundreds of thousands dead and contributed to a devastating destabilization of the Middle East is not a story that can be addressed within a museum designed to memorialize. Perhaps most shocking is the museum's display, in its main Foundation Hall, of a brick from the Abbottabad compound, where Osama bin Laden was killed in 2011, along with a jacket worn by one of the Navy SEALs of that operation and a U.S. Central Intelligence Agency 'challenge coin' awarded for its completion, as if they provide a simple historical closure to the meaning of 9/11. It is difficult in this context not to see the lives of the almost 3,000 people who died on that day as justification for the actions that followed their deaths.

The vision of the future constructed in the museum is sadly embodied in that brick, a future of revenge and seemingly morally justified ongoing destruction and conflict. Exceptionalist narratives are thus quite powerful in the harnessing of memory towards political aims, and they are disabling to the capacity to imagine different kinds of futures without ongoing conflict. Clearly, the memorialization of 9/11 has enabled further violence and cannot engage with modes of forgiveness, reconciliation or any movement towards peace.

THE GRIEVABLE LIFE

Forms of cultural memory activate discourses of morality. Thus, in providing spaces for memories to be shared, for mourning and experiencing loss, memorials and memory sites can allow for engagements with questions of empathy, the valuing of life and the moral obligations we have to each other in shared humanity. Remembrance can enable a *moral* obligation not to forget traumas, not to forget the dead and, by implication, not to forget why they died. It is often through design that these kinds of moral stances are conveyed. A memorial like the Vietnam Veterans Memorial, for instance, lists of the names of the Americans who died in the war. In so doing, it asks visitors to mourn the dead as individuals and as a collective. But it is the form of the memorial's design that can be seen as encouraging a moral stance about those lost lives. The memorial's black granite walls are cut into the ground, drawing visitors down into a space of contemplation and conveying a sense of loss. In its defiance of the triumphal codes of monuments, which on the Washington Mall are designed in white stone to be seen from a distance, the Vietnam Veterans Memorial makes a statement against war, conveying through its form that the war was not worth the loss it produced.

We might think that all memorials engage in the moral stance that deaths must be mourned and that violent conflict does not warrant the lives it takes. But a significant number of memorials are built in response to wars, in which the dead have been effectively nationalized. War memorials memorialize those who died on one side of a conflict, and any memorial that speaks to lives lost on both or many sides of a conflict is extremely rare. Here, Judith Butler's concept of the grievable life can help us to see how memory practices can often divide the dead into those who are grievable and those who are not. Butler argues that it is precisely within the experience of mourning and loss that we come to fully engage with the question of humanity, of what counts as human. Thus, the question, 'what counts as human' becomes the question 'whose lives count as lives?', which in turn takes us to 'what makes for a grievable life?' (Butler 2004, 20). A life of value is thus a life worth grieving, a life whose loss can 'undo' us in mourning.

The world is, of course, filled with examples of disparate mourning, of designations of some lives as grievable and other lives as ungrievable, hence unmourned. In its inclusion and exclusion, memorialization often participates in designating distinctions of the dead into, for instance, victims and perpetrators, the named and unnamed, and the innocent and the complicit. Memorialization can be an expensive, involved and complex project, so cultural memory in official forms is often in the province of societies and nations with resources. A significant amount of memorialization takes place within the official context of nations which have political stakes in designating the dead within terms of patriotism. For instance, it is a strange outcome of the events of 9/11 that those who died that day are often described as American patriots, even though several hundred of them were not U.S. citizens. While the Vietnam Veterans Memorial names the Americans who died in that war, because it is a national memorial on the Washington Mall, it cannot even begin to acknowledge the 3 million Vietnamese who died, for whom it was a war of colonialism, invasion and occupation. Artist Chris Burden responded to the memorial in 1991 by creating a work titled The Other Vietnam Memorial, which displays Vietnamese names printed on copper panels—why, he asked at the time, are we celebrating our dead, who were the aggressors? (Forgery 1997, D7).

Conflicts over naming occur quite often with memorials, often with debates about who is officially part of those designated to be mourned. In The Eye That Cries (El Ojo Que Llora) memorial in Lima, Peru, designed by Lika Mutal, which pays tribute to the victims of the violence perpetrated by military government and the Shining Path guerrillas with whom it was at war from 1980 to 2000, the stones of the memorial unintentionally included the names of some Shining Path prisoners who were killed while in prison. Yet the fraught debate about their inclusion, which resulted in incidents of the memorial being vandalized, provoked a broader discussion about loss (Hite 2012, 42–62). As Butler (2004) writes, 'The differential distribution of public grieving is a political issue of enormous significance. . . . Why is it that governments so often seek to regulate and control who will be publicly grievable and will not? . . . Why is it that we are not given the names of all the war dead, including those the US has killed, of whom we will never have the image, the name, the story, never a testimonial shard of their life, something to see, to touch, to know?' (38–39). So it is that memorials are always as much about forgetting as remembering, forgetting certain dead while memorializing others. Naming is always shadowed by the unnamed. Yet any movement toward peace would need a recognition of loss on both sides of a conflict.

REPARATION AND VULNERABILITY

Can memorialization be deployed in ways that do not create competing frameworks of those who can and cannot be grieved? Butler writes about the difficult of fully accepting the precarity of life and the state of vulnerability that is inherent to cycles of violence. Thus, the vulnerability exposed in an event like 9/11 is to some extent unbearable and must be screened over and transformed into something else, such as militaristic responses and securitization. The memorial and museum at Ground Zero are shadowed by the newly completed 1 World Trade Center, which, as the most expensive and securitized building ever constructed, is an emblem of the nation's desire to mask and counter vulnerability rather than to make sense of it. In addition, the arbitrariness of life, embodied in this case in the compelling and devastating stories told of those ordinary people caught up in history on that day, the arbitrary difference between those who lived and those who died, is deeply threatening to our sense of security and capacity to make sense of life. What would it mean to actually sit with that vulnerability, to understand the degree to which it demands that we not only confront precarity and arbitrariness but also fully come to grasp our interdependence? Butler (2004) asks, 'Is there something to be gained from grieving, from tarrying with grief, from remaining exposed to its unbearability and not endeavoring to seek a resolution for grief through violence? . . . If we stay with the sense of loss, are we left feeling only passive and powerless, as some might fear? Or are we, rather, returned to sense of human vulnerability, to our collective responsibility for the physical lives of one another?' (30). Confronting our collective vulnerability is a crucial issue of our times, in particular as we face futures of global conflict and climate change–induced catastrophe.

These formulations point to the capacity to feel our connection to the other and, in mourning, to consider the loss of others as well as our own. It is a deeply radical act to mourn a stranger, one of the most powerful acts of humanity. Years ago, while researching the AIDS Quilt, I found a letter that I have never forgotten from a family who worked on a quilt panel for someone they had never met which stated, 'Through our work and discussion we have come to love Rodney. Though we know virtually nothing about him, we have all come to think of him with a special fondness'. The process of making a quilt panel is a kind of tarrying of grief; it is about taking time with mourning since it takes a while to produce a panel sewing by hand. To mourn a stranger is to experience that shared sense of vulnerability.

The question of mourning the other has, of course, much larger political consequences, in particular in terms of considering how memorialization can lead to reparative practices rather than to revenge. Here, the work of countermemorials and the alliance of memorialization with human rights discourse opens up in some ways a means to move beyond competitive memory and the valuing of some lives over others towards reparative connections. In general, countermemorial strategies emerge not in the immediate aftermath of tragic events but rather in second- and third-generation contexts and when memorialization is taking place with some distance of time. Since the 1990s, there have been a number of what James Young (2000) calls countermonuments and countermemorials constructed in Germany which not only memorialize but also address the question of memory itself. These works are as much about the creation of a space for debate about memory and the past as they are about memorialization. For instance, Jochen Gerz and Esther Shalev Gertz's 1986 *Harburg Monument against War and Fascism and for Peace*, commissioned by the city of Hamburg and constructed in a nondescript plaza in a suburb, consists of a large 44-foot pillar of aluminium that residents were encouraged to scrawl inscriptions on. As it filled with writings, it was lowered into the ground, finally disappearing completely in 1993; all that remains is the top of the pillar and a plaque. The memory of what is written about the past, fascism and peace is there, hidden from view yet present in a way that integrates memory as a shadow into the present.

Countermemorials, like Chris Burden's alternative Vietnam memorial, are often conceived as responses to memorial projects that can perpetuate violence. In 2007, artist Joseph DeLappe created the virtual exhibition and memorial competition iraqimemorial.org as a response to the online publication of the 5,201 proposals for the World Trade Center Memorial Competition in the fall of 2003. His aim was to create a mirror call for proposals to memorialize the many more Iraqi civilians who had died in the Iraq War. He states, 'How do we respond as artists (is it possible to respond)—to the deaths of Iraqi civilians that are occurring as the result of the actions of our government?' (Peraica 2008). The proposals, which number more than 180, aim to render these invisible dead present in some way. To mention just a couple, Peter Janssen and Ward Janssen's The Circle, 27.5 kilometres long (which represents one millimetre for each Iraqi), is drawn around the centre of Baghdad, demarcated by a thin copper wire. The artists write, 'Anyone entering or leaving the city central areas will always have to cross the circle and might for a short moment reflect on those compatriots who did not survive the Iraq tragedies but also on his or her 27,500,000 fellow citizens, fellow mourners'. Nadia Awad's This War, featuring thousands of life-size figures of detainees, civilians and children who have been mutilated by the war, is constructed of the reeds from southern Iraq, their heads covered in white sheets. 'I envision these thousands of reed figures floating down the Potomac River and wafting past Capitol Hill in quiet confrontation with the architects of the War'. The project of counting haunts many of these proposals, demonstrating the need to render the dead present in a context of war in which they have literally not been counted. The iraqimemorial.org project participates in a mourning of strangers by rendering visible not only those caught up in the U.S. invasion of Iraq but also those defined within the codes of war as the enemy: in suggesting that we should mourn the civilians who were killed by the U.S. invasion and occupation, it asks us to mourn across the borders of humanity that are constructed in wars.

This brings us back to the grievable life and the necessary work of aligning memorialisation with a sense of all lives as valuable. Many of the memorialisations taking place in Latin America stand out in their connection of the memory of state terrorism and torture in the past to human rights struggles in the present. Because the memorialization in Argentina and Chile, for instance, is about the disappearance and torture of people, most of them young, by military dictatorships and because many of the memorial projects were begun 15 to 20 years after these regimes had left power, these memorial projects were spawned in part through the work of human rights organizations. In some of these contexts, practices of protest were transformed into memory rituals. Thus, in Argentina, the Madres de Plaza de Mayo have marched every week since 1977 in front of the government building, with images of their disappeared children, and over time their performance of protest became one of memory (it is also, perhaps inevitably, now one of tourism). Other sites in Argentina, such as Olimpo in Buenos Aires, have transformed former detention and torture sites into community centres that address contemporary immigrant communities and human rights in addition to memorializing those who died there.

Museums of memory are proliferating throughout the Americas in Chile, Argentina, Peru, Colombia, Uruguay and El Salvador. These museums bear witness to the deaths of tens of thousands who were tortured and murdered and disappeared under political regimes over the past several decades, and many situate their exhibitions in relation to human rights. In Chile, the government inaugurated a national Museum of Memory and Human Rights to remember the time of the country's military dictatorship (1973–1990), in which tens of thousands were tortured and thousands killed. The Museo de la Memoria y los Derechos Humanos begins with the day of the military coup d'état in 1973 (coincidentally on September 11) and places Chile's attempts to come to terms with the violations in a larger regional and international context. What would it mean for the 9/11 Memorial Museum to have a similar mission? If the 9/11 museum could tell the history of 9/11 in a meaningful way, it too would have to address the question of human rights—not only to see terrorism as violence against human rights but also to examine the abuses of human rights committed by the United States in response to that day's tragedy. The framework of human rights allows us to see how the tragic deaths of those ordinary people who were caught up in history on September 11, 2001, are connected to the tragic deaths that have followed from it. Such a reframing would move towards reparation, towards the goals of peace, rather than revenge.

Precarious life. Vulnerability. Human rights. And irony. It is perhaps ironic that I argue that it is both irony (in the form countermonuments and counter-memorials) and the largely unironic framework of human rights that allow us to transcend the competitive and exceptionalist narratives of memory and to deploy memory as a means towards peace rather than towards further conflict. Yet the mode of irony in cultural memory projects is essentially about demanding a deep and layered understanding of the stakes of memory and a critique of the capacity of memory to carry too much power. Similarly, human rights demand a connection of memory to present struggles, not as an entity separated off from contemporary struggles. These modes offer ways for the deep, meaningful and affective expressions of memory and loss to produce forms of reparation, to remind us that the capacity to grieve the other is one of the acts that makes us most human. It is in their capacity to generate debate, to open up discussions about what conflict has meant, to encourage us to mourn the other, that memorial projects can aid in the project of peace.

REFERENCES

Butler, Judith. 2004. *Precarious Life: The Powers of Mourning and Violence*. London: Verso.

Forgery, Benjamin. 1997. 'One Monument Too Many'. *Washington Post*, 6 November, D7.

Hite, Katherine. 2012. *Politics and the Art of Commemoration: Memorials to Struggle in Latin America and Spain*. New York: Routledge.

Huyssen, Andreas. 2003. *Present Pasts: Urban Palimpsests and the Politics of Memory*. Stanford, CA: Stanford University Press.

Peraica, Ana. 2008. 'An Interview with Joseph DeLappe'. 16 January. http://victims.labforculture.org.

Rieff, David. 2016. *In Praise of Forgetting: Historical Memory and Its Ironies*. New Haven, CT: Yale University Press.

Rothberg, Michael. 2009. *Multidirectional Memory: Remembering the Holocaust in the Age of Decolonization*. Stanford, CA: Stanford University Press.

Sturken, Marita. 2015. 'The 9/11 Memorial Museum and the Remaking of Ground Zero'. *American Quarterly* 67, no. 2 (June): 471–90.

Young, James. 2000. *At Memory's Edge: After-Images of the Holocaust in Contemporary Art and Architecture*. New Haven, CT: Yale University Press.

testimony in human rights trials

ESMA ruling 2017 (?)

Chapter Six

Justice in the Land of Memory

Reflecting on the Temporality of Truth and Survival in Argentina

Natasha Zaretsky

The Park of Memory is a serene space, situated on the edge of Buenos Aires' River Plate. Upon entering, one can see various sites of memory—metal rods uncannily reverberating in the wind, geometric sculptures and other material interventions in the landscape. A wall stretches towards the water's edge, inscribed with rows of names, documenting the people disappeared and killed during the 1976–1983 military dictatorship in Argentina. Thirty years after the end of the dictatorship, I walked along that path with an Argentine friend, searching through the rows of names until she found the one she knew. The park had provided visitors with blank sheets of white paper, which she used to gently position over her friend's name, slowly tracing the edges of the letters in memory of that friend, killed in those years of state violence.

These traces of memory represent the remains of a violent past, rendered visible by the sites and practices of cultural memory created in Argentina in response to terror. Along the water's edge, one can also find a walking path with signposts and maps, detailing the repression and terror of that time. One sign depicts multiple outlines of people, along with the number 30,000—the estimated number of disappeared. Yet another sign, hauntingly, presents the profile of one person in a single airplane, linking this park and this space to the histories of bodies thrown into the River Plate during the infamous death flights—when those considered subversive were 'disappeared' into the water.[1]

This Park of Memory forms part of a complex topography of memory and citizenship in Argentina, sites of memory to the victims of state violence in Argentina. During the dictatorship, remembering the victims of state repression was a powerful form of dissent: family members of the disappeared used the memory of victims to challenge the attempts to silence and elide their experience and, further, to 'disappear' the very effects of state violence.[2] This continued during the years of democracy after the dictatorship ended in 1983,[3] when, despite a landmark truth commission (the 1984 CONADEP), subsequent amnesty laws led to years of impunity.

It is during those years without substantive justice that Argentina became what I would call a 'land of memory'—a nation of memory-based protests. As sociologist Elizabeth Jelin (2003, 2017), argues, the memory of repression became a critical site of contestation between civil society and the state and an important ground for building democracy. These protests also helped herald an era of reform. The amnesty laws were finally overturned in 2003, allowing justice to return to the land of memory, with hundreds of human rights trials that have been launched—enabling the state to hold perpetrators accountable for past crimes against humanity through a process of retributive justice that many have been waiting for and demanding for decades.

These forms of justice offer avenues to reckon with a violent past and achieve a measure of accounting, sustaining the human rights movements in their advocacy against impunity. Yet as these trials unfold, it is imperative to explore what they ultimately mean within the broader framework of recovery from past violence. For decades, Argentines turned to memory and testimony as mechanisms of survival when retributive justice was untenable—and, certainly, memory and truth have historically served as core tenets of transitional justice efforts (Hayner 2001; Hinton 2010). However, now that retributive justice has become possible through trials of perpetrators, what role does cultural memory have?

This chapter examines the lived experience of justice in the land of memory that Argentina has become, exploring the continued need for cultural memory and a truth that transcends juridical understandings. I suggest that such memory offers critical insights into the social value and import of these juridical spaces, especially when considered within the broader framework of collective repair. This view of memory resists and challenges normative assumptions and understandings of the process of recovery—teleological framings of progress that serve as the foundation of transitional justice and peace studies more broadly, as noted by Alexander Hinton, Giorgio Shani, and Jeremiah Alberg (see the introduction). Indeed, the processual and often uneven nature of cultural memory in Argentina reveals the plurality and contingency of survival, also evident in the spaces that trials and testimony provide for social repair and trauma. This therefore generates opportunities to rethink peace and consider how these processes challenge any normative assumptions of a simple progress in the aftermath of state violence.

In this way, memory, as Hinton, Shani, and Alberg suggest in the introduction, is inherently subversive to teleology precisely because of its plurality. Yet, as Marita Sturken (in this volume) notes, a greater proliferation of memory does not necessarily generate peace or greater understanding; further, silence, as Leigh Payne (in this volume) argues, can also present an important form of communication. Yet, while state violence and trauma can pose certain limits to dialogue and understanding, even generating paralysis, other forms of expression, such as the arts, can provide meaningful forms of exchange (see Zerubavel, in this volume). Indeed, by turning to cultural practices on the ground (see also Sawhney, in this volume), the dynamics of lived experience suggest that these memorial challenges can yield meaningful engagement with a complex past.

Such processes of cultural memory in Argentina are the focus of this chapter, drawing on ethnographic readings of memory as situated in contemporary juridical testimonies of state violence. These public spaces of witnessing offer new opportunities for engaging with a complex past, renewing its meaning in the present in an active process that suggests an important part of peace in Argentina hinges on public spaces of memory in civil society. I begin with an overview of the history of memory-based human rights groups that arose in response to state violence. I then review the current state of justice, including an analysis of the human rights trials. I also examine the continued salience of memory and testimony within this context of justice, exploring its significance as a space of citizenship and healing. I conclude by contemplating the complex temporalities of survival in Argentina, including what they reveal about broader issues pertaining to transitional justice and the continuing importance of truth and memory to understanding peace and the aftermath of mass violence.

THE LAND OF MEMORY

In the years of repressive state violence during a military dictatorship (1976–1983) that some scholars call genocide,[4] Argentines turned to memory as a form of protest and dissent. Groups like the Mothers of the Plaza de Mayo, whose children were disappeared, took to Buenos Aires' central plaza to protest the repression of the state, marching every week. Such practices of memory became especially important in response to the overwhelming silence of the dictatorship. During those years, as Elizabeth Jelin and Susana Kaufman note, memory became a key space for society to make sense of and resist that violence, suggesting that the contradictions and tensions evident in the uses of memory offer valuable insights into Argentine society (Jelin and

Kaufman 2000, 90). Further, this attention to the processual nature of cultural memory has become the hallmark of memory studies (Hirsch 2012; Olick 2003; Sturken 2007; Zerubavel 1995), emphasizing how societies collectively construct a sense of the past, including the contestations and conflicts inherent to negotiating the meaning of violence.

The significance of such memory work in Argentina hinged on the silences central to state terror. The detentions, tortures and disappearances were waged in a clandestine way, with the military in power attempting to disappear not just human beings but also the truth of that time. Indeed, in many ways, the power of the state's repressive apparatus depended on the terror and fear of the populace—a silence disrupted by the protests of the Madres and the work of other human rights organizations, like the Asamblea Permanente de Derechos Humanos (Permanent Assembly for Human Rights). These social movements actively resisted the official narratives denying human rights abuses and crimes against humanity underway. The Madres, for instance, used their protests in public spaces like the Plaza de Mayo to challenge the notion that their children had simply disappeared and to defend their rights to know the truth of what happened. Through their protests and advocacy, they also inscribed memory into public spaces and the political ethos of democratic Argentina.

Some form of accounting, however, became critical to the transition from violence to democracy. One of the first acts of newly elected President Alfonsín was to create the CONADEP—the National Commission on the Disappeared, created in 1983 to investigate and document the systematic abuses committed by the state from 1976 to 1983. As one of the first truth commissions in the world, the CONADEP[5] served as an important model for transitional justice, seeking to address the patterns of human rights abuses without rendering Argentina vulnerable to another military coup. It thus offered a possible model for national repair and sustainable transition into democracy. Yet for many of the human rights groups, actively remembering their children and the victims of the dictatorship remained imperative, as did the possibility for justice and greater accountability, especially pressing with the institution of amnesty laws that heralded an era of impunity in the 1990s.

In those years without justice, memory took on an even more prominent role in Argentine politics. In addition to the Mothers of the Plaza de Mayo, other human rights groups were also active, such as the Abuelas de Plaza de Mayo (Grandmothers of the Disappeared), whose mission was to search for their grandchildren, kidnapped by the state or born while their parents were detained. Many of those children were then adopted to military families, and some have since been reunited with their biological families since then through DNA matches (Gandsman 2012). H.I.J.O.S. (an organization representing children of the disappeared) was formed in 1995 to demand justice for the perpetrators of the crimes against their parents. They chose another modality of protest, also occupying public spaces, but instead of marching in the central plaza of Buenos Aires, they turned to 'escraches'—noisily marching down the streets where perpetrators lived to call out their presence and render visible that which otherwise may vanish under the surface of everyday life.[6]

Memory thus came to shape civil society in powerful ways that would later lead to political changes, especially under the leadership of Néstor Kirchner (2003–2007) and, later, Cristina Fernández de Kirchner (2007–2015). During that time, the state incorporated the memory of repression into their human rights platform. In 2002, for instance, 24 March became a national holiday, the National Day of Memory for Truth and Justice. Additionally, those terms—'Memory', 'Truth' and, 'Justice'—became engraved in pillars at important sites like the ESMA, where thousands of victims were kidnapped and tortured, in a space located within the periphery of Buenos Aires. That very site became officially known as the 'ex-ESMA' also called the Space of Memory, and lies adjacent to the Park of Memory; it would also house the offices of the human rights groups noted above as well as the archive, Memoria Abierta (Open Memory), which has created a significant collection of testimonies related to the state violence.[7] This attempt to reinforce memory in the social landscape developed throughout Argentina, with various official sites of memory installed,[8] signalling the ongoing salience of memory to Argentine politics and citizenship.

JUSTICE RETURNS: AN ANALYSIS OF HUMAN RIGHTS TRIALS

While memory and truth became significant parts of civil society, they have always existed in a state of constitutive tension with justice—or the lack of justice—in the decades that immediately followed state violence. In 1985, the 'Trial of the Juntas' prosecuted just nine high-ranking military officers, with five ultimately sentenced and four acquitted. Yet even those trials lost their meaning shortly thereafter when two amnesty laws: the Full Stop Law in 1986 (limiting prosecution to lawsuits indicted within 60 days of the law's enactment and effectively silencing the 600 pending charges) and the Due Obedience Law in 1987 (essentially giving a blanket amnesty to everyone involved). Then, in 1989–1990, the subsequently elected President Menem pardoned those officers who had been sentenced or court-martialed.[9]

In the period of impunity that followed, memory and truth became even more significant in the place of a delayed justice. Other forms of testimony would also take on a new significance, including the 1995 publication of *The Flight* by journalist Horacio Verbitsky, which detailed the account of Adolfo Scilingo, a retired naval officer who had admitted to personally pushing 30 people to their deaths from the death flights he operated. In this account, Scilingo, unsparingly, detailed what he witnessed and observed in those flights, and, as Leigh Payne (2008) notes, this was a confession without remorse—a different form of testimony than that provided by victims and one that was predicated on the expectation that he would not suffer any consequences for telling his story.

Less than 10 years thereafter, such a confession would be less likely due to changes in the judicial sphere that would expose perpetrators to being held accountable for such crimes. In 2003, the Argentine government overturned the amnesty laws that were instated in the late 1980s.[10] Additionally, that year, the Supreme Court of Argentina permitted extraditions for crimes against humanity. This, then, opened the door for trials of those perpetrators who had been living without accountability for decades. The first such trial took place in 2006, focusing on Miguel Etchecolatz. Since then, there have been more than 140 related to crimes against humanity and more than 500 convictions, with trials taking place throughout the nation, including Tucumán, Córdoba and Buenos Aires (Human Rights Watch 2016).

Perhaps one of the most significant trials that emerged focused on the crimes that took place at the notorious ESMA, where an estimated 5,000 people were tortured and disappeared, a site of extensive repression. After decades of advocacy, the ESMA megatrial began in 2012, with 68 former officials facing 800 charges, including kidnapping, torture and murder. Some of the most notable accused being tried include Alfredo Astiz and eight death flight pilots. On 29 November 2017, the ESMA megatrial came to a close, with 29 perpetrators sentenced to life in prison and 19 receiving sentences of eight to 25 years for their role in the brutal repression during the dictatorship.

In this way, with the ESMA trial and other trials, it seems as if justice had arrived in the land where memory predominated, along with a strong affirmation of what is known as the 'right to truth'—a precedent developed in response to the phenomenon of forced disappearance and one that is supported by the American Convention for Human Rights and further reaffirmed through the transitional justice mechanisms (such as the CONADEP) and, now, the juridical sphere through these trials.[11] These trials certainly represent a significant step forward in the path towards justice and accountability for the perpetrators and the state.

These processes of transitional justice are part of global efforts underway in various nations trying to move forward following periods of state violence and genocide (Hayner 2001; Hinton 2010). Yet, while a global phenomenon, there are also quite specific contingencies to consider, including how local contexts and cultures shape the lived experience of justice, as suggested by Hinton (2010) and the work of legal anthropologists like Sally Engle Merry (2006). Focusing on local contexts and contingencies also dovetails with what Leonardsson and Rudd (2015) reference as the 'local turn' in studies of peace building, with an emphasis on 'voices from below' and local agency in understanding postconflict societies.[12] This reinforces the significance of an ethnographic approach to redefining universalizing categories (such as peace and justice) that can otherwise flatten lived experiences. Indeed, anthropologists, traditionally concerned with the voices of various subjects 'on the ground', can contribute in important ways to studies of peace and transitional justice (see Hinton 2010, 2; see also the introduction).

By focusing on such processes of recovery and the pluralities of lived experience, additional questions can emerge, as Hinton (2018) suggests, in relation to the normative assumptions underlying what he coins the 'transitional justice imaginary'. This includes teleological notions of progress and a 'utopian better future' (7), ascribing possibilities of transformation that may never actually be possible; such an imaginary then becomes a 'justice façade', in Hinton's words, that might conceal more than it reveals about societies attempting to rebuild following genocide and state violence.

In Latin America, these desires for a better future also resonate with the significance of 'truth'. Truth commissions or processes have become an important political and social force in the region over the past 30 years. The 1983 CONADEP was one of the first truth commissions in the world and the first to generate a report that became a best seller (Robben 2010). Since then, truth commissions have proliferated in Latin America, taking on particularly powerful weight in the aftermath of authoritarian rule and state violence.

From Argentina and Chile to Brazil, Guatemala, and Peru, truth has emerged as an important space for accounting for past violence. In response to state terror, torture, disappearances, and genocide, communities of survivors, and victims, and concerned citizens, have turned to truth as a grassroots response as they seek to advocate for justice and resist the official erasure of their experience; states have also engaged truth as a form of transitional justice, using truth commissions and other modalities of truth (such as the opening of state archives) to transition from conflict or violence into democracy (Hayner 2001). During times when justice and prosecution of perpetrators of abuse may not appear possible, truth commissions have developed as official paths forward (noting, of course, the teleological assumptions this implies as well, following Hinton 2018); it also becomes a way to achieve 'restorative justice'—a way to restore the order disrupted by political violence. Moreover, some scholars, like Martha Minow (1998), argue that truth commissions may offer a more effective way of acknowledging past violence and help-ing victims heal, more effective, perhaps, than trials would on their own. Of course, such commissions, as instances of transitional justice, should also be critically assessed for the normative assumptions framing the possibilities for repair they entail (following Hinton 2018).

In Argentina, as Robben (2010, 2018) argues, the desire for retributive trials has animated transitional justice efforts and human rights advocacy (in contrast to the experience of Chile, for instance, where an emphasis on reconciliation dominated). However, more than spaces of retribution, in what follows, I argue that trials also serve as dialogic spaces of memory that con-tinue to be critical to the renewal of civil society and sustaining peace and the fabric of a society in repair.

BEYOND JUSTICE: TRAUMA AND DIALOGIC MEMORY IN THE ESMA TRIALS

Part of the significance of truth commissions for recovery relies on the under-standings of surviving trauma and the particular role of testimony in societies following genocide and other forms of political violence.[13] Scholars of trauma and political violence understand testimony and narrative to hold a central place in survival and reconciliation—allowing individuals[14] and nations to heal and move forward. The struggle to find one's voice when reaching the edge of experience and the paradoxical necessity of finding that voice for survival are well covered in the literature on psychological trauma, violence and war.[15] This necessity for a listener and recognition can also extend be-yond the psychoanalytic encounter to apply to other instances like truth com-missions, such as the CONADEP.[16] Transitional justice, as Martha Minow (1998) reminds us, offers a space for collective healing. In these moments of testimony, the listener is the critical interlocutor, then, of the narrative that is central to moving forward from trauma, reinforcing the dialogic nature of posttrauma narratives and survival itself.[17] Yet testimony also operates *within* juridical spaces as well—with trials revealing new openings for a collective, public memory.

In what follows, I offer reflections on the patterns emerging in the testi-monies during the ESMA trials (2012–2017). These trials certainly provide evidence that seeks to prove the crimes that were committed at this site of torture and repression. Yet the testimonies that emerge during the trials also reveal a more plural, contingent accounting, a witnessing to both the violence that took place and the *aftermath* of that violence—to the memories of those crimes as they have impacted people's lives. These testimonies, I suggest, expose the complex articulations of memory and justice in the juridical space of the trial, offering evidence and traces of history as well as memory.[18]

Many of the accounts, presented decades after the violence, offer evidence of the systematic nature of the abuses that took place at the ESMA. For instance, in Andrés Ramón Castillo's testimony of 3 October 2013, he described the role of doctors during torture sessions as follows:

> He stated that there was at least one doctor present at his kidnapping. The doctors, he clarified, were there to make sure that the person kidnapped made it out alive to the clandestine center of detention, torture and extermination. Once at the center, the doctors took part in the torture sessions, so that the kidnapped could be tortured without dying as long as the torturers wanted. One of the doctors he saw at the ESMA was Magnacco.
>
> He also stated that the ESMA doctors participated in the systematic appropriation of babies. The Marines spoke about their '*Sarda*' (in relation to maternity). As this room was close to the bathroom, they could see what happened inside when they walked by. Some time later, the guards began to show them the newborn babies. He remembers seeing around 15. '*El Gordo Selva*' ('Fat Selva') was in charge of finding clothes for the baby, and also of later stealing those same babies. At the ESMA they said that the babies would be given to someone, but they never said to whom.

This appears to be a straightforward witness statement—describing what Castillo observed at the ESMA, including providing specific details of names of those involved.

Yet, in addition to those who witnessed the violence in the ESMA, the trials also presented witnesses with access to any accounts that related to those implicated in the ESMA crimes. For instance, on 15 October 2014, they interviewed Geronimus Wiedenhoff, a pilot for a Dutch airline who gave his witness statement from the Netherlands, about a cockpit conversation he had with Julio Poch, who had also been a fighter pilot in Argentina during the dictatorship years. This account reveals the unexpected manifestations of the violence from the past and the tensions that inform new spaces of witnessing:

> The prosecutor asked [Wiedenhoff] to relate the conversation he had with Julio Poch in an airplane cockpit on April 15, 2005. The witness stated that the conversation took place in the cockpit, in an Amsterdam–Tenerife flight, which was the first flight he shared with Poch. They had to return to Amsterdam because there was a problem with the aircraft. The plane was repaired in Amsterdam and they were able to complete their flight. Wiedenhoff commented that in flights like this one, there is time to talk, so they talked about Argentina and about Julio Poch's time as a fighter pilot.

Wiedenhoff asked Julio about the *Madres de Plaza de Mayo*. Julio looked at him directly and said, in English: 'They should have killed them all. They should have buried [them]'. After having stated this in English, he was asked to translate into Dutch, so that the interpreter could legally offer a translation in Spanish.

Wiedenhoff continued with his statement and said that he was astonished and frightened by Poch's reaction. . . . They did not talk about that subject for the rest of the flight. They might have spoken about something else, but that subject was closed. They landed and then returned to Amsterdam, in a normal flight.

While this account offers testimony about one of the accused perpetrators, Julio Poch, it also tells us more: about the ways in which violence creates new forms of witnessing in unexpected places, just as the process of testimony reveals its dialogic and negotiated nature.[19]

This process becomes more complex, however, for survivors. Even as the official acknowledgement of their traumas may help society move forward, it can also prompt a renewed form of trauma in some cases. In these moments, we see how individual and national healing may also be in tension. One witness, María Elena Monti, testified in June 2015 about the challenges of survival. From her testimony, she described leaving Buenos Aires after seeing her brother being kidnapped by the state and then returning tortured. Fleeing from place to place to avoid such detention, she eventually left the city altogether. Yet her family continued to suffer constant 'surveillance' and worse: 'they received constant threatening telephone calls, telling them that they would "disappear them all."' She thus lived in a state of internal exile in various cities, coming to see her family again only in the late 1980s. She would discover the story of how her mother died through a newspaper account:

On June 22, 1983, there was an article in the newspaper *Clarín* with the title: 'No Irregularities at the Morgue'. The article offered explanations of 106 cases of death 'subversives' killed in 'shoot-outs'; her mother was one of the cases. María Elena had been told that her mother died of cardiac arrest; she was seen lying on the street around her house. She would later learn that heart attack was caused after the kidnapping during a torture session.

In addition to describing her own experience of living in hiding, she also described the impact of not being able to know about the whereabouts of her family—part of the lived experience of that trauma to which this testimony also attests.

Another account from Isabel Teresa Cerutti, on 3 October 2013, also details the ways in which her understanding of what is happening as a first-person survivor occludes certain possibilities of knowing. Her partner, Ernesto Berner, was kidnapped, and she testified to her experiences. The proceedings chronicled in the Argentina Trial Monitor describe Cerutti testifying as follows:

At the time of Ernesto's kidnapping, Isabel was three months pregnant. That is why she was kept after her son was born. During that time, she had little contact with her family. They few times they saw each other they met in different places. Once her son was born, she reestablished contact with her mother-in-law. . . . Isabel went first to '*El Banco*' ('The Bank') and then to '*El Olimpo*' ('The Olimpo'). After Isabel was freed, she learned that her mother-in-law had been kidnapped one week before her own kidnapping.

At the time of Ernesto's disappearance, Isabel thought that he had been taken to '*El Atlético*' since it was known to be a clandestine center of detention, torture and extermination. Only after the Impunity Laws were rescinded she learned that he had not been to '*El Atlético*'. The Argentinian Forensic Anthropology Team told her that, and her only reaction was to become mute and pale; she could not ask anything. Some time later, she was able to talk to survivors who told her that they had seen him on January 11, in the basement, sitting in a chair located close to an 'operating room', as if waiting for his turn.

Thus, her perspective as a witness is situated in a particular way, with the past never fully accessible to her alone; part of the trauma appears in the way she realizes the shifting and evolving nature of her own knowledge about what happened to her. Yet this also demonstrates how she relies on others to shape her own sense of the past, signalling another way of framing collective memory.

What is of note in these testimonies is that they are plural and contingent—revealing multiple contours of the violence and its aftermath as well as the ongoing trauma of uncertainty.[20] While this evidence may be used for prosecuting the perpetrators accused of the crimes at the ESMA, it is also clear that they offer a vision of testimony as a dialogic and collective process, thereby expanding the boundaries of witnessing as well as its survival. This, then, has implications for how we understand the reshaping of the collective, so critical to the question of accounting as well as repair in the wake of state violence.

This additional reparative role of juridical spaces may be especially important since no single process can fully resolve the loss at the heart of this violence. This is not to diminish the significant advances, which must be acknowledged: in addition to the trials and the significant public memory projects underway, other advances include the recovery of more than 100 grandchildren abducted during the time of the dictatorship. But this is a process of recovery that must continue, as a full resolution is never possible. Further, the juridical processes that have developed are not perfect; there are trial delays and other challenges, some more notable, like the disappearance of Julio Lopez, a torture victim and witness, his vanishing still unresolved (Human Rights Watch 2016).[21]

Given the fractured nature of survival, we can see an added significance to understanding how memory continues to operate in these juridical spaces and how trials afford new opportunities for collective accounting and a dialogic process of recovery. This further reinforces the need for a local framework for understanding justice (following Hinton 2010) and peace (following Leonardsson and Rudd 2015) and, further, suggests the valuable contribution of anthropology and ethnography to understanding the lived experiences of these processes. While testimony serves a pivotal role in transitional justice and truth commissions, it also offers insights into the value of juridical spaces in the aftermath of state violence: sustaining the possibility of repair critical to citizenship, even many years after the violence.[22]

CONCLUSION: REFLECTING ON THE TEMPORALITIES OF SURVIVAL

Since the ESMA megatrial began in 2012, hundreds of witnesses have offered their testimonies, demonstrating the radical plurality of the experience of repression at the ESMA. In November 2017, after five years, the trial came to a close, with more than 40 convictions, reinforcing the systematic pattern of crimes against humanity that hundreds of victims suffered during Argentina's dictatorship. In addition, by looking at sites of retributive justice as also restorative, we can see the ongoing value of testimony as a dialogic process for the victims and survivors and as part of a complex work of social repair essential to sustaining civil society in contemporary Argentina.

This also suggests the complex and uneven evolution of democracy in the wake of state violence. Even 40 years after the dictatorship, fissures remain, with certain tensions emerging between memory and justice. The human rights landscape has shifted in Argentina with the presidency of Mauricio Macri, elected in 2015. In May 2017, for instance, a ruling (known locally as the '2x1' ruling because of the reduction in sentencing) by the Supreme Court of Argentina seemed to open the door for lessening sentences of perpetrators and, from a symbolic perspective, treating crimes against humanity as ordinary crimes.[23] Many feared that the significant reforms of the early twenty-first century could potentially become eroded as the perpetrators convicted of crimes may now seek lessened sentences and what this might signal in terms of a possibly shifting landscape about the cultural significance of the dictatorship.

In response, significant protests that cut across a range of groups in civil society brought thousands of citizens to the streets of Buenos Aires, demonstrating the precarious nature of memory and, perhaps, time itself. This stands in contrast to the flattening of the past embedded in the premises of what Hinton (2013) describes with 'transitional justice time' where 'violent pasts are delimited and narrowed' (87). The dynamic nature of that past as it moves in and out of the scope and visions of contemporary needs suggests a temporality that resists any simple teleologies.

For the 2017 protests surrounding this 2x1 ruling—the protests that called 'never again' to impunity—involved an active disruption of time, suturing the present to the past; remembering and memory became profoundly articulated with processes of retributive justice and societal repair and peace. These embodied disruptions can tell us something about how violence operates through time, challenging temporal coherence and order both during the period of repression and in the aftermath.

This process of disruption continues to become manifest through the testimonies and proceedings emerging through the human rights trials, representing the plural nature of memory as an evolving social process that offers a contingent, dialogic sense of the past. Of course, an important distinction is that these trials offer a justice that had previously existed as a possibility on the horizon and now represents a tangible form of accounting. This chapter suggests that these trials have become another site of memory, along with the monuments, memorials, and national days of remembrance, which Argentines traverse as they move through time.

Indeed, such forms of accounting also address the struggle for repair at the heart of survival. Through these ESMA testimonies, we also see fractured temporalities that allow us to consider the possibilities of restoration and repair *within* retributive models of justice, to consider the value of juridical spaces as sites where memory and narrative are produced and a certain rendering of the collective becomes manifest.

Such opportunities for actively engaging with the past become even more significant for a society that remains in a state of perhaps perpetual transition from political repression and violence, revealing the ongoing salience of memory for sustaining democracy, recovery, and survival. In understanding peace on the ground as a lived experience, these insights also suggest the need to study it as a local process, one that needs to be renewed in and through civil society in a plurality of sites, where repair can be operating through sites of memory as well as justice.

NOTES

1. For a detailed account of one of these death flights, see Verbitsky (1996). Additionally, for an analysis of the confession from Adolfo Scilingo (one of the pilots

of the death flight) described in Horacio Verbitsky's account within the context of perpetrators' narratives, see Payne (2008).

2. We also see such attempts at erasure functioning through other modalities, including language and discourse (see Feitlowitz 1998).

3. During the military dictatorship, tens of thousands of people, including students, priests, psychoanalysts, teachers, and other citizens, were systematically kidnapped, tortured and killed for being allegedly 'subversive' to the national order (CONADEP [1985] 2003). Much of this torture happened in clandestine detention centers, like the ESMA (the Navy School of the Mechanics), located inside the boundaries of Buenos Aires, where an estimated 5,000 people were tortured, disappeared, and repressed. In 2004, this site of torture and death was transformed into the ex-ESMA—Space of Memory and Human Rights (El Espacio de Memoria y Derechos Humanos).

4. Daniel Feierstein (2014) makes the argument that the state violence in Argentina should be considered genocide if we take the definition of genocide defined in critical genocide studies (see, e.g., Hinton, La Pointe, and Irvin-Erickson 2014), which would include the intent to destroy any group in whole or in part (be that group defined politically or in other social categories).

5. See Crenzel (2009) for a comprehensive analysis of the CONADEP.

6. See Taylor (2006) for an analysis of the representational practices of H.I.J.O.S. See also Taylor (1997) and Navarro (1989) for analysis of previous protests of the Madres.

7. Although this chapter focuses largely on memory-based social movements, there were also other nongovernmental organizations, like the Centro de Estudios Legales y Sociales (CELS), which served an important role in advocating for and documenting human rights abuses.

8. See 'Sitios de Memoria' (n.d.).

9. For a detailed account of the history of human rights during that time, see Brysk (1994).

10. The Supreme Court of Argentina found the amnesty laws to be unconstitutional in 2005, which opened the door for prosecutions of those responsible for the repression during the 'Dirty War'. Importantly, they also found that statutes of limitations did not apply to these crimes, as they were crimes against humanity. See Supreme Court of Argentina (2010).

11. For an overview of the significance of the 'right to truth' to the rule of law in Latin America more broadly, see Inter-American Commission Human Rights (2014).

12. For more analysis of the 'local turn', see Hughes, Öjendal, and Schierenbeck (2015).

13. See also Friedlander (1992).

14. Cathy Caruth has written extensively on the nature of individual trauma. See Caruth (1995, 1996). In addition, the work of Susan Brison (2002) and Judith Herman (1992) speaks importantly to the importance of testimony in the wake of trauma, and the work of Dori Laub (1995) has been significant in understanding the struggles for survivors of genocide.

15. For issues relating to articulation and war remembrance, see Ashplant, Dawson, and Roper (2000); see also Robben and Suárez-Orozco (2000).

16. See Minow (1998).

17. See Caruth (1996).

18. A large number of the testimonies are compiled in the proceedings described in the Argentina Trial Monitor (ATM), a joint collaboration between Rutgers University's Center for the Study of Genocide and Human Rights and Argentina's Universidad Nacional de Tres de Febrero. The ATM translates proceedings of the ESMA trials to generate an English-language archive of the testimonies produced during this historic trial.

19. For an analysis of the evolution of testimony as a genre, see Wieviorka's (2006) work on Holocaust testimony and archives.

20. It is also of interest to note that the ATM proceedings are in the third person—chronicles of the witnesses' accounts rather than direct transcripts. This offers another layer of testimony, with implications for theorizing witnessing and archives that will be pursued in other work.

21. Impunity also plagues Argentina in other cases, such as the still-unresolved AMIA Bombing; see Levine and Zaretsky (2015).

22. For a more in-depth discussion of transitional justice, see Roht-Arriaza and Mariezcurrena (2006).

23. For additional analysis of the social impact of the 2x1 ruling, see Zaretsky (2017).

REFERENCES

Ashplant, Timothy G., Graham Dawson, and Michael Roper, eds. 2000. *The Politics of War Memory and Commemoration*. London: Routledge.

Brison, Susan J. 2002. *Aftermath: Violence and the Remaking of the Self*. Princeton, NJ: Princeton University Press.

Brysk, Alison. 1994. *The Politics of Human Rights in Argentina: Protest, Change, and Democratization*. Stanford, CA: Stanford University Press.

Caruth, Cathy, ed. 1995. *Trauma: Explorations in Memory*. Baltimore: Johns Hopkins University Press.

———. 1996. *Unclaimed Experience: Trauma, Narrative, and History*. Baltimore: Johns Hopkins University Press.

Castillo, Andrés Ramón. 2013. Proceedings in *Argentina Trial Monitor*. 3 October 2013.

Cerutti, Isabel Teresa. 2013. Proceedings in *Argentina Trial Monitor*. 3 October 2013.

CONADEP. [1985] 2003. *Nunca Más: Informe de la Comisión Nacional sobre la Desaparición de Personas*. Buenos Aires: Eudeba.

Crenzel, Emilio. 2009. *La historia política del Nunca Más: La memoria de las desapariciones en la Argentina*. Buenos Aires: Siglo XXI Editores.

Feierstein, Daniel. 2014. *Genocide as Social Practice: Reorganizing Society under the Nazis and Argentina's Military Juntas*. Translated by Douglas Andrew Town. New Brunswick, NJ: Rutgers University Press.

Feitlowitz, Marguerite. 1998. *A Lexicon of Terror: Argentina and the Legacies of Torture*. Oxford: Oxford University Press.

Friedlander, Saul, ed. 1992. *Probing the Limits of Representation: Nazism and the Final Solution.* Cambridge, MA: Harvard University Press.

Gandsman, Ariel. 2012. 'Retributive Justice, Public Intimacies and the Micropolitics of the Restitution of Kidnapped Children of the Disappeared in Argentina'. *International Journal of Transitional Justice* 6, no. 3: 423–43.

Hayner, Priscilla B. 2001. *Unspeakable Truths: Facing the Challenge of Truth Commissions.* London: Routledge.

Hermán, Judith Lewis. 1992. *Trauma and Recovery.* New York: Basic Books.

Hinton, Alexander Laban, ed. 2010. *Transitional Justice: Global Mechanisms and Local Realities after Genocide and Mass Violence.* New Brunswick, NJ: Rutgers University Press.

———. 2013. 'Transitional Justice Time: Uncle San, Aunty Yan and Outreach at the Khmer Rouge Tribunal'. In *Genocides and Mass Atrocities in Asia: Legacies and Prevention,* edited by Deborah Mayersen and Annie Pohlman, 87–98. London: Routledge.

———. 2018. *The Justice Façade: Trials of Transition in Cambodia.* Oxford: Oxford University Press.

Hinton, Alexander Laban, Thomas La Pointe, and Douglas Irvin-Erickson, eds. 2014. *Hidden Genocides: Power, Knowledge, Memory.* New Brunswick, NJ: Rutgers University Press.

Hirsch, Marianne. 2012. *The Generation of Postmemory: Writing and Visual Culture after the Holocaust.* New York: Columbia University Press.

Hughes, Caroline, Joakim Öjendal, and Isabell Schierenbeck. 2015. 'The Struggle versus the Song—The Local Turn in Peacebuilding: An Introduction'. *Third World Quarterly* 36, no. 5: 817–24.

Human Rights Watch. 2016. 'Argentina'. In *Human Rights Watch World Report.* New York: Human Rights Watch.

Inter-American Commission Human Rights. 2014. *The Right to Truth in the Americas.* http://www.oas.org/en/iachr/reports/pdfs/right-to-truth-en.pdf.

Jelin, Elizabeth. 2003. *State Repression and the Labors of Memory.* Translated by Judy Rein and Marcial Godoy-Anativia. Minneapolis: University of Minnesota Press.

———. 2017. *La lucha por el pasado. Cómo construimos la memoria social.* Buenos Aires: Siglo XXI Editores.

Jelin, Elizabeth, and Susana Kaufman. 2000. 'Layers of Memories: Twenty Years after in Argentina'. In *The Politics of War Memory and Commemoration,* edited by Timothy G. Ashplant, Graham Dawson, and Michael Roper, 89–110. London: Routledge.

Laub, Dori. 1995. 'Truth and Testimony: The Process and the Struggle'. In *Trauma: Explorations in Memory,* edited by Cathy Caruth, 61–75. Baltimore: Johns Hopkins University Press.

Leonardsson, Hanna, and Gustav Rudd. 2015. 'The "Local Turn" in Peacebuilding: A Literature Review of Effective and Emancipatory Peacebuilding'. *Third World Quarterly* 36, no. 5: 825–39.

Levine, Annette H., and Natasha Zaretsky, eds. 2015. *Landscapes of Memory and Impunity: The Aftermath of the AMIA Bombing in Jewish Argentina.* Leiden: Brill.

Merry, Sally Engle. 2006. *Human Rights and Gender Violence: Translating International Law into Local Justice*. Chicago: University of Chicago Press.

Minow, Martha. 1998. *Between Vengeance and Forgiveness: Facing History after Genocide and Mass Violence*. Boston: Beacon Press.

Monti, María Elena. 2015. Proceedings in *Argentina Trial Monitor*. June 2015.

Navarro, Marysa. 1989. 'The Personal Is Political: Las *Madres de Plaza de Mayo*'. In *Power and Popular Protest*, edited by Susan Eckstein, 241–58. Berkeley: University of California Press.

Olick, Jeffrey K., ed. 2003. *States of Memory: Continuities, Conflicts, and Transformations in National Retrospection*. Durham, NC: Duke University Press.

Payne, Leigh. 2008. *Unsettling Accounts: Neither Truth or Reconciliation in Confessions of State Violence*. Durham, NC: Duke University Press.

Robben, Antonius C. G. M. 2010. 'Testimonies, Truths, and Transitions of Justice in Argentina and Chile'. In *Transitional Justice: Global Mechanisms and Local Realities after Genocide and Mass Violence*, edited by Alexander Laban Hinton, 179–205. New Brunswick, NJ: Rutgers University Press.

———. 2018. *Argentina Betrayed: Memory, Mourning, and Accountability*. Philadelphia: University of Pennsylvania Press.

Robben, Antonius C. G. M., and Marcelo M. Suárez-Orozco, eds. 2000. *Cultures under Siege: Collective Violence and Trauma*. Cambridge: Cambridge University Press.

Roht-Arriaza, Naomi, and Javier Mariezcurrena, eds. 2006. *Transitional Justice in the Twenty-First Century: Beyond Truth versus Justice*. Cambridge: Cambridge University Press.

'Sitios de Memoria'. n.d. *Secretaria de Derechos Humanos, Argentina*. https://www.argentina.gob.ar/derechoshumanos/sitiosdememoria. Accessed 21 September 2018.

Sturken, Marita. 2007. *Tourists of History: Memory, Kitsch, and Consumerism from Oklahoma City to Ground Zero*. Durham, NC: Duke University Press.

Supreme Court of Argentina. 2010. *Delitos de lesa humanidad: Informe sobre la evolución de las causas*. Buenos Aires: Supreme Court of Argentina.

Taylor, Diana. 1997. *Disappearing Acts: Spectacles of Gender and Nationalism in Argentina's 'Dirty War'*. Durham, NC: Duke University Press.

———. 2006. 'DNA of Performance'. In *Cultural Agency in the Americas*, edited by Doris Sommer, 52–81. Durham, NC: Duke University Press.

Verbitsky, Horacio. 1996. *The Flight: Confessions of an Argentine Dirty Warrior*. Translated by Esther Allen. New York: New Press.

Wiedenhoff, Geronimus. 2014. Proceedings in *Argentina Trial Monitor*. 15 October 2014.

Wieviorka, Annette. 2006. *The Era of the Witness*. Translated by Jared Stark. Ithaca, NY: Cornell University Press.

Zaretsky, Natasha. 2017. 'In Argentina, a Call for "Never Again", Again'. *Latin America Goes Global*. 12 May. http://latinamericagoesglobal.org/2016/03/2859.

Zerubavel, Yael. 1995. *Recovered Roots: Collective Memory and the Making of Israeli National Tradition*. Chicago: University of Chicago Press.

Chapter Seven

Negotiating Difference and Empathy

Cinematic Representations of Passing and Exchanged Identities in the Israeli–Palestinian Conflict

Yael Zerubavel

In conflicts involving clashing narratives of victimhood, violence, and dislocation, traumatic memories reinforce the attachment to the past and the lack of readiness to feel empathy towards the other's perspective or to agree to necessary compromises in advancing peace negotiations. The Israeli–Palestinian conflict is a case in point. Conflicting narratives of trauma and loss that Jews and Palestinians produced are based on their historical experiences and deeply entrenched in their national memories. For Jews, the memory of a long history of persecutions by non-Jews, culminating in the Holocaust, accounts for the critical need to return to their homeland and establish the state of Israel. For the Palestinians, the 1948 Nakba represents the loss of their homeland and the creation of the refugee problem, and the Israeli occupation of the post-1967 years has deepened their sense of victimhood (Auron 2013; Zertal 2005; Zerubavel 1995, 2006). These counternarratives thus lock Palestinians and Jews in a continuing cycle of violence and distrust that prevents them from moving forward in negotiating peace.

This chapter draws on an approach to peace studies that focuses on the local level of the peace-building process in contrast to the top-to-bottom approach that assigns peace negotiations to global powers, national governments and elites (Hughes, Öjendal, and Schierenbeck 2015; Leonardsson and Rudd 2015). Although the present discussion does not address peace negotiations specifically, it does share the concern of other chapters in this volume about the relation of traumatic memory, silence and forgetting and the ability to move towards peace.[1] This chapter thus focuses on individuals and everyday practices as important dimensions in transforming the processes that may reshape the cultural predisposition towards bridge building. My claim is that the portrayal of identity exchanges between members of opposing national groups in film allows the characters (and, vicariously, the viewers) to experience everyday life from the perspective of the other and may thereby contribute to empathy building and fostering human contacts. The close examination of films that portray the interaction at the local level also suggests the challenges and limitations of identity exchange as well as its potential failure to enhance empathy with the other.

Various coexistence forums involving Israeli and Palestinian activists, academics, artists, youth groups and others have pursued dialogues at the sub-governmental, local level for greater understanding and empathy across the national divide. An experimental textbook, *Learning Each Other's Historical Narrative* (2002, 2006), created by teams of Palestinian and Israeli educators, mutually acknowledges the gaps between their respective historical narratives and allows students to address and explore those differences. A similar challenge is presented around other conflict situations that produced oppositional educational narratives (Bekerman, Zembylas, and McGlenn 2009). The arts are a particularly important venue for depicting human experiences in conflict situations, exploring the impact of war and trauma and probing into existential and moral dilemmas that people face in these situations.

Through the theme of identity changes and exchanges, films may open up the possibility of exploring the perspective and experiences of those positioned across a national and religious divide through the theme of identity changes and exchanges. This chapter addresses three cinematic representations of a process of identity exchange between Israeli Jews and Palestinian citizens of Israel or Palestinians from the Occupied Territories. The theme of identity change was central to Zionist ideology as it advocated for the transformation of exilic Jews into native Hebrews and regarded this transformation as one of its fundamental achievements. The early Zionist immigrants to Palestine looked to their biblical ancestors and ancient heroic figures for inspiration to model this transformation. They viewed Palestinian Arabs and, in particular, the Bedouins as closer to the model of their own biblical ancestors (Zerubavel 2008). Israeli literature and culture of the 1940s and the 1950s focused on the new 'mythological Sabra', the native Hebrew who represented the counterimage to the exilic Jew, and celebrated the successful accomplishment of a profound identity change (Zerubavel 2002). Since the 1970s, however, Israeli literature and film became preoccupied with examining Israeli Jewish identity, exploring and articulating doubts about the extent to which it represents a profound transformation and increasingly suggesting a return to the Jewish character and roots. Identity politics reinforced this trend, focusing on diversity and hybrid identities, most visibly in reference to Mizrahi (Middle Eastern) Israeli Jews and Palestinian citizens of Israel (Rouhana 1997, 2017; Shenhav 2006; Shenhav and Hever 2012).

The three films examined here present a range of identities involved in the act of identity exchange and the circumstances surrounding it. The first film, *Fictitious Marriage* (1988), directed by the Israeli Jewish director of Mizrahi descent Haim Bouzaglo, features a Middle Eastern Israeli Jew who passes as a Palestinian from the Occupied Territories. The second film, *A Borrowed Identity* (2014), directed by the Israeli Jewish director of European origin Eran Riklis and based on fictional works by the Israeli Palestinian author Sayed Kashua, features an Israeli Palestinian who assumes the identity of an Israeli Jew. The third film, *The Other's Son* (2012), directed by the Jewish French director Lorraine Lévy, examines an identity exchange between an Israeli Jew and a Palestinian from the West Bank that resulted from human error when they were babies. The plot revolves around the implications of the error when it comes to light as the two 18-year-old young men must redefine their identities.

The films differ significantly in the circumstances, motivation, self-reflection and outcome of identity exchanges between Palestinians and Israeli Jews yet share the profound interest in exploring the implications within the context of the Israeli–Palestinian conflict. Whether the characters choose to pass as members of the other group or are misidentified, this representation allows these characters to assume the perspective of the other and provides social critique through estrangement. More poignantly, the films explore the significance of collective identities as well as both the ability and the constraints involved in moving across the national and religious divide, especially in a conflict situation. The films also serve to probe the challenge of sustaining human bonds in an ongoing conflict situation.

FICTITIOUS MARRIAGE

Hayim Bouzaglo's *Fictitious Marriage* (*nisu'im fictivim*)[2] opens with a farewell scene, setting the stage for a journey: a young man takes leave of his wife and two young children while a cab is waiting to drive him from Jerusalem to the airport to fly to New York. The opening scene introduces the expectation that the film would follow the traveller's experiences abroad, yet the plot subverts this anticipation. At the airport, the man abandons his briefcase, and after passing through the security checks, he sneaks out of the airport and takes a cab to Tel Aviv, thus embarking on a different journey. Although he remains within the country, the airport serves as the liminal space of an indiscreet 'nonplace' (Augé 1995) where he sets out on a journey of identity transformations (Van Gennep 1960). The police investigation following the discovery of a missing passenger and his deserted briefcase reveals only skimpy details about him: a high school teacher, Eldad Nattan, lives in a middle-class neighbourhood in Jerusalem. The film does not provide a clear explanation for his decision to forgo his trip to New York beyond his wife's brief comment on the impact of his recent service of military reserve duty and his own vague reference to his state of confusion.

In brief and elusive phone calls, Eldad Nattan pretends to his wife that he is calling from New York, but his lie contains a grain of truth since Tel Aviv emerges as a stand-in for America. The taxi driver brings him to 'California Hotel'; the young receptionist mistakenly identifies him as an Israeli who lives in America returning for a home visit, while he gives her a fictitious New York address, and she introduces herself as 'Judy', using the American-ized version of her Hebrew name Yehudit. Obsessed with American culture, she serves as his guide in the consumer-oriented Americanized culture of Tel Aviv. Instead of being a tourist abroad, he now becomes a tourist in his own country (MacCannell 1999), and his trip to America is realized without leav-ing its borders. When 'the tourist' suggests to her that she may be able to get a green card in America through a 'fictitious marriage', she misinterprets it as a marriage proposal and boasts to the Arab coworker, 'It is not simply a marriage; it is a fictitious marriage!' Like the fantasy video game that the two play, their relationship is based on fantasy, luring images and misunderstand-ings, which he fails to acknowledge and she fails to grasp.

This comic subplot around his transformation into a tourist in his own country presents a critique of Israeli materialism and provincialism, leading to a more complex and powerful identity change. Revealing his confusion and lack of purpose to an old man in a casual conversation, Eldad receives the advice to find meaning in the simple acts of daily living. In the early morning, he appears dressed up in shabby clothes and holding a plastic bag in his hand, looking like a transitory worker. Sitting in a park and eating an Arab 'bagel', he is misidentified by Palestinian workers who look for a job as one of their own, and when they climb on a pickup truck for work, they invite him to join them. Without correcting their mistake, Eldad joins them. Given his Middle Eastern background and some knowledge of Arabic, he passes as a Palestin-ian, but in order to minimize the risk of being found out, he pretends to be mute. There is an ironic twist in the Israeli man seeking personal redemption through manual work: the idea was the cornerstone of the Zionist pioneers' ideology in the early twentieth century, but in the post-1967 reality, Eldad can more easily achieve it by passing as a Palestinian.

From this point on, Eldad moves between his two fabricated identities. It soon becomes clear that the film focuses on his second, more challenging journey as a Palestinian labourer. He observes his society from the perspec-tive of the marginalized Palestinian, the ultimate 'other' who, as an illegal labourer, must hide from the law. Eldad experiences how Israeli Jews treat the Palestinians as a group of people who lack individuality or as nonpersons: the laborers are horded onto a truck to be transported to work; they sleep in a storage place on the floor, and the guard locks the door at night as if they were prisoners or animals; and Jews disparage the Palestinians and the quality of their work, assuming they do not understand Hebrew or not caring if they do. When a provocative female artist living next door to the construction site desires to have sex with a Palestinian, she lets them choose the man for her, revealing that she considers them interchangeable. Ironically, when the random lot, unbeknownst to her, leads to the selection of the Jew disguised as a Palestinian, her deliberate desire to transgress the ethnic boundaries is subverted, and another fictitious encounter is created.

The Israeli Jew's success in passing as a Palestinian worker culminates in an invitation by a 'fellow' Palestinian worker to visit his family in Gaza. The journey out of the borders of Israel thus ends up in the Occupied Territories, now experienced from the perspective of the occupied watching Israeli soldiers patrolling the street. This passage into the Palestinians' private space represents a new phase in his relations with them, yet it ultimately leads to the unravelling of his fictitious identity. When the female artist asks him to take a shower to remove the smell of his fishing expedition in Gaza and gives him clean clothes, he is visually transformed back into a middle-class Israeli Jew. This change of appearance foreshadows his internal transformation when, standing at the window and watching a child swinging on a tire, he remembers seeing the Palestinians loading boxes and a similar tire onto their car in Gaza. Seized with terror that the boy might be sitting on a tire filled with explosives, he runs out in panic screaming in Hebrew, 'A bomb! A bomb!' while waving the kids and their mothers away.

Nothing was found hidden inside the tire, but the scream shatters his fictitious identity as a mute person and a Palestinian as well as the apparent comradeship and trust he had formed with his coworkers. In the powerful segment that follows it, the camera moves back and forth between the Palestinians standing on the scaffolds speechlessly staring at him in disbelief and the exposed Israeli who stares back at them in silence without offering any explanation or apology. The sharp contrast between the commotion and panic triggered by his scream and the frozen silence that follows underscores the rupture that it introduces. The scene brings home the powerful grip of fear, violence and mistrust that undermines the ability to build human relations within the context of the Israeli–Palestinian conflict.

The closing scene shows the teacher returning to his family and home in Jerusalem, carrying gifts to his children. Unaware that the police informed his wife that he never left the country and that she participated in the unsuccessful search to locate him, he keeps the pretence of having returned from New York. His wife, on her part, does not confront him about it. Thus, the two collude in maintaining their silence about what took place since he left home, adding another twist to the theme of 'fictitious marriage'.

The transition in and out of identities demonstrates their potential fluidity and defies the tendency to essentialize Israeli identity and its inherent contrast to its two 'others', the exilic Jew and the Palestinian. The two identity exchanges nonetheless indicate different forms of passing. From a Zionist perspective, posing as an émigré from Israel (*yored*, literally, 'one who goes down') implies a moral and historical regression, yet in the context of post-1967 Israel and the excessive admiration of all things American, this transition becomes a form of 'passing up' (Aharoni 2009). In sharp contrast, however, the transition from a middle-class professional Israeli Jew to an illegal, blue-collar construction worker from the Occupied Territories implies a double 'passing down' (Bardenstein 2005). The film suggests the cultural closeness of Middle Eastern Jews and Arabs that challenges the essentialized dichotomy between Israeli Jews and Palestinians. The key character thus gives up his Israeli Jewish affiliation, middle-class comfort and his voice (an essential tool for a teacher) to become a voiceless manual worker who appears to passively follow others. In contrast to the stereotype of the mythological Sabra who pursues his goals with resilience, courage and determination, he is led by circumstances more than by a premeditated design, becoming a sort of 'tourist' in his wandering in and out of the fictitious realities of his assumed identities. These identity exchanges resemble brief experiments more than profound transformations, failing to introduce a significant change in his life or a better understanding of either self or the 'other'. The film thus weaves together the critique of contemporary Israel life and the decline of human values, the growing consumerism and anomie and the corrupt impact of the occupation on post-1967 Israeli society.

A BORROWED IDENTITY

Eran Riklis's film *A Borrowed Identity* (*aravim rokdim, zehut she'ula*) presents a different take on identity exchange from the perspective of a Palestinian citizen of Israel. An award-winning director, Riklis was selected to direct the film, which is based on two semiautobiographical Hebrew novels by the Palestinian Israeli writer and journalist Sayed Kashua, who adapted his works to the screen.[3] The film revolves around a precocious Israeli Arab boy named Eyad who leaves the Arab town of Tira, where he grew up to pursue his studies in an elite Jewish school in Jerusalem. The first part of the film is marked by Kashua's signature self-mockery and satirical approach to the portrayal of Israeli Arabs' attempts to negotiate between the Palestinian and Israeli societies. A typical scene comically features an Arab teacher introducing the Palestinian historical narrative to his students at the local school, only to quickly switch over to the official Israeli map and historical narrative when a visitor steps into the classroom. A more poignant scene, which inspired the title for Kashua's (2004) novel *Dancing Arabs* (and the original film title), takes place during the Gulf War, depicting Israeli Arabs dancing on rooftops upon hearing about Iraqi SCUDs directed at Tel Aviv.

Eyad is accepted to a prestigious liberal boarding school in Jerusalem attended by privileged middle-class Israeli Jewish students. Standing out among his peers with his Arabic name and accent, unfashionable clothes and lack of familiarity with Jewish teenagers' norms, Eyad becomes deeply aware of his otherness. In one of the film's most evocative scenes, he confronts his teacher and classmates during a Hebrew literature class discussion focused on the Jewish heroine of Amos Oz's canonical novel *My Michael* (1968) and her fears and sexual fantasies about her Arab childhood playmates. Eyad's animated intervention shifts the discussion from the Jewish woman's perspective to that of the Arabs. As time passes, Elad acquires native fluency in Hebrew, becomes better acquainted with his school culture and develops a close friendship with a girl in his class. Incidents outside of his school nonetheless serve as grim reminders of his otherness when Jewish teenagers from another school bully him or when Israeli soldiers stop to interrogate him upon hearing him speak in Arabic.

Eyad enters two sets of relations with peers that shape his future. When his school's social service program assigns him to help a Jewish boy of his age, Yonatan, who suffers from muscular dystrophy, the two boys who share the experience of being outsiders and different soon develop a close friendship. At some point, Yonatan tells his friend, 'Sometimes I forget you're an Arab', to which Eyad revealingly replies, 'Me too'. As Yonatan's health further deteriorates, his mother asks Eyad to move in with them to help care for her disabled son. The other significant relationship he develops is that with a female classmate, yet when the girl's mother finds out about it, she threatens to take her daughter out of school. Instead, Eyad volunteers to drop out of school to let his girlfriend complete her studies there. Although the two secretly remain romantically involved, his girlfriend eventually breaks off their relation to ensure her eligibility for a coveted position in the military intelligence. Whereas parental authority fails to separate them, the military service succeeds. As a high school dropout and an Arab, Eyad works as a dishwasher in a Jewish restaurant. When he learns from Palestinian coworkers that Arabs have no chance of being promoted to better positions, he applies to a waiter

position using Yonatan's name and address and is accepted. Although Yonatan's mother confronts him about borrowing her son's identity without his
or her permission, she allows him to maintain this borrowed identity in order
to help him advance.

The film focuses on Eyad's dual identities in Jerusalem as he takes care of
Yonatan and studies for his high school diploma. When his friend dies, the
borrowed identity evolves into a complete identity change. He and Yonatan's
mother take her son's body to a Muslim cemetery, wrapped in a cloth that
Eyad's devout Muslim grandmother kept from her pilgrimage to Mecca, to be
buried as if it were Eyad. Yonatan's burial thus provides the official closure
to Eyad's Arab identity that was fading in reality, allowing him to openly
embrace Yonatan's Jewish identity as his own.

A Borrowed Identity thus presents a prototypical case of passing up by a
member of a discriminated minority group who wishes to benefit from the
majority's privileges and avoid the prejudice and obstacles directed at members of his group. He can achieve this with the help of the secular, liberal
Jewish mother whose support expresses her gratitude to Eyad for the friendship and kindness he showed her terminally ill son and her commitment to
help him out of his predicament as an Israeli Arab. In contrast to *Fictitious
Marriage*, this film shows the possibility of creating a personal bond and
friendship in a society ridden by discrimination aggravated by the Israeli Palestinian conflict. In some respects, *A Borrowed Identity* follows Elia Kazan's
Gentleman's Agreement (1947), which offered a critique of anti-Semitism in
postwar American society. As in his earlier films, Riklis chooses the personal
and humanistic approach to the Israeli–Palestinian conflict, focusing on individuals' struggles and readiness to take personal risks in the face of prejudice,
hatred and inhumane bureaucratic procedures. Yet *A Borrowed Identity* does
not fully engage in the complexities of the process of identity exchange. The
film abandons Eyad's biological family and gives no account about whether
they are aware of his borrowed identity or believe his official death and its
impact on them. Moreover, his choice of passing as a Jew may have worked
out for him personally but can hardly be taken as a solution of a situation that
led him to embark on this route in the first place.

Indeed, the history of the screening of the film reveals the difficulties that
its distributors faced given the unfolding political events. The film was selected to open the prestigious Jerusalem Film Festival in the summer of 2014,
but when extreme violence erupted between Israel and the Palestinians (from
the Palestinians' capturing and killing of three Jewish youth to Israel's 'Operation Protective Edge' in Gaza), the film distributors postponed its screening to the late fall. The English title of the film was changed from *Dancing
Arabs* to the more neutral *A Borrowed Identity*, whereas the Hebrew title

combined the original and the new titles. The film received mixed reviews by critics and provoked some powerful anti-Arab statements on Israeli social media,[4] illustrating the negative emotions and inflammatory attitude towards both the Palestinians and the left-leaning, liberal Israeli Jews that the film set out to explore.

THE OTHER SON

Unlike the two Israeli films, which examined voluntary acts of identity change, Lorraine Lévy's *The Other Son* (*Le Fils de l'autre*) explores the case of an accidental identity exchange between two babies during an emergency evacuation from a Haifa hospital. The error comes to light 18 years later when medical tests prior to the military draft reveal that the young man who has been raised as an Israeli Jew could not be the son of his parents. A further investigation reveals that in the havoc created on that day, the hospital handed the Jewish baby to a Palestinian family from the West Bank and the Palestinian baby to a Jewish family from Israel. The hospital's director arranges a meeting with the two sets of parents in which he admits this past error. The discovery forces the families and their sons to come to terms with this misidentification and renegotiate their respective identities, family ties and national identification.

The Other Son follows the sons and their families confronting this unsettling and highly ambiguous situation within the context of the Israeli–Palestinian conflict. The young men, who grew up with a clear sense of identity in their respective communities—Yassin (the biological Jew) as a Palestinian and Joseph (the biological Palestinian) as an Israeli Jew—were socialized to consider the other community as their enemy. They now face the challenge of accepting their own blood ties with that community. At the age they legally turn from children to adults, they sort out their conflicting national identities to make a new sense of themselves and their multiple familial connections across the national divide. This fluid situation similarly challenges their families to navigate their relationship with the son whom they continue to raise as their own and their biological son who has been raised with a different religious and national identity. *The Other Son* introduces a situation that challenges the essentialized view of Palestinian Arab and Israeli Jewish identities and the tensions between them as well as the possibility of fostering a new sense of identity and familial bonds across the national divide within a conflict situation.

The film, created by a female director, presents gender as a more critical variable than national identity in determining the parents' initial responses to their son's mistaken identity. The two mothers show greater readiness to face the new situation as they look at the photos of the 'other sons' during their first meeting at the hospital, while the fathers are reluctant to assimilate the new information. When the Jewish mother calls the Palestinian mother and invites their family to come for a visit, the husbands grudgingly go along with this plan. Still, they are less inclined to open up to their newly discovered biological sons and cannot keep the national conflict from entering their inter-action. The situation is aggravated by the fact that the Palestinian family lives under Israeli occupation, while the Jewish father is a high-ranking military officer. During the visit, a political debate soon erupts between the fathers, while others attempt to diffuse the tension. The most extreme response to the new situation on the Palestinian side comes from Yassin's older brother, who now rejects him as 'one of them' and accuses his parents for going over to visit 'the occupiers'. On the Jewish side, the most extreme view is articulated by the family's rabbi, who informs Joseph that he must undergo an official conversion if he wishes to be considered a Jew. The shocked young man reminds the rabbi that he was his best student and challenges the logic of his response, asking if his parents' biological son who grew up as a Muslim is more Jewish than he is. The rabbi's unequivocal legalistic response, 'this is the way it is', unsettles Joseph without offering any guidance for the complex psychological, social and religious issues that the young man faces.

Adjusting to the new situation, Joseph decides to give up his earlier plan to volunteer for a highly select combat unit and forgo the military service, which is mandatory for Israeli Jewish men but voluntary for Arab citizens. Given his father's military career and the importance of military service for high school graduates, this decision also separates him from his father and his own peers who are about to be enlisted in the army. When his family goes to the synagogue on the Sabbath, Joseph travels by himself to the West Bank to visit his new family. Surprised by this unannounced visit, his Palestinian mother invites him to join them for dinner. The scene around the family's dinner table, with the son who is a stranger and does not speak their language, sensitively highlights the psychological, cultural and political challenges they all face. The awkward gathering changes when Joseph begins to sing an Ara-bic song he just learned by himself. His gesture communicates his desire to feel closer to his Arab family and its culture. It also reveals his love of music, which he unknowingly shares with his biological father and brother. As they join his singing and play their instruments, the music becomes an alternative language of intimacy between them and diffuses the strangeness that marked their earlier interaction.

In time, the strongest bond is formed between the two sons, who wish to learn more from each other about the life that could have been their own and work through the tensions that underlie their shifting identities. Their ambiguous sense of self is fraught with tensions as it is challenged by their cultural heritage and the violent reality of the Middle East, but their budding relation helps both negotiate the fluid situation. In a highly symbolic scene, as the two young men watch their reflection in the mirror, one of them notes that they are like Isaac and Ishmael. The analogy to the biblical ancestors who retrospectively represent brotherhood between a Jew and a Muslim offers a familial metaphor that provides an alternative interpretive framework to the Israeli–Palestinian conflict. Joseph intimates to Yassin the new sense of liminality that he experiences: 'I can't feel Jewish anymore, but I don't feel Arab'. Yassin, who begins to visit Joseph in Tel Aviv, appears to share this ambivalence. Their favourite meeting place is the beach, the unstructured liminal space, which is critical for an identity transformation (Van Gennep 1960).

Eventually, even the more reluctant male family members, the two fathers and the Palestinian brother, gradually accept the situation and open up to interacting with 'the other son' and 'the other family'. The Israeli Jewish and the Palestinian Muslim fathers meet in a café, and the Israeli officer arranges work permits for his new Palestinian relatives. The Palestinian brother shakes hands with Joseph's father when he sees him walking by himself at night beyond the Israeli checkpoint looking for Joseph, who was visiting his Palestinian family. When the Palestinian brother joins Yassin on a visit to Tel Aviv and the three young men spend time on the beach, hooligans attack Joseph at night, and Yassin and his Palestinian brother rescue him. The scene with the two of them around Joseph's bed in the hospital represents their new affinity as 'brothers' beyond the distinctions of blood and national ties.

The film does not provide closure and leaves the viewer to imagine how the process might be developed from this point on. The end suggests that the young people whose lives became entangled through an accidental identity exchange at birth were learning to accept the fluidity of their identities and family ties with the support of their mothers and, more gradually, that of the other family members. Significantly, the film presents an optimistic take on the two families' readiness to accommodate and rebuild their bonds in spite of the ongoing national conflict and without external forces that further complicate this process.[5]

CONCLUSION

The three films discussed in this chapter illustrate different takes on the meanings and complexities of the process of identity exchanges between

Israeli Jews and Palestinians. Whether they feature an identity change that results from a deliberate action, incidental circumstances or a human error, their focus on identity change raises the possibility of malleable identities, and their plot reveals some of the challenges and constraints following such transition. *A Borrowed Identity* explores the case of 'passing up', which involves a gradual and deliberate process that culminates in a complete identity exchange as an Israeli Palestinian buries himself to fully assume the identity of an Israeli Jew. *Fictitious Marriage* presents the opposite process of 'passing down' for a limited time without indicating clearly if the transition was premeditated or the outcome of an incidental mistake. Yet once he is misidentified as a Palestinian, he actively embraces this identity until the imagined state of emergency, and his fear for the children's lives breaks through his pretence. *The Other Son* differs from both films in featuring an unknown identity exchange between Palestinian and Jewish babies that forces the individuals unintentionally involved to negotiate their personal, familial, religious and national affiliations.

In itself, the exploration of identity exchange does not imply an optimistic take on the conflict or the ability to resolve it. Neither the linear progression from one identity to the other that *A Borrowed Identity* presents nor the circular movement that *Fictitious Marriage* depicts offers an alternative to the binary opposition between Jews and Palestinians or the prejudice and hostility that feeds into the Israeli–Palestinian conflict. It may be telling that it took a French director to offer the possibility of creating personal relations and human ties across the national divide, drawing on her position as an outsider to the conflict, as she acknowledges in an interview (Ward 2013).

The featuring of identity exchanges between Israeli Jews and Palestinians challenges the common tendency to essentialize those identities as inherently opposed to each other and demonstrates the spectrum of identity formations that display their fluidity. As Carol Bardenstein (2005) points out, the cinematic representations suggest that such exchanges may be more easily attainable between those who are placed closer to each other on that identity continuum between European (Ashkenazi) Jews, Middle Eastern (Mizrahi) Jews and Palestinian citizens of Israel and other Palestinians.[6] In addressing this theme, the films open for the viewer the possibility to rethink the essentialized Jewish/Palestinian dichotomy that bolsters the conflict.

The cinematic engagement with the theme of identity exchange reveals the human dimension of the impact of the conflict on the lives of individuals whose identities shift, providing a venue for experiencing empathy with the other. The films offer a social critique of the prejudice, social stereotypes and violence that prompt a young Palestinian Israeli to borrow his dying Jewish friend's identity and ultimately have it replace his own or an Israeli man of

Middle Eastern origins to suspect Palestinian coworkers whom he befriended as terrorists. The discussion of the cinematic portrayal of identity exchanges thus contributes to the broader discussion of hybrid-identity formations as well as sheds light on the possibility of fostering human relations and personal ties between Israelis and Palestinians as a way of building trust and moving forward in peace building.

NOTES

1. See this volume's introduction and the discussion of these issues in the chapters by Payne, Sturken, and Zaretzky.

2. The film received several awards and was recently mentioned by a prominent Israeli film critic in a select list of Israeli films (Klein 2017).

3. The script combines parts of two of Sayed Kashua's Hebrew novels, *Dancing Arabs*, which he published in 2002 (English translation 2004), and *Second Person Singular*, which he published in 2010 (English translation 2012). In 1986, Anton Shammas, an Israeli Palestinian writer, published his pathbreaking Hebrew novel *Arabesques* (English translation 2001), in which mirroring and exchanges of identities are abundant (Hochberg 2010; Levy 2014).

4. Positive responses to *Borrowed Identity* included reviews by major film critics (Duvdevani 2014; Klein 2014), yet others wrote mixed or negative reviews (Kiniso 2014; Libergal 2014; Shamir 2014). The social media were filled with negative and hateful responses, some of which were triggered by the title (Kalderon 2014).

5. The film has received positive reviews of its noted sensitivity to cultural differences and its focus on the personal dimensions of the conflict (Mintze 2012; Morris 2012; Scott 2012).

6. Both Bardenstein (2005) and Preminger (2012) include in their discussion the theme of identity exchange in cross-casting, which the present chapter does not address.

REFERENCES

Aharoni, Mattan. 2009. 'Cultural Encounter, Peeling Off and Acquiring New Identities in the Film *Fictitious Marriage*'. *Selil: A Digital Magazine for History, Film, and Television* 3 (Summer): 51–65. (in Hebrew)

Augé, Marc. 1995. *Non-Places: Introduction to an Anthropology of Supermodernity*. London: Verso.

Auron, Yair. 2013. *The Holocaust, the Rebirth and the Nakba*. Tel Aviv: Resling. (in Hebrew)

Bardenstein, Carol. 2005. 'Cross/Cast: Passing in Israeli and Palestinian Cinema'. In *Palestine, Israel, and the Politics of Popular Culture*, edited by Rebecca L. Stein and Tel Swendburg, 99–124. Durham, NC: Duke University Press.

Bekerman, Zvi, Michalinos Zembylas, and Clair McGlenn. 2009. 'Working toward the De-Essentialization of Identity Categories in Conflict and Postconflict Societies: Israel, Cyprus, and Northern Ireland'. *Comparative Education Review* 53, no. 2: 213–34.

Duvdevani, Shmulik. 2014. 'Dancing Arabs: Leave the Populism, Watch the Film'. *Yediot Ahronot*, 30 November. http://www.ynet.co.il/articles/0.7340.L-4597476.00.html. (in Hebrew)

Hochberg, Gil. 2010. 'To Be or Not to Be an Israeli Arab: Sayed Kashua and the Prospect of Minority Speech-Acts'. *Comparative Literature* 62, no. 1: 68–88.

Hughes, Caroline, Joakim Öjendal, and Isabell Schierenbeck. 2015. 'The Struggle versus the Song—The Local Turn in Peacebuilding: An Introduction'. *Third World Quarterly* 36, no. 5: 817–24.

Kalderon, Aviad. 2014. 'Facebook Protest against the Film "Dancing Arabs—A Borrowed Identity"'. *Walla*, 20 November. http://e.walla.co.il/item/2803598. (in Hebrew)

Kashua, Sayed. 2004. *Dancing Arabs*. New York: Grove Press.

———. 2012. *Second Person Singular.* New York: Grove Press.

Kiniso, Shani. 2014. 'Dancing Arabs—A Borrowed Identity: A Review'. 6 December. http://srita.net/2014/12/06/dancing_arabs_review. (in Hebrew)

Klein, Uri. 2014. 'Why It Is Important to Watch *Dancing Arabs*'. In *Ha'aretz*, Gallery, 27 November. http://www.haaretz.co.il/gallery/cinema/movie-reviews/.premium-1.2496629. (in Hebrew)

———. 2017. 'Israeli Films Which Every Israeli Film Buff Should Watch'. *Ha'aretz*, *Gallery*, 1 May. http://www.haaretz.co.il/gallery/cinema/.premium-1.4058361. (in Hebrew)

Learning Each Other's Historical Narrative: Palestinians and Israelis. 2002, pt. 1. 2006, pt. 2. Beit Jallah, Palestinian National Authority: Peace Research Institute in the Middle East.

Leonardsson, Hanna, and Gustav Rudd. 2015. 'The "Local Turn" in Peacebuilding: A Literature Review of Effective and Emancipatory Local Peacebuilding'. *Third World Quarterly* 36, no. 5: 825–39.

Levy, Lital. 2014. *Poetic Trespass: Writing between Hebrew and Arabic in Israel/Palestine*. Princeton, NJ: Princeton University Press.

Libergal, Ofer. 2014. 'Without Cipralex: Dancing Arabs—A Borrowed Identity without Balance'. 27 November. http://e.walla.co.il/item/2804939. (in Hebrew)

MacCannell, Dean. 1999. *The Tourist: A New Theory of the Leisure Class*. Berkeley: University of California Press.

Mintze, Jordan. 2012. 'The Other Son (Le Fils de l'autre): Film Review'. 19 April. http://www.hollywoodreporter.com/review/film-other-son-le-fils-de-l-314229U.

Morris, Wesley. 2012. '"The Other Son" Is a Switch from Usual Mideast Melodrama'. *Boston Globe*, 25 October. http://archive.boston.com/ae/movies/2012/10/25/the-other-son-switch-from-usual-mideast-melodrama/dFHSrlr4NcqcswFu0EXNuJ/story.html.

Oz, Amos. 1968. *My Michael*. Tel Aviv: Am Oved. (Hebrew).

Preminger, Anat. 2012. 'The Arab Other in Israeli Cinema and Discourse'. *Journalism and Mass Communication* 2, no. 2: 412–20.

Rouhana, Nadim N. 1997. *Palestinian Citizens in a Jewish Ethnic State: Identities in Conflict*. New Haven, CT: Yale University Press.

———, ed. 2017. *Israel and Its Palestinian Citizens: Ethnic Privileges in the Jewish State*. Cambridge: Cambridge University Press.

Scott, A. O. 2012. '"The Other Son", about the Palestinian-Israeli Divide'. *New York Times*, 25 October. http://www.nytimes.com/2012/10/26/MOVIES/THE-OTHER-SON-ABOUT-THE-PALESTINIAN-ISRAELI-DIVIDE.HTML?_R=1.

Shamir, Oron. 2014. 'Dancing Arabs: To Dance between Identities'. *Achbar Ha'Ir*, 27 November. http://www.mouse.co.il/CM.articles_item.519.209.77464.aspx. (in Hebrew)

Shammas, Anton. 2001. *Arabesques*. Berkeley: University of California Press.

Shenhav, Yehuda. 2006. *The Arab Jews: A Postcolonial Reading of Nationalism, Religion and Ethnicity*. Stanford, CA: Stanford University Press.

Shenhav, Yehuda, and Hannan Hever. 2012. '"Arab Jews" after Structuralism: Zionist Discourse and the (De)formation of an Ethnic Identity'. *Social Identities* 18, no. 1: 101–18.

Van Gennep, Arnold. 1960. *The Rites of Passage*. Chicago: University of Chicago Press.

Ward, Sarah. 2013. 'Interview with Lorraine Lévy, Director of *The Other Son*'. *Trespass Magazine*, 13 May. http://www.trespassmag.com/interview-with-lorraine-levy-director-of-the-other-son.

Zertal, Idith. 2005. *Israel's Holocaust and the Politics of Nationhood*. Cambridge: Cambridge University Press.

Zerubavel, Yael. 1995. *Recovered Roots: Collective Memory and the Making of Israeli National Tradition*. Chicago: University of Chicago Press.

———. 2002. 'The Mythological Sabra and Jewish Past: Trauma, Memory, and Contested Identities'. *Israel Studies* 7, no. 2: 115–44.

———. 2006. 'Patriotic Sacrifice and the Burden of Memory in Israeli Secular National Hebrew Culture'. In *Memory and Violence in the Middle East and North Africa*, edited by Ussama Makdisi and Paul A. Silverstein, 77–100. Bloomington: Indiana University Press.

———. 2008. 'Memory, the Rebirth of the Native, and the "Hebrew Bedouin" Identity'. *Social Research* 75, no. 1: 315–52.

Chapter Eight

Silence

'Do Not Confuse It with Any Kind of Absence'

Leigh A. Payne

'There is no such thing as silence', composer John Cage famously quipped (Gann 2010). Remembering to not repeat the past, in contrast, is built on the foundation of overcoming silence about that violent past. 'Speaking truth to power' is the call behind victim-oriented approaches in peace studies. They emphasize verbal testimony, public truth telling, and official claim making to give voice to the voiceless and to advance justice for atrocities committed. 'Never again!' is the cry made out loud and often in human rights mobilizations to avoid in the future the horrors of past violence. To suggest that there is no such thing as silence in the aftermath of violent conflict challenges the core orientation of peace studies to struggle against oblivion and forgetting.

Yet Cage is certainly right that complete silence—a silence capable of obliterating sound or memory—does not exist. The capacity to mobilize for peace emerges not out of total silence but from fractured silence, a silence that cannot be kept, that has already begun to break. The battle to speak out and to make known coexists in violent regimes and situations alongside active silencing efforts. This kind of silence resembles Cage's 4'33" silent composition;[1] even imposed silence fails to obliterate expression.

Cage's composition further highlights the 'purposeful use' (Hogan, cited in Glenn and Ratcliffe 2011, 5) of silence to effectively make a point, to draw attention to expression—musical or not—that might not otherwise be heard. This type of silence—that even Cage acknowledged—not only exists but also may even improve on sound, on language. In the words of Susan Sontag ([1969] 2002), silence overcomes the limitations of language in expressing 'unspeakableness, indescribability, ineffability'. In remembering past violence, silence may sometimes provide the only way to communicate the lived horrors and their haunting. At other times, it provides a better, more effective way of expressing the events of the past and the hopes for the future. Some silences work on behalf of victims and survivors of those atrocities, providing protection from greater harm. Silence is sometimes a 'chosen instrument of power' (Parrott 2012, 383) that has been used to suppress expression; it can be—and has been–an effective instrument in the struggle against forgetting. It is, as such, worth keeping, respecting, and even admiring, like 4′33″, because of what it allows us to hear, to know, if we listen closely.

To rethink peace studies is to remain open to silence as an effective, powerful, acceptable and appropriate form of expression. Silence is not the same as silencing expressive acts that remember the past. It is not always about forgetting and oblivion. It is sometimes a deliberate and purposive strategy used by victims, to be heard, to be safe, to be respected, to be understood, to have dignity restored. Silence is, in the words of Ashis Nandy (in this volume), one of the unexamined 'black holes' of peace studies. As Adrienne Rich (2008) has written, 'Silence can be a plan, rigorously executed, the blueprint to a life . . . do not confuse it with any kind of absence'.

SILENCE AND SILENCES

Silence, as Cage portrayed in 4′33″, is not an absence of sound or expression. At times, it is omission, leaving something out. At other times, it constitutes nonverbal forms of communication, the expression of ideas and emotions without words. It is not easily or comfortably defined, in Foucault's (1978) words, as a 'binary division to be made between what one says and what one does not say' (27). There are, instead, 'different ways of not saying such things, how those who can and those who cannot speak of them are distributed, which type of discourse is authorized, or which form of discretion is required in either case. There is not one but many silences, and they are an integral part of the strategies that underlie and permeate discourses'.[2]

In the promotion of peace and in memory studies, the most constant and enduring characteristic of silence is how it has been used in conscious and unconscious efforts to forget the past, to turn the page and to move on. Silence is equated with silencing, the harmful and dangerous power to suppress expressions of pain and wrongdoing, as explored in Nitin Sawhney's chapter in this volume. The power of silence in obliterating language is also evident in the notion of the 'inexpressibility of pain' (Scarry 1985), the incapacity of words to effectively communicate atrocity. Memory politics and peace studies have struggled with these dual notions of silence: its necessity because language fails to communicate atrocity and the need to overcome silence to communicate atrocity so that it will not occur again. In *Maus*, also discussed in Beverley Curran's chapter in this volume, Art Spiegelman (1991, 393) reflects on the struggle over and against silence. The figure representing his therapist questions the enterprise since books have not brought change and cannot represent those who did not survive to tell their stories.

As the excerpt from *Maus* suggests, the limitations of language show where silence exists, why it is sometimes more expressive than verbal communication but also how difficult it is to respectfully preserve when it shares the desire to fill a void in memory and knowledge. This chapter explores the potential power and uses of silence in the service of memory against forgetting. It suggests that even in silence—especially with particular types of silences—hearing, listening and understanding the past occurs. It suggests that the promotion of peace may depend as much on these silences as on speech.

SILENCE AS THE ONLY POSSIBLE WAY

When speaking out is too dangerous, silent expression becomes the only possible form of expression. Art, performance and the media emerge during dictatorships when words are censored or forbidden.[3] That these forms persist into the democratic period attests to their continued power to speak and to be heard by new generations: a persistent struggle of 'never again!' The Mothers of the Plaza de Mayo, explored in Natasha Zaretsky's chapter in this volume, still walk quietly every Thursday afternoon in front of the Argentine presidential palace, 33 years after the end of the dictatorship. They wear their signature white head scarves representing the diapers of their disappeared children. They still bear photos of their disappeared children calling for their reappearance alive.

This silent vigil continues to have power and has even spread to other parts of the world.[4] Stencils of bicycles used by the disappeared students still appear on Rosario's (Argentina) city walls, a silent reminder of a lost generation. The appearance of life-size paper silhouettes that appeared overnight during the Argentine civil-military dictatorship, quietly and clandestinely denouncing the disappearances, have been incorporated into a 'siluetazo' art and memory project by Eduardo Gil today (Romero 2013). Quiet bones from the Cambodian killing fields are still piled up at the former Tuol Sleng prison, now a museum, nearly four decades after Pol Pot was deposed. Bones are visited in churches and other sites of the Rwandan genocide. In the former Villa Grimaldi Torture Center, now the International Peace Park in Santiago, Chile, rose bushes have been planted in the past few years, each one named after a woman tortured there. The smell of roses amid the sounds of horror are the enduring memories of victims of that place long after the regime responsible and the building itself cease to exist.

In *Trauma, Taboo, and Truth-Telling*, Nancy Gates-Madsen (2016) explores quiet reflective memorial sites aimed at individual mourning and remembrance and society-wide attention to the loss, a silent call for 'never again!' They are intentionally and deliberately silent. They recognize the need for stillness to absorb the magnitude of the loss. Lima's 'Crying Eye' memorial site represents the Earth Mother (Pachamama) with a stream of constant tears. The visitor reaches her by following a circular path lined with stones engraved with the names of the dead and disappeared in Peru's armed conflict. The names of the disappeared appear without sound and permanently in the Forest of Memory in Tucumán, Argentina (Milton 2005). One of the trees was planted by poet Juan González in memory of his detained and disappeared son Hernán. González's 'poetry against the dictatorship', like the tree he planted, reflect silent grief, protest and memory in their titles: 'The Cry in the Heavens' and 'Tribulations of Language'.[5] The work of Marcelo Brodsky (2007) also represents a silence through reflection, sometimes literally so. He photographs two students looking at his piece, the Buenos Aires National High School (Colegio Nacional de Buenos Aires), in which they silently examine the photograph, appearing to be superimposed on the ghosts of those students who disappeared from the school during the dictatorship.

These are silent and sacred reflections on the enormity of loss, grief and mourning that extend beyond time. The silent spaces they create provide a societal equivalent of private memorial services, calling for a moment of silence to remember. Public and collective rituals reenact those ceremonies. Six moments of silence occur during the memorial events surrounding 9/11 corresponding to specific tragedies on that day. The United Kingdom comes to a near standstill on the eleventh hour of the eleventh day of the eleventh month to remember the tragedy of World War I. Ephratt (2008, 1918) states that 'in cases of extreme emotional experience . . . or in cases of nonverbal experience such as absence and loss (death), silence is to be seen as the preferred mode of expression, but in many such cases also as the most authentic and most adequate, hence the only possible way to communicate the emotional experience' (1918).

Whether these sacred and silent spaces are the *only* way or even the best way of expressing tragedy is often questioned. Marita Sturken's chapter in this volume examines the contention over memorialization. Incidents of politically infused vandalism, such as the orange pro-Fujimori dictatorship paint thrown on the Crying Eye monument, are not necessarily the most troubling acts. The impulse to destroy sacred spaces of memory may reinforce their power to communicate. More concerning is disrespect, disregard and disengagement. Disrespect involves carrying away bones as tourist souvenirs in Rwanda. When graffiti artists tag, throw up and bomb (Ross 2016) the

Women in the Memory Monument in Santiago, they disregard its value and meaning. The space and its significance are rendered banal—a mere tourist site or urban space—disengaged from remembrance to not repeat the past.

SILENCE AS EFFECTIVE EXPRESSION

That silent spaces do not reach everyone does not take away from their capacity to communicate to many the unspeakable loss, indescribable pain, ineffable harm. Silence expresses what is not there, what is no longer with us, what continues to have power over us in memory.

Silence is a speech act. We recognize this in our everyday language. We say, 'silence gripped'. The artist Alec Von Bargen tries to capture that grip of silence—a way of feeling, of overcoming numbness—in his work: 'I believe that as a society we have become immune to the suffering, the solitude, the silent pleas of others. We are saturated by images . . . which we generally can't directly relate to so we tend to simply turn the page'.[6] John McPhee (2015) shares this view about silences when he claims that 'it's what you leave out' that makes for effective communication and commands attention. Still others refer to 'silence's power to speak . . . more poignantly than words themselves often have the capacity to enjoin' (Slattery 2007, 73). In silence is the 'potential to profoundly disrupt, shift, and deploy power' (Glenn 2004, 332).

All these authors speak to the dangers of an excess of words and memory. Consider Borges's (1954) story *Funes, el memorioso*. Borges writes, 'The truth is that we all live by leaving behind' (113). He goes on to say, 'To think is to forget a difference, to generalize, to abstract. In the overly replete world of Funes there were nothing but details, almost contiguous details' (115). Borges thus agrees that omission—leaving out or silencing some of the details—enables us to focus on the important ones.

Images play a role in paring down distracting details. A person, a face, one moment effectively communicate an enduring sense of loss. In Spain's *guerra de esquelas*, relatives placed in newspapers more than 400 notices for those killed in the Civil War 70 or more years after their death (Fernández de Mata 2009). Similarly, Cecilia Sosa (2007) writes of the remembrances of the dead and the disappeared that appear daily in Argentina's *Página/12* newspaper: 'They always draw your attention to see them appear as you turn the page, in a space between news stories. Young faces, smiling. Longed for in their absence, year after year'.[7] Schindel (1997) refers to these remembrances as 'the words of faces' (las palabras del rostro). She says, 'There are the faces. Eloquent in their timeless muteness, the photos as a visible expression of a crime [the regime] tried to hide'. The faces taunt, they defy, they assert themselves soundlessly.

They express with a silent look full of expression that the past will not be forgotten.

The emotional power of eye contact, even in still images, has been verified in psychological (and advertising) studies. 'The magnetic and mesmeric nature of eye contact' activates 'parts of the brain that allow us to more acutely and accurately process another person's feelings and intentions' (Murphy 2014). It is thus no wonder that the silent eyes of the dead and disappeared speak to us in powerful and emotive ways and that their photographs are so frequently used to express loss and atrocity.

Alejandro Baer's (2005) work on video testimony highlights the communicative and epistemological value of the unspoken: 'face, gestures, pauses, silences, and hesitations' (123). Baer writes that facial expressions wear the signs of the event: 'the face remembers (as it re-lives the "unrepresentable" occurrences) and tells the story. The video recording captures the visual drama of the testimony. Facial expressions, emotions, and subtle body language' (122). Citing Levinas (1996) and Chalier (1995), Baer writes that the face creates a 'unique communicative connection' between the speaker and the listener that words on a page or even spoken words without images cannot achieve. The visual, the traces of the horror, are seen, felt and experienced. The observer is there, a witness (123). Baer (2006) has written that 'there are truths that are so profound that they can only be transmitted through silence' (102). Yael Zerubavel builds on this possibility or impossibility of meaningful dialogue in her chapter in this volume.

The power of silence to communicate the truth and memory of past atrocity to an otherwise unconnected audience relies on the subconscious effect of the transmission of memory through silent facial expression. Silence can also involve a deliberate act of resistance and protection that can serve memory politics and promote peace. As Jill Parrott (2012) states, 'Keeping silent as a matter of self-restraint is a powerful move—it involves the choosing of one's rhetorical weapons, which are (in this case) protective gear' (386).

SILENCE AS PROTECTIVE GEAR

Several observers recall the appearance, in the years before the Argentine coup but after repression had already begun, of a sign hung on the Buenos Aires obelisk landmark with the words 'Silence is health'. It was intended to quell traffic-related noise, but observers felt it carried a more sinister message about the dangers—in the form of violent reprisals—of speaking out.[8]

Believing that silence is a healthy alternative is not the exclusive domain of politically powerful repressors and suppressors of speech and memory.

Silence is considered to have healing powers to deal with 'chaos and sorrow', as one advertisement for a silent retreat professed. The retreat claimed to appeal to 'everyone willing to put aside past memories and beliefs and open to the path of truth' (Landrith 2016). This statement challenges—and appears to criticize—the memory politics orientation around finding truth through memory and testimony. The retreat suggests that what might be good for societies emerging from atrocity—excessive dwelling on the past—can be harmful to individual victims of wrongdoing. It contends that individuals who let go of the traps of the past—who leave behind recrimination and embrace silence—will live healthier and liberating lives.

The dilemma for victims is not always one of denunciation versus healthy silence. Denouncing violence may always seem like the right thing to do for the collective good, to make violence visible and actionable, to prevent their reoccurrence. Victims of violence are often coerced into contributing to this greater societal goal and to overcome the very high personal costs they anticipate. Victims of sexual violence in making public the wrongdoing they experienced face trauma in the retelling, stigma, voyeurism, blame, doubt and distrust. They usually fail to control the story once it is out. Moreover, justice and nonrepetition is not a guaranteed outcome. These calculations may explain why sexual violence is one abuse over which silence prevails in memory politics. While the victims of sexual violation make testimony, their testimony often leaves out—silences—specific details.[9] Their silence is not the same as an absence of truth about the past; instead, sexual violence becomes part of a 'public secret'. The silence surrounding the sexual violence experienced by individuals may provide—or may at least be perceived as providing—a better possibility of protection than compelling individuals to speak out before societies are capable of hearing and understanding what happened to them.[10]

Although not the accused, victims of sexual violence often feel that they are on trial (Mack 2011). In this context, they sometimes exert a 'right to remain silent'. They are not legally compelled to speak out, and their reason for refusing to do so acknowledges that 'anything said can and will be used against the individual in court'. The *Miranda* warnings, similar to 'pleading the fifth' (referring to the U.S. Constitution's Fifth Amendment right to a fair trial), protect the individual from being compelled to speak. Silence affords protection. Kathleen Cavanagh (2002, 492) summarizes the two protections embodied in the right to silence: from a forced confession and from self-incrimination. Victims, but particularly victims of sexual violence, often need these protections from coerced testimony and stigma. Silence allows them the freedom to opt 'out of oppressive familial and state structures', to return to their communities with their dignity intact (Mack 2011, 211).

Silence in this form could be considered a subversive act. Recognizing the potential social harm of the 'right to remain silent', the United Kingdom does not guarantee such protections (Cavanagh 2002, 495). Cavanagh states, 'The erosion of the right to silence is just one casualty in the "war on terrorism"' (513). With the Northern Ireland conflict, Cavanagh notes the suspension of legally protected silence, also used elsewhere, in which the rights of the individual are denied in favour of the rights of societies and states to seek protection from violence through speech, even coerced speech.[11]

Memory entrepreneurs may overlook the incompatibility between individual and victims' protections (through silence and from public spectacle) and societal needs (truth and nonrepetition).[12] They could point to the so-called comfort women who overcame the fear of stigma to receive compensation and acknowledgement for the systematic use of sexual violence and enslavement in World War II. They might not see the danger in suspending individuals' 'right to silence' to promote the needs of societies for denunciations and collective remembrance.

Yet David Rieff (2016a, 2016b) has recently cast doubt on the social value of public remembrance; he suggests that memory politics has gone too far and calls for silence and forgetting. 'We have been taught to believe that the remembering of the past and its corollary, the memorializing of collective historical memory, has become one of humanity's highest moral obligations', he states (2016a), before advancing the idea of collective forgetting and silence as a surer path to ending past violence. Against the 'terror of forgetting' that Rieff poses (2016a). 'the terror of remembering too well, too vividly'. 'Given humanity's tendency towards aggression', Rieff argues, 'it is at least possible that forgetting . . . may be the only safe response. . . . To put the dilemma even more bluntly, remembrance may be the ally of justice, but it is no reliable friend to peace, whereas forgetting can be'.

Rieff's position seems to be a throwback to an earlier era in which forgetting for the sake of peace and stability was viewed as preferable to perpetual memory and contention. The threat of plunging countries back into conflict is the sort of 'functional silencing' that governments have used to avoid accountability and continued conflict. Social science quantitative analysis disproves this assumption by showing that trials and contention contribute to peace, democracy and human rights (Dancy et al. in press; Kim and Sikkink 2010; Olsen, Payne, and Reiter 2010). And yet societies—like Spain—continue to promote silence to avoid the assumed return to bloodbath.

C. M. Hardt's (2005) documentary film *Death in El Valle* recounts the filmmaker's successful efforts in finding her grandfather's killer in the Spanish Civil War. After she triumphantly presents her evidence to her mother, aunts and uncles, she is surprised by their reaction. They did not want to know. They explain to her that with the knowledge, they will be forced to avenge their father's death. With no possibility of trial, they would have to take violence into their own hands. Violence begets violence. Living with the silence and the pretence of not knowing, therefore, protects against that violence.

SILENCE AS POWER

Returning to Cage, it would be absurd on the one hand to contend that 'there is no such thing as silence' in memory politics. On the other, like Cage, an interrogation of silence in memory politics and peace studies reveals powerful forms of expression about the violent past.

The power of silence resides in omission, allowing for stronger emotive expression. Silence fills in where there is an absence of words and strips down where there is an excess. Sontag ([1969] 2002) contends that 'we lack words and we have too many of them'. She goes on to claim, 'Words are crude, and they're also too busy—inviting a hyperactivity of consciousness which is not only dysfunctional in terms of human capacities of feeling and acting, but which actively deadens the mind and blunts the senses'. Silence, in contrast, intensifies sensation;[13] its power is in that capacity to make us feel.

Everyday usage recognizes the power of silence. 'There are no words' and 'I am speechless' are common expressions that reveal silence's power to express emotions where words cannot. Silence surrounds taboos acknowledging their power in the memory narrative. These events are known—public secrets—but are expressed in their absence. Once they are invoked in spoken narrative, they no longer have that power. The silence expresses the power that certain acts continue to have.

Yet for silence to be powerful and therefore effective, it has to be heard. In this way, silence corresponds to an effective form of speech 'that compels listeners, one that is heard', not one that can be 'tuned out' (hooks 1989, 6). This is why Cage's 4′33″ composition has effect, as the audience is called together to listen to what the silence expresses. Similarly, in ceremonies or rituals, silent reflection is evoked; it does not evolve naturally or organically. The power of silence lies in its capacity to disrupt or interrupt, to be set apart. Similarly, when speech is expected and does not occur, silence's power is in defiance, a refusal to comply.

Memory politics, moreover, concede to victims, survivors and their defenders the moral authority—the power—to silence aspects of the violent past. They possess the power to clear away, omit, silence narratives about the past that jeopardize the 'never again!' agenda. Such an act occurred in

2006 when the government of Nestor Kirchner excised from the Argentine National Truth Commission (CONADEP) Report—23 years after it was written—references to the 'two-demons' theory. The silencing obliterated the military's justification for its coup and repressive regime in the name of establishing order when the left took up arms against the state.[14]

In sum, silence—when it is chosen and not imposed, when it is used purposefully (Glenn 2004, 13)—has the power to effectively express and protect. Its power to communicate advances the memory politics of—and promotion of peace through—'never again!' In that sense, and as Adrienne Rich (2008; see also Glenn 2004, 1) so eloquently states,

> Silence can be a plan
> rigorously executed
>
> the blueprint to a life
>
> It is a presence
> it has a history a form
>
> Do not confuse it
> with any kind of absence

NOTES

1. See Cage's 4'33", directed, photographed and edited by Joel Hochberg, soloist William Marx, McCallum Theatre, Palm Desert, California, uploaded 15 December 2010 to https://www.youtube.com/watch?v=JTEFKFiXSx4 (accessed 14 April 2016).

2. See more at http://percaritatem.com/2010/01/09/foucault-on-what-is-said-in-silence/#sthash.koeDb7gb.dpuf.

3. One current example is Chinese photographer Xiaobo Liu, whose artist husband has faced imprisonment for open calls for democracy and human rights. Liu has chosen a 'silent protest' art form using black-and-white photographs of dolls, 'the size of infants but with adult faces—faces that show pain or terror, frozen cries, a hint of biliousness. . . . Some of the dolls appear to be imprisoned; others appear to be the victims of violent trauma and massacre' (Link 2012, 6–7).

4. A novel shows the power of the Madres symbol by suggesting that 'extras' might have to fill in when the aging mothers die and the day and time might be changed for greater touristic convenience (Bilbija and Payne 2011, 30; Shua 1997). For parallel types of movements, see Women in Black (Pryor 2011).

5. For information on the Memory Forest, see http://signodisociado.blogspot.com.ar/2009/01/el-bosque-de-la-memoria-tucuman.html. For information on Juan González and his poetry, see http://www.lagaceta.com.ar/blogs/toukouman/631970/

poesia-versus-dictadura-juan-gonzalez-tribulaciones-lengua.html (accessed 13 April 2016).

6. 'The Art of Silence and Remembering through the Works of Alec Von Bargen'. See https://www.cobosocial.com/art-and-design/art-silence-10-ways-seeing (accessed 15 April 2016).

7. In this review of a collection of the remembrances, *Poesia diaria*, Virginia Giannoni, who collected the images and edited the collection, remarked, 'It always struck me how they interrupted reality, these words that expressed so much pain, on paper that could be used to wrap up potatoes'.

8. Writer Uki Goñi (2015), for example, writes, 'During these long walks, I came across a disturbing sign of the times that I should perhaps have heeded better. On the broad 9 de Julio Avenue that divides Buenos Aires in half—"the widest avenue in the world", according to some Argentines—stands a giant white obelisk that is the city's most conspicuous landmark. In 1974, the landmark lost its virginity in the strangest of ways. A revolving billboard was suspended around the Obelisco, snugly encircling the huge white phallus. Round and round the ring turned, inscribed with an Orwellian message in bold blue letters on a plain white background: "Silence Is Health"' (from https://faustasblog.com/2015/05/argentina-silence-is-health [accessed 13 April 2016]). Marguerite Feitlowitz (1998, 34) has also written about the sign and its message.

9. See, for example, Theidon (2015).

10. The renowned human rights professor David Weissbrodt of the University of Minnesota Law School, in a discussion at the UMN Human Rights Salon on 12 April 2016, suggested that silence over torture and legal wrongdoing in Guantanamo resembles this form of cautionary or protective silence. He contends that moving forward with legal cases in Guantanamo would likely backfire due to a general unwillingness to accept wrongdoing in the U.S. war on terror. Evidence is actively gathered for future litigation. That evidence constitutes a public secret: widely known but not openly acknowledged.

11. Oren Gross (1998) argues that emergency conditions might warrant some suspension of these rights, but 'this accommodation ought to take place within the confines of legality' . . . that balance 'state security with the demands of individual freedoms, liberties, and rights'. See also Cavanagh (2002, 513).

12. Another way to think about this notion of compelling speech is around the expressive function of law and courts. Antony Duff (2011) and others recognize the communicative effect or expressive function of law and criminal punishment. Is there also a 'silencing' effect of law and criminal punishment? Considering sexual violations, for example, the exoneration of alleged rapists, particularly in intimate or date-rape cases, communicates to victims the impossibility of conviction. Silence may thus prove more effective in protecting the victim than trial that leads to the exoneration of the rapist.

13. See the review of Sara Maitland's 'A Book of Silence' in 'Out of This World', *Economist*, 15 November 2008, 105.

14. A few years later, two former members of the armed left spoke out, seemingly resurrecting the two-demons theory. They admitted to their role in violating

human rights. They further contended that the failure to advance accountability on both sides of the violence was tantamount to a cynical process of 'victors' justice'. Against this claim was the evidence of the justice meted out by the civil-military dictatorship against the 30,000 dead and disappeared. The arguments of the former armed militants thus had to be 'de-authorized'. As illegitimate voices in memory politics, they could not be heard and could not harm the clear narrative about the past (Payne 2016).

REFERENCES

Baer, Alejandro. 2005. *El testimonio audiovisual: Imagen y memoria del Holocausto.* Madrid: CIS and Siglo XXI.

———. 2006. *Holocausto: Recuerdo y representación.* Madrid: Editorial Losada.

Bilbija, Ksenija, and Leigh A. Payne. 2011. 'Time Is Money: The Memory Market in Latin America'. In *Accounting for Violence: Marketing Memory in Latin America,* edited by Ksenija Bilbija and Leigh A. Payne, 1–40. Durham, NC: Duke University Press.

Brodsky, Marcelo. 2007. *Buena Memoria.* Buenos Aires: La Marca Editora.

Borges, Jorge Luis. 1954. *Funes, The Memorious.* In Jorge Luis Borges, *Ficciones.* Translated from the original Spanish (*Funes, el memorioso* [1944]) by Anthony Kerrigan. Buenos Aires: Editorial Sur.

Cavanagh, K. A. 2002. 'Emergency Rule, Normalcy Exception: The Erosion of the Right to Silence in the United Kingdom'. *Cornell International Law Journal* 35, no. 3 (Winter): 491–513.

Chalier, Catherine. 1995. *Levinas. La utopia de lo humano.* Barcelona: Riopiedras.

Dancy, Geoff, et al. In press. 'Behind Bars and Bargains: New Findings on Transitional Justice in Emerging Democracies'. *International Studies Quarterly.*

Duff, R. A. 2011. 'Responsibility, Citizenship and Criminal Law'. In *Philosophical Foundations of Criminal Law,* edited by R. A. Duff and Stuart Green, 125–48. Oxford: Oxford University Press.

Ephratt, Michal. 2008. 'The Functions of Silence'. *Journal of Pragmatics* 40: 1909–38.

Feitlowitz, Marguerite. 1998. *A Lexicon of Terror: Argentina and the Legacies of Torture.* Oxford: Oxford University Press.

Fernández de Mata, Ignacio. 2009. 'In memoriam . . . esquelas, contra-esquelas y duelos inconclusos de la Guerra Civil Española'. *Historia Antropología y Fuentes Orales* (HAFO), issue 42, 93–128. http://www.politicasdelamemoria.org/wp-content/uploads/2009/01/In-memoriamSmall.pdf-1170.compressed.pdf. Accessed 26 August 2017.

Foucault, Michel. 1978. *The History of Sexuality.* Vol. 1. Translated from the French (*Histoire de la sexualité*) by Robert Hurley. New York: Random House.

Gann, Kyle. 2010. *No Such Thing as Silence: John Cage's 4'33".* New Haven, CT: Yale University Press.

Gates-Madsen, Nancy. 2016. *Trauma, Taboo, and Truth-Telling: Listening to Silences in Postdictatorship Argentina.* Madison: University of Wisconsin Press.

Glenn, Cheryl. 2004. *Unspoken: A Rhetoric of Silence*. Carbondale: Southern Illinois University Press.

Glenn, Cheryl, and Krista Ratcliffe, eds. 2011. *Silence and Listening as Rhetorical Arts*. Carbondale: Southern Illinois University Press.

Goñi, Uki. 2015. Faustasblog.com/2015/05/argentina-silence-is-health. Accessed 13 April 2016.

Gross, Oren. 1998. "'Once More unto the Breach': The Systemic Failure of Applying the European Convention on Human Rights to Entrenched Emergencies'. *Yale Journal of International Law* 23, no. 2: 437–501.

Hardt, Cristina M, dir. 2005. *Death in El Valle/Muerte el El Valle*. Film. United States: Death in El Valle, Inc./SG&A Campaigns. http://www.muerteenelvalle.com/SP/Home/Home.html. Accessed 26 August 2017.

hooks, bell. 1989. *Talking Back: Thinking Feminist, Thinking Black*. Boston: South End Press.

Kim, Hun Jun, and Kathryn Sikkink. 2010. 'Explaining the Deterrence Effect of Human Rights Prosecutions for Transitional Countries'. *International Studies Quarterly* 54: 939–63.

Landrith, Sharon. 2016. 'Love Arising from Stillness: A 5-Day Silent Retreat'. Omega Institute catalog,16.

Levinas, Emmanuel. 1996. *Ética e infinito*. Madrid: Visor.

Link, Perry. 2012. 'Silent Protest'. *New Republic* 243 (16 February): 2. http://web.b.ebscohost.com.ezp1.lib.umn.edu/pov/detail/detail?sid=81dcbc76-e999-4c19-b11c-28b8a9e00b5a%40sessionmgr102&vid=0&hid=125&bdata=JnNpdGGU9cG92LWxpdmU%3d#AN=70594903&db=pwh. Accessed 13 April 2016.

Mack, Katherine. 2011. 'Hearing Women's Silence in Transitional South Africa: Achmat Dangor's *Bitter Fruit*'. In *Silence and Listening as Rhetorical Arts*, edited by Cheryl Glenn and Krista Ratcliffe, 195–213. Carbondale: Southern Illinois University Press.

McPhee, John. 2015. 'Omission: Choosing What to Leave Out'. *The New Yorker*, 14 September.

Milton, Cynthia E. 2005. 'Naming'. In *The Art of Truth-Telling about Authoritarian Rule*, edited by Bilbija, Ksenija, Jo Ellen Fair, Cynthia E. Milton, and Leigh A. Payne, 104–9. Madison: University of Wisconsin Press.

Murphy, Kate. 2014. 'Psst. Look Over Here'. *New York Times*, 16 May. http://www.nytimes.com/2014/05/17/sunday-review/the-eyes-have-it.html?_r=1. Accessed 15 April 2016.

Olsen, Tricia D., Leigh A. Payne, and Andrew G. Reiter. 2010. *Transitional Justice in Balance: Comparing Processes, Weighing Efficacy*. Washington, DC: United States Institute of Peace Press.

Parrott, Jill M. 2012. 'Power and Discourse: Silence as Rhetorical Choice in Maxine Hong Kingston's *The Woman Warrior*'. *Rhetorica* 30, no. 4 (Autumn): 375–91.

Payne, Leigh A. 2016. 'Left Unsettled: The Inconvenient Confessions to Past Violence from Guerrilla Movements'. Paper presented at the Latin American Studies Association, New York, 26–30 May.

Pryor, Ashley Elliott. 2011. 'Gesturing toward Peace: On Silence, the Society of the Spectacle, and the "Women in Black" Antiwar Protests'. In *Silence and Listening as Rhetorical* Arts, edited by Cheryl Glenn and Krista Ratcliffe, 180–94. Carbondale: Southern Illinois University Press.

Rich, Adrienne. 2008. 'Cartographies of Silence'. https://poetrying.wordpress.com/2008/12/15/cartographies-of-silence-adrienne-rich. Accessed 26 August 2017).

Rieff, David. 2016a. 'The Cult of Memory: When History Does More Harm Than Good'. *The Guardian*, 2 March. http://www.theguardian.com/education/2016/mar/02/cult-of-memory-when-history-does-more-harm-than-good?utm_source=Sailthru&utm_medium=email&utm_campaign=Democracy%20Lab%20Weekly%20Brief%2C%20March%207%2C%202016&utm_term=%2ADemocracy%20Lab

———. 2016b. *In Praise of Forgetting: Historical Memory and Its Ironies*. New Haven, CT: Yale University Press.

Romero, Ivana. 2013. 'El día en que los desaparecidos tomaron forma de silueta de papel'. *Tiempo*, 27 May. http://tiempoargentino.com/nota/48710/el-dia-en-que-los-desaparecidos-tomaron-forma-de-silueta-de-papel. Accessed 13 April 2016.

Ross, Jeffrey Ian, ed. 2016. *Routledge Handbook of Graffiti and Street Art*. London: Routledge.

Scarry, Elaine. 1985. *Body in Pain: The Making and Unmaking of the World*. New York: Oxford University Press.

Schindel, Estela. 1997. 'Palabras del rostro: Una lectura de los avisos de desaparecidos de Página/12'. *El Ojo Mocho. Revista de Crítica Cultural* 11 (September–October): 116–17.

Shua, Ana María. 1997. *La muerte como efecto secundario*. Buenos Aires: Editorial Sudamericana.

Slattery, Dennis Patrick. 2007. 'The Subtle Power of Silence'. *Mythopoetry Review* 30 (November). https://www.mythopoetry.com/mythopoetics/review_sardello_slattery.html. Accessed 26 August 2017.

Sontag, Susan. [1969] 2002. 'The Aesthetics of Silence'. In *Styles of Radical Will*, 3–34. New York: Picador, 1969.

Sosa, Cecilia. 2007. 'Nomeolvides'. *Página/12*, 16 September. https://www.pagina12.com.ar/diario/suplementos/radar/9-4115-2007-09-16.html.

Spiegelman, Art. 1991. *Maus: A Survivor's Tale, II: And Here My Troubles Began*. New York: Pantheon.

Theidon, Kimberly. 2015. 'Hidden in Plain Sight: Children Born of Wartime Sexual Violence'. *Open Security*, 30 September. https://www.opendemocracy.net/opensecurity/kimberly-theidon/hidden-in-plain-sight-children-born-of-wartime-sexual-violence.

Part III

Rethinking Peace

Translation

Jeremiah Alberg

This project began with a seminar held in Tokyo called 'Rethinking Peace Studies I: Translation'. The connection between peace studies and translation is not immediately apparent, but with a little reflection, the connections become obvious. While this volume is not the first to reflect explicitly on the connection between translation and peace studies, there is not a lot of research out there. I did find that just a few years ago, Hillary Footitt, writing in the *Journal of War and Cultural Studies*, pointed out the need to reconceptionalise the space of war from the nation-state to more 'multivocal translational spaces'.[1] She was calling for translations studies to become an integral part of war and cultural studies since one has to translate identities and espouse 'a conscious interdisciplinarity which might lead us to focus more on the performative than the representational' (209). Much of what she calls for finds a positive response in the following chapters. The authors offer a variety of reflections on the ways that we 'translate' identities so that what 'gets through' in all the changes and transformations still has a valid claim to standing for the original. I draw attention to Footitt's suggestion that we focus more on the performative than the representational. I think that this focus is clear throughout most of this collection, as authors have sought to resolve different dilemmas faced by peace studies by turning to the performative aspects of discourse, art and politics.

It is not accidental that we are growing in our awareness of translation and its connection with other disciplines. I think it is of a piece with feminist studies, postcolonial studies and area studies. The dominating forces of discourse are becoming more transparent, and the complexity of our situations, be they on a domestic, local, national or international level, demand recognition. We cannot ignore those who deserve a place at the table but do not understand the language being spoken at that table.

Part III

Translation presumes a lack of mutual understanding. It works to overcome this lack in full knowledge that in doing this, it runs the risk of replacing what is a 'mere' lack with a positive misunderstanding and thus leaving the parties in a putatively worse position than they were before. I wrote that they 'run the risk', but I mean that inevitably this too is at least a part of the outcome. One does not overcome the lack without also creating misunderstanding. The road to mutual understanding is always long and almost always crooked. We do not move from mutual incomprehension to comprehension except through miscomprehension. It is part of the human condition.

Translation is a fundamental human reality. I 'translate' what I want to express for any given audience and thus speak differently to my children than I do to my wife, even when using the same language to talk about the same thing. I think it goes even deeper. The fundamental substitution of word for object, of a symbol standing for something else, is the primary form of translation. We sidle up to reality through the symbolic process, and at its root it is a translation.

The contributions in this part construe translation in wide way. One could be forgiven for thinking that Chiba's contribution concerning the crisis of Japan's pacifist constitution due to the Abe administration's attacks on it is a straightforward piece of political philosophy with some historical background. Indeed, it is this, and thus it highlights how deeply translation enters into our understanding of things like politics and history. He carefully considers the array of historical influences related to pacifism that were translated during the Meiji and Taisho periods and thus entered into the Japanese intellectual universe at the time that nationalistic and militaristic ideologies were ascendant. He also considers the way that the Abe government is using translation to obfuscate its movement away from constitution and the pacifism that is essential to it.

My own contribution can, like Chiba's, give the impression of being at a remove from translation studies. But in our past, humans learned to allow one thing to 'stand for' or mean another thing. One form this takes is sacrificial violence in which an innocent victim is substituted for the community. This helps us to understand in a new way the old Italian saying: '*Traduttore, traditor*' (translator, traitor). It is not simply that the act of expressing something said in one language in another language always distorts. Rather, it points to the fundamental reality that the first substitution involved a misrecognition—the victim was killed because it was believed that the victim's death would bring us peace. The truth, that the victim's substitutionary death brings peace, is indissolubly connected with the lie of the violence that kills him or her. Beginning to undo this fundamental distortion is the first step to a more fundamental solution to the problem of violence.

Curran gives us the most straightforward and thus the most dialectical and compelling use of translation. She analyzes the 'translational text' of *Maus*. Her brilliant take on this brilliant work makes us aware of all of the levels that translation works on: interlinguistic as well as intralingual, cross-cultural as well as intrapersonal. There is also the intersemiotic level. It is not accidental that the greatest cataclysm of the twentieth century calls forth such incredible demands on translation. I do not think it is accidental that one of the best ways of dealing with the Holocaust turns out to be translating it into the comics form. Only by using all the guile and genius at his disposal is Spiegelman able to give expression to that which is beyond expression and help us to approach this horrifying reality. Curran provides expert guidance in helping us to accompany him.

With all of its pitfalls, translation still aims at getting the message through, preserving the identity in the midst of change, allowing communication to continue. It is a noble and yet, at the same time, a mundane task.

NOTE

1. Hilary Footitt, 'War and Culture Studies in 2016: Putting "Translation" into the Transnational', *Journal of War and Culture Studies* 9, no. 3 (2016): 209, doi:10.108 0/17526272.2016.1192421.

Chapter Nine

A Translational Comics Text and Its Translation

Maus *in Japanese*

Beverley Curran

Waïl S. Hassan (2006) describes translational texts as 'performances of inter-linguistic, cross-cultural communication, operating on several levels of mediation and contestation' (753). Such texts are sites of interlingual intervention where knots of social unease continue to be scrutinized and reconsidered. A translational comics text, such as Art Spiegelman's *Maus*, draws attention to other forms of mediation at work, including the 'visual language set in motion with and against the verbal' (Chute 2010, 3), the unspoken and the friction created among space, time and movement through the comics form. This translational text's performance is not only interlinguistic and cross-cultural but also intralingual and intrapersonal as well as intersemiotic. *Maus* is an intralingual translational text that makes visible two different experiences that have led to the conversations in two different Englishes between Vladek, an Auschwitz survivor, and Artie, his cartoonist son. Vladek's English is inflected with Polish, but when *Maus* depicts memories in which he was speaking Polish, they are rendered in 'standard' American English. It is an interlingual translational text in its strategic use of different languages in the story; that is, in addition to the range of Englishes, there is also the presence of German, Polish, Yiddish and Hebrew. As a translational comics, its hybrid and artisanal form of image, narration and dialogue is an intersemiotic, or media, translation whose performance challenges 'a stable, centred sense of knowledge and reality' (Pratt 1991, 37).

In visual terms, the translational is marked by the use of masks. Spiegelman summarizes his comics as a story of his father told in animal figures, but Ono Kosei, the Japanese translator of *Maus*, points out that it is not a comics which depicts humans as animals; its use of animal 'mask play' is what makes *Maus* such an inspired work (Ono 2014): we witness the performance of engaging with a survivor's tale, both what is told and what is suppressed or concealed. *Maus* uses the culture of comics to record traumatic testimony, and the material medium of comics gives *Maus* the visual capacity to foreground the temporal complexity of the story in the structural juxtaposition of moments in time that allows different pasts and presents to coexist in order to register change.

Maus has been translated into more than 30 languages, including Japanese. Spiegelman speculated on the possibility that the Japanese translation by Ono, a prolific comic translator and researcher, did not receive much attention, possibly because 'Jews are totally exotic' and because the comics translation did not conform to manga reading conventions (Baccolini and Zanettin 2008, 116). Yet Spiegelman (2004) himself makes an explicit connection between Hiroshima and the Holocaust—'the twentieth century's other central cataclysm' (n.p.)—in his introduction to a new collaborative English translation of Keiji Nakazawa's 1972–1973 manga *Hadashi no Gen* [*Barefoot Gen*], describing the sustained and selective killing project of the Holocaust and the sudden extermination of the atomic bombings of Hiroshima and Nagasaki as distinct but contiguous. This chapter discusses the translational nature of *Maus* and then considers some examples of how it is interlingually translated into Japanese. In the process, the hybrid nature of *Maus* is examined in order to reconsider translational comics texts as a form of engagement within and among multiple modes of personal, historical and traumatic memory and as a medium ideal for autobiography and bearing witness.

TRANSLATIONAL EFFECTS

Translational texts grapple with how to tell a story; that is, the language that is used is never taken for granted but rather is a conscious choice that has intended and unintended consequences. As a translational comics text, *Maus* is located not only on linguistic or cultural fault lines but also on 'that faultline where World History and Personal History collide' (Spiegelman 2014, n.p.) This is a story not about the Holocaust but rather about how a son survives the effects of a Holocaust survivor's trauma by telling his father's story, so it grapples with the urge to translate the father's words into standard English and with guilt about unintended effects of stereotypical characteristics. That is, it performs the awareness of active agency with a will towards transformation as well as an awareness of the loss of control that takes place in the circulation of discourse. As such, it exhibits an important characteristic of the translational text, which 'undercuts the myth of autonomous cultural and civilizational identities' (Hassan 2006, 755). Ethical and aesthetic limitations of Holocaust representation were at the heart of the controversy of *Maus*: should a comic book be a form that a Holocaust survivor's tale takes? In discussing *Maus* as a translational text, it is attention to the formal translation of Holocaust testimony to a comics text which shows 'enough to begin to know what you're missing' (Clifford 1997, 39) and more:

> The story of *Maus* isn't just the story of a son having problems with his father, and it's not just a story of what his father lived through. It's about a cartoonist trying to envision what his father went through. It's about choices being made, of finding what one can tell, and what one can reveal and what one can reveal beyond what one knows one is revealing. (Spiegelman 2011, 73)

Integral to this project to not only retrieve but also create memory is the task of the translational comics artist to make simultaneously present, through intralingual translation of English to English in the conversations between father and son, different times and places that are present, absent and unfolding and to evoke interlingual translation, as the father relates in his later-acquired English in the present what happened to him, family and friends in the past in other places and in other languages: it is not only a question of who speaks but also a question of how. And, crucially, it is the hybrid medium of comics that in its visual staging and performance articulates 'what language can only point at' (Spivak 2000, 403).

COMICS AS A TRANSLATIONAL ZONE

Maus is an example of what Emily Apter (2013) has called translation zones, where 'discrete languages contained within perimeters of standardized usage' give way 'to plurilingual process, that is to say, languages-in-translation: pidgins, creoles, idiomatic sampling, loan words, calques, code-switching, and the burgeoning ciphers of finance capitalism' (100). As a *translational* zone, comics thickens the linguistic contours with its 'architectonic' approach to plural temporalities in which the languages are spoken. Spiegelman's (2011) decision to be a cartoonist 'had something to do with finding a zone that was not my parents' zone. It was my assimilation into American culture that was closed to my parents, and it gave me a zone of safety from them' (37). The opacity of comics that excluded his father as reader was a 'picture window onto American culture' (37) for Spiegelman. In particular, Harvey Kurtzman's *Mad* comics work was central to developing the particular translational zone in which Spiegelman works. For example, there is Kurtzman's 1954 cartoon of Mickey Rodent, which shows how quickly a character—or person or social group—can be translated simply by renaming.

It is not only the renaming or the text that needs to be considered in a close reading of a translational comic text. The analysis of Bernard Krigstein's work in 'An Examination of "Master Race"', an article by John Benson, David Kasakove and Art Spiegelman (1975), shows the attention paid to the art. Before offering a detailed and careful reading of the visual, the article points out that the text of the comic 'was written as it was printed before the artist ever saw it' (41). The artist is engaged in an intersemiotic translation of a prior text that unleashes more breadth and density as it exceeds not only the story about the haunting effects of the Holocaust but also the single reading associated with a disposable commodity like the comic book. In *Maus*, Spiegelman thickens the story that is Vladek's 'survival tale' through his recasting of it in comics form.

The play and transgression of underground comics also informs Spiegelman's approach to making *Maus*. The three-page prototype of *Maus*, which first appeared in the 1972 underground comics *Funny Animals*, shows that, from the beginning, Spiegelman was interested in the play of language heard and seen: visually, we recognize difference in the spelling of 'Maus' instead of 'mouse', but aurally, the two words sound the same. At the same time, there is a blurring of the written and the drawn. The merging of phonetic English and German, which continues in *Maus*, is a gesture that 'not so much eliminates the English as . . . contaminates it, associating it with, rather than opposing it to, the essential languages of the Holocaust' (Rosen 1995, 252), and counters the idea of English as the language of the Allies and therefore resolved of any connection. The three-page tale of a Holocaust survivor is being told to a young boy named Mickey, firmly situating the story in an American cultural setting where the most popular mouse is a Disney construction. In short, *Maus* is from the onset 'invested with the history and aesthetics of the cartoon' (Doherty 1996, 77), including commercial mainstream and counterculture American comics and German anti-Semitic cartoons. In the early 'Maus', the English used by 'Poppa' is not yet a temporal marker as it becomes in *Maus* to distinguish past experience played out in languages other than English and the accented English in which the father tells his son Mickey a bedtime story about his experiences. In the later *Maus* comics, unaccented English marks the fluency of languages spoken at a time when masks and seamless passing are crucial to survival and the fear of an accent works to suppress speech. In looking at this prototype and the later *Maus*, it is poignant to see that both begin with a son calling on his father to tell him a story.

Before *Maus* was released in two volumes in 1986 and 1991, the initial five chapters of the six that make up *Maus I* appeared serially between 1980 and 1985 in *RAW*, the 'comix' magazine cofounded and coedited by Spiegelman and Françoise Mouly. At every stage, the form that a story takes—how comics tells a story—has been a preoccupation. Spiegelman prefers the term 'comix' (or 'commix') or 'co-mix' to undermine the stubborn idea that hu-mour is the key element and instead foregrounds the synthesis of words and pictures to tell a story of any scale as a 'three-dimensional narrative': 'Such a form . . . recognizes that part of any narrative will be this internal register of knowledge—somewhere between words and images—conjured in the mind's movement between itself and the page' (Young 2000, 55). This is a triangula-tion that resonates with Jakobson's idea of intrapersonal translation as a part of every act of mis/understanding.

Comics is particularly enabling for a subject like the Holocaust because, as a translational zone that occupies psychic as well as material locations, it reminds the reader that it is artisanal:

> One's own mark—offering up a facsimile of one's own handwriting—makes it more like looking into an actual journal, like Anne Frank's or maybe Alfred Kantor's notebook drawings of Auschwitz. This approach led me to abandon most of my art supplies for *Maus*, to work on typing paper. Using stationary store supplies, boned paper, typewriter correction fluid and a fountain pen made it more like writing, like offering up a manuscript, something made by hand. (Spiegelman 2011, 174)

The do-it-yourself nature of the comics marks *Maus* as a slow translational text that took time to create and that takes time to read due to its volume, reduced and expanding panels, multiple scripts and voices and the density of visual discourse.

The linguistic interruptions that characterize a translational text are found in *Maus* in the visual skewing, which is part of the artisanal nature of the comics that prioritizes selective placement over production conformity. Go-ing through the pages, the eye finds skewed objects that interrupt the varied grids of the visual paragraphs. These objects are initially ephemera, like posters and train tickets. They then start to include photographs and comics depictions of Artie's mother Anja and, later, of her passport, a map of Poland and diagrams and other views. We see them predominantly as markers that punctuate Vladek's story, so it is startling to see the ephemera of marketing join this collection late in *Maus II*, when Artie is being pitched a licencing deal. The skewed poster reads, 'MAUS You've Read the Book. Now Buy the Vest!' (Spiegelman 1996, 202), and the do-it-yourself labour of love has been positioned as a crass commodity.

TRANSLATING THE TRANSLATIONAL

Ono Kosei, the Japanese translator of *Maus*, is well known for his translations of comics, which include Marvel works and Winsor McCay's *Little Nemo*, as well as his research on international comics and animation. Ono first met Spiegelman in 1980 in Tokyo, and they bonded over comics; within 10 minutes, they had already talked about Little Nemo and Donald Duck. It is interesting to examine how a translator of Ono's experience and expertise approaches the interlingual translation of a translational comics text like *Maus*.

One of the most striking choices made by the translator is to limit the linguistic variation in the speech of Vladek and Artie. This is significant because *Maus* is an accented cultural production 'driven by the aesthetics of juxtaposition' (Naficy 2001, 6) that uses not only the voices of exilic and diasporic displacement but also those of the comics tradition and its artisanal production mode. The resonating auditory effects draw attention to what Hamid Naficy has observed in the accented cinema of exilic and diasporic filmmaking where the 'accent permeates the . . . deep structure: its narrative, visual style, characters, subject matter, theme, and plot' (23). However, the structure of comics, Spiegelman argues, exceeds the cinematic in its ability to juxtapose moments of time: 'In a story that is trying to make chronological and coherent the incomprehensible, the juxtaposing of past and present are always present—one doesn't displace the other as it happens in film' (Spiegelman 2011, 166). The attention to how language use also marks different temporalities (that are always present) is linked to the structure of a comics page as a 'visual paragraph' (167):

> Comics pages are structures made up of panels, sort of the way the windows in a church articulate a story. Thinking of these pages as units that have to be joined together, as if each page was some kind of building with windows in it, was something that often happens overtly in *Maus*, and sometimes is just implicit in the DNA of the medium. (166)

The variations in Vladek's language not only mark the movement from one place to another that is part of his survivor's tale but also present the inner language that Roman Jakobson (1971) called intrapersonal translation, which inflects how memories are passed on:

> Any sign requires an interpreter. The perspicuous type of semiotic communication involves two separate interpreters, the addresser of a message and its addressee. However . . . inner speech condenses the addresser and the addressee into one person, and the elliptic forms of intrapersonal communication are far from being confined to verbal signs alone. The mnemonic knot on a handkerchief made by Russians to remind themselves to accomplish an urgent matter is a typical example of an inner communication between the earlier and the later self. (702)

The linguistic variations in *Maus* are part of the whole project of the connections between the father and the story as he tells it and the son and how he tells it. The structure of the translational comics text signifies that this is a story that is intrinsically 'a merger of different sign systems' (Jakobson 1971, 705).

I would like to now consider a couple of visual paragraphs from *Maus* and then examine Ono's interlinguistic translation. These two pages are the opening spread of 'The Honeymoon', the second chapter of *Maus I: My Father Bleeds History*. Before entering the frames, we are told that Artie has been visiting his father Vladek 'quite regularly to hear his story', but the first thing he asks is 'about Mom.' In the top single framed drawing, we see Artie about to sit down at the kitchen table, placing a cup next to his book and pen, while his father counts out portions of pills, '. . . 11 . . . 12 . . . 13', part of a habit of sorting that is repeated throughout the text, an unconscious memory in Piercian semiotics, which does not preserve actual or factual circumstances of learning and is recalled only when being performed. The counting is linked to the numbers tattooed on Vladek's arm and on the sorting and classification that were part of his experience of the Holocaust.

The second of four tiers has three frames which show only Vladek, who continues to count; in the first, we 'hear' his distinctive syntax that shows past linguistic habits constructing his sentences in English: 'I'm making into daily portions my pills . . . 14 . . . 15 . . .'. He continues to count his pills orally in the second framed drawing ('. . . 16 . . . 17 . . . 18 . . .'), and then in the third, he verbally adds what the pills are for ('it's 6 pills for the heart, 1 for diabetes . . . and maybe 25, or 30 vitamins') while visually we see him counting on his fingers. The third tier has two frames: the first shows Artie with pen poised drinking coffee while his father talks about his distrust of doctors and their drugs ('junk food'). In the pair of panels that form the bottom tier, Artie now has a cigarette in his mouth and pen in hand as he returns to the subject of his mother: 'About Mom. . . . Did she have any boyfriends before she met you?' Vladek answers, 'Not *romantic* . . . but one tall boy from Warsaw', and in the final frame of the first page, he confides with an emphatic frown of disapproval, 'He was . . . a *Communist*!' As we look at this visual paragraph, we see panes in the windows and the panes of the cupboard as well as the panes on Vladek's housecoat; in this way, the tiered structure of the page is also found within the framed drawings. The gutters that separate and support the frames also function like the ellipses found within each framed drawing.

On the second page of this early chapter, the number and size of framed drawings changes, and so does the site of the story. The top of the four tiers on this page shows two drawings of Vladek at the table. In the first, he continues to count as he begins his story about Anja and the boy from Warsaw. We read what Vladek says, but we may not know exactly how he pronounces 'Sosnowiec', the name of the Polish town where he lives with Anja after they marry. In the second, he waves his hands, showing all 10 fingers as he explains that he did not know the boy was a communist at the time: 'I *always* kept far away from Communist people'. The second tier or sentence of this visual paragraph is a single drawing that is located in Poland and the past. We see two kinds of animals: the police are pigs, which marks them as Polish in the context of *Maus* but also is visual play on a derogatory term for police found throughout 1960s underground comics and beyond. The white uniforms of the police and their vehicle contrast with the dark coats and hats of the Jewish mice, gathered in the right half of the drawing. Vladek, who has just returned from a business trip, is among the crowd and being addressed: 'Hey Vladek. . . . They just arrested the seamstress that lives down your hall. . . . She had some secret Communist documents!' The next tier is also a single panel and shows Vladek entering a room, cluttered with patterns, where he finds his in-laws. Together, they explain, 'The police were *here*!' 'Looking for Anja!' The bottom tier is supported by two framed drawing that have uneven dimensions that unsettle the visual paragraph and make it appear unsteady. We learn in the first of the two final panels that Anja has told her parents that 'that boy from Warsaw brings Communist messages', and in a dramatic disclosure in the final frame, we learn that Anja 'translates them into German and passes them on!' The transmission of secret messages takes place generationally from Anja to her parents and then back to Vladek and interlingually from Polish to German. Below this second drawing is a line that not only unsettles the visual structure of this page but also brings us back to the present by accenting Vladek's English: 'Anja was involved in *conspirations*!' We are aware that the conversations we have just been reading in English have been translated and took place in Polish.

When these two pages are translated into Japanese, there are intended and unintended translation effects that are experienced in visual as well as linguistic terms. If we look at the visual paragraph, we see the density of the kanji characters that create visual constellations within the translated text. If we compare the constellations on the two pages—one page located in the 'present' in Vladek's kitchen in New York and the other moving into a Sosnowiec of the 1930s—the precision and density of the kanji clusters give a different sense of the two worlds: the first visual paragraph is full of kanji clusters related to the body and its ailments: 心臓病 · *shinzoubyou* (heart disease), 糖尿病 · *tounyoubyou* (diabetes), 体調 · *taichou* (physical condition), 医者 · *isha* (doctor) and 健康 雑誌 · *kenkouzasshi* (health magazines). On the second page, where Vladek visually returns to the past, the kanji makes different associations: 逮捕 · taiho (arrest), 秘密書類 · himitsu shorui (secret documents), 警察 · keisatsu (police) and 陰謀 · inbou (conspiracy). The dense compression of the kanji on the page draws our eyes to create a powerful visual linkage.

Another cluster of words are visually linked because of their rendering in the phonetic katakana script, the Japanese writing system used primarily for marking imported words: mama (ママ), papa (パパ), vitamin (ビタミン), junk food (ジャンクフード), boyfriend (ボーイフレンド), romantic (ロマンチック), Warsaw (ワルシャワ) and communist (コミュニスト). Katakana is a phonetic reading of words, so they are accented but retain the distorted echo of their vocalization in English or, in the case of the city of Warszawa, in Polish. On the second page, the katakana words are names of people and places that we may not be familiar with. In addition to the rendering of the names of Anja (アンジャ) and Vladek (ヴラデック), there is the town of Sosnowiec (ソスノヴェツ) in addition to Warsaw and four more appearances of "communist" in katakana script. The katakana distances these terms but provides support to pronouncing these terms phonetically. It is interesting to see that they fall into two rough groups: one contains terms that are part of a global lexicon of concepts and geographic names, while the other is local.

Another way that Ono's translation further inflects these pages is related to Vladek's counting. In addition to the numbers that we see in the framed drawings, Ono adds another in the unframed entry point to the first visual paragraph by translating the innocuous 'For the next few months' as '2 ~ 3 か月'. This again suggests the translator's awareness of the significance of numbers, the iteration of the one tattooed on Vladek's arm and the escalating numbers of bodies sorted, confined and killed.

Ono's translation of these two visual paragraphs also resituates Vladek's memories from somewhere else where he spoke languages other than English to a place in the past. Using the pronoun *washi* represents him as an old man, the Japanese translation distances the narrative, marking it as another time rather than another time and place. In a sense, this can be a subtle way to link the story of the Holocaust to that of the traumatic war memories of an older generation in Japan.

THE TRANSLATOR IN THE TEXT

While Anja's activities as a translator are depicted as dangerous, Vladek presents his own languages as survival skills. As he explains to his son, 'You must know everything to survive' (Spiegelman 2011, 54), be it a foreign language or how to repair a shoe. When as a Polish soldier he is captured by German soldiers in 1939, he is able to speak German, and this keeps him from being beaten. Later, when he is released and returns to Poland, he finds that the German tongue offers protection in public spaces from being identified as

Jewish. Vladek always rides in the German sections of segregated streetcars ('The Germans paid no attention of me. . . . In the Polish car they could *smell* if a Polish Jew came in' (Spiegelman 1996, 142). When things get worse and Anja and Vladek have no place to go, Vladek says to her, 'Stay calm. . . . Walk as if we're just strolling . . . and speak German' (146). The first actual German 'spoken' in the text is 'Er verblutetet' ('His blood ran out') (52), referring to a German soldier shot by Vladek when he was a Polish soldier. In Ono's translation, German is replaced by Japanese in the translation of this phrase, although in other parts of the text, the German remains.

At Auschwitz, the cultural capital of Vladek's ability to speak both English and Polish increases when he finds himself selected to teach the block supervisor English. Near the end of *Maus II*, in the immediate and chaotic wake of the war, Vladek meets American soldiers and winds up able to stay with them in return for 'keep[ing] the joint clean': 'So we worked for the Americans and they *liked* me that I can speak English. . . . They gave to us food cans and gifts and called to me "Willie"' (Spiegelman 1996, 272). The arrival of the American forces in Japan signalled occupation, not liberation, so images on this page of *Maus* where the soldiers offer chocolate, take charge and converse casually in English resonate in the cultural memory of Japan in a strikingly different way; they arrive, of course, in the wake of the devastation of Hiroshima caused by American bombs. Along with this association come others: Artie smokes like a chimney or, more precisely, like the chimneys at Auschwitz. Does it take much more imaginative slippage to blow the smoke into the shape of an atomic mushroom cloud?

CONCLUSION

Maus draws attention to the crucial dimension of form in the construction and performance of any translational text. After all, how a story is told changes the story. Our relationships to our languages and the languages of our relationships are complex in themselves and are further complicated by our shifting locations in time and space. As *Maus* grapples with how the son deals with the story of his father, it simultaneously performs the absence of the son's mother and what has been left unsaid or misunderstood. This translational comics text in Japanese returns us to its mediated story and how to rethink it in a number of associative ways. We recognize in the process, practice and production of translation and the readers that it assembles the performativity that Judith Butler (2015) has described as 'a way of naming a power language has to bring about a new situation or set into motion a set of effects' (28).

ACKNOWLEDGEMENTS

I gratefully acknowledge the support of a Grant-in-Aid for Scientific Research (C26503012) from the Japan Society for the Promotion of Science, which enabled research and writing of this chapter as part of an ongoing project on contemporaneous translation.

REFERENCES

Apter, Emily. 2013. *Against World Literature: On the Politics of Untranslatability.* London: Verso.

Baccolini, Raffaella, and Frederico Zanettin. 2008. 'The Language of Trauma: Art Spiegelman's *Maus* and Its Translations'. In *Comics in Translation*, edited by Frederico Zanettin, 99–132. Manchester: St Jerome.

Benson, John, David Kasakove, and Art Spiegelman. 1975. 'An Examination of "Master Race"'. *Squa Tront* 6 (1975): 41–47.

Butler, Judith. 2015. *Notes toward a Performative Theory of Assembly.* Cambridge, MA: Harvard University Press.

Chute, Hillary L. 2010. *Graphic Women: Life Narrative and Contemporary Comics.* New York: Columbia University Press.

Clifford, James. 1997. *Routes: Travel and Translation in the Late Twentieth Century.* Cambridge, MA: Harvard University Press.

Doherty, Thomas. 1996. 'Art Spiegelman's *Maus*: Graphic Art and the Holocaust'. *American Literature* 68, no. 1 (March 1996): 69–84.

Hassan, Waïl. 2006. 'Agency and Translational Literature: Ahadaf Soueif's "The Map of Love"'. *PMLA* 121, no. 3 (May 2006): 753–68.

Jakobson, Roman. 1971. 'Language in Relation to Other Communication Systems'. In *Selected Writings II: Word and Language*, 697–708. The Hague: Mouton.

Naficy, Hamid. 2001. *An Accented Cinema: Exilic and Diasporic Filmmaking.* Princeton, NJ: Princeton University Press.

Ono, Kosei. 2014. 'Dai 57 kai shinyakuhan Little Nemo no tame no manga ni yoru yobun'. Mainichi nanikawoomoidasu: Ono Kosei no jigen drift, Ono Kosei jiden blog. 4 July.

Pratt, Mary Louise. 1991. 'Arts of the Contact Zone'. *Profession* (1991): 33–40.

Rosen, Alan. 1995. 'English as a Metaphor in Spiegelman's *Maus*'. *Prooftexts* 15, no. 3 (September 1995): 249–62.

Spiegelman, Art. 1986. *Maus: Auschwitz wo iki nobita chichioya no monogatari* [*Maus: A Survivor's Tale*]. Translated by Ono Kosei. Tokyo: Shobunsha.

———. 1991. *Maus II: Auschwitz wo iki nobita chichioya no monogatari* [*Maus: A Survivor's Tale and Here My Troubles Began*]. Translated by Ono Kosei. Tokyo: Shobunsha.

———. 1996. *The Complete Maus.* New York: Penguin.

———. 2004. '*Barefoot Gen*: Comics after the Bomb, an Introduction by Art Spiegelman'. In *Barefoot Gen, Vol. 1: A Cartoon Story of Hiroshima*, by Keiji Nakazawa, translated by Project Gen. San Francisco: Last Gasp.

———. 2011. *MetaMaus: A Look inside a Modern Classic, Maus*. New York: Pantheon.

———. 2014. *In the Shadow of No Towers*. New York: Pantheon.

Spivak, Gayatri Chakravorty. 2000. 'The Politics of Translation'. In *The Translation Studies Reader*, edited by Lawrence Venuti, 397–416. London: Routledge.

Young, James E. 2000. 'Against Redemption: The Arts of Counter Memory'. In *Humanity at the Limit: The Impact of the Holocaust Experience on Jews and Christians*, edited by Michael A. Signer, 44–62. Bloomington: Indiana University Press.

Chapter Ten

To Arrive Where We Started

Peace Studies and Logos

Jeremiah Alberg

LOOKING BACK AND LISTENING

The history of how this chapter came to be written has direct bearing on how it is to be read. It was conceived in relation with the project 'Rethinking Peace Studies' and born directly out of it. It was written based upon reflections sparked by the three conferences with the themes 'Translation', 'Memory' and 'Dialogue' that were held in November 2014 (Tokyo), March 2015 (New York) and November 2015 (Sri Lanka), respectively. It was first presented as a paper at the culminating conference of the 'Rethinking Peace Studies' project, which was held in Tokyo in June 2016. The themes of translation, memory and dialogue are constitutive parts of the theory that I describe in this chapter. The ultimate goal of these activities is to change the nature of the discourse surrounding peace studies. The first place in which this change occurs is my own discourse. This chapter tries to extend an anthropology to include discourse on peace building and peacekeeping.

Translation can be fruitfully understood as an act of creative imitation and substitution in which the translator seeks to imitate the original but to imitate it in other languages. By putting translation first, we are warned against the search for a 'pure' origin that would found our identity over against some imagined 'other'.

As several of the chapters of this volume attest, memory is central to peace. What we choose to remember and to forget, the way we choose to remember and whose memories are honoured and whose are erased affect the possibility of peace. In the theory that I outline in this chapter, memories are emptied of their poison when one looks back on one's desire and its object and recognizes the role of the mediator or the other in the generation and maintenance of the desire. To see the truth of desire is to see the way in which the mediator or model conferred on the object a value that the object itself did not possess. The truth is that the object desired was desired for the ontological weight one believed it could bestow and that belief is false.

With the possibility of creatively translating what was originally an exclusion of the other into a fuller reality that includes the other and with the possibility of healing memories of the poison they contained by recognizing one's complicity in the other's violence, we become capable of dialogue—capable of seeing the other as other and not merely as an extension of myself. The other becomes like me in becoming different from me. The similarities no longer frighten me. With the possibility of dialogue comes the possibility of peace. Other contributors have shown how these possibilities are realized in various media and contexts. Curran's contribution highlights the way in which a comics translates not only language but also images, history and relationships. Sturken shows the delicate interplay between what we remember and how we memorialize. I believe that René Girard has a voice here because he is able to help us understand the violent roots of systemic distortions in our translations as well as our memories. We are not so much lying as misrecognizing something, and this misrecognition gives birth to wrong translations and false memories.

LEAVING THE BEATEN PATH

The task of rethinking something is well served by an oblique path. It is the 'beaten path' that we are trying to leave and forge a new way. At the same time, we worry that the 'new' way only ends at the familiar destination of more violence.

To rethink something is difficult and to rethink the study of peace even more so. The desire for peace is one of the deepest desires of humanity, and many people of moral stature have turned their minds to this problem. Here, I voice a doubt that accompanies this whole project: 'What can I contribute that is new to a conversation of such worth and history?' Returning to the fount of the problem is a way to draw out forgotten possibilities.

Our default rationality is tainted by violence. Here I will show that, while we all share a rationality formed by violence (we are children of the logos of violence), there exists another rationality that subverts this violent rationality from within. This other rationality allows us to understand reality in another way. The other rationality gives new meanings to translation, memory and dialogue. There is another logos.

Violence and peace are human problems. They presume an anthropology. Animals do not wage war, nor do they develop weapon systems. They have no armies or generals, no United Nations. Animals do not build monuments to fallen heroes or write great novels titled *War and Peace*. Violence and its counterpart, peace, are human realities. An adequate theory of violence and peace must meet the conditions of the anthropological theory that underlies it. Thus, peace studies presupposes a fundamental anthropology. I will give a brief account of the anthropological principles we possess for explaining the problem of human violence.

THE WAY AHEAD

The anthropology that I propose is the mimetic theory developed by the philosopher and literary critic René Girard in a series of writings that began with the publication of *Mensonge romantique et vérité romanesque* (English title: *Deceit, Desire, and the Novel: Self and Other in Literary Structure*) in 1961 and extends through *Achever Clausewitz* (English title: *Battling to the End*), published in 2007. In those 45 years, Girard expounded a theory of human desire and human violence. He elaborated the resolution of this violence through the scapegoat and the revelation of that resolution through the Judeo-Christian scriptures. His insights were culled from the great works of European literature, and he extended these insights through historical, ethnological and anthropological studies. He then demonstrated that these insights are contained within the Bible, and he applied his analysis to modern history and the rise of terrorism. Girard's work is an interdisciplinary methodology that peace studies can use profitably.

TOWARDS MIMETIC THEORY

Mimetic Desire

Girard's so-called mimetic theory begins with something simple, something that most people can understand and accept: human desire is imitated desire. That is, human desire is not a straight line from the desiring subject to the desired object but is triangular in structure. In addition to the subject and the object, there is a model that communicates to the subject what is desirable. In most cases, the model does this by possessing or at least desiring the object. Girard distinguishes biological drive from desire; the former is a need and its fulfilment, while the latter has no determinate object. The subject does not know what he or she wants until told by another.

The human capacity for imitation was noticed in antiquity. In his *Poetics*, Aristotle (1984, bk. IV) wrote of the human being 'one of his advantages over the lower animals being this, that he is the most imitative creature in the world, and learns at first by imitation'. What was left unnoticed or at least unremarked upon was the fact that this mimesis extended to desire. Mimetic desire is clearly visible in children. A child plays in a room filled with toys. Another child enters. What toy does the second child desire? We know the answer: the toy of the first child. And is the first child willing give the toy to the second child? No. Suddenly, this toy acquires great value.

Girard's insight was to uncover this concealed triangular structure in literature. Almost all drama includes the theme of imitative desire. Cervantes, Shakespeare, Flaubert, Stendhal, Proust, and Dostoyevsky (the main writers whom Girard has analysed) reveal its operation through their novels and plays. Freud was also on its trail in *Totem and Taboo*, hence the '*vérité romanesque*', or 'novelistic truth', in the French title of his first work. In contrast, other, less great literature serves to confirm readers in their belief in the autonomy of their own desire—of its spontaneous emergence, free from any social influence, hence the '*mensonge romantique*', or the 'romantic lie'. This lie is an act of translation. We translate our borrowed desire into our own original, spontaneous desire.

Mimetic desire is recognizable in children but less so in adults, in ourselves. We accept the perennial delusion that our desires are for objects: desirable in and of themselves. We refuse to see how the person who is the model of our desires works in our own lives. As I said, I think that this refusal is based on an act of translation and is the first difficulty of our 'default' rationality. Thanks to Freud, it is not as difficult to admit that we are not always aware of what is driving us as it once was.

At the Crossroads of Mimetic Conflict

Simply as a matter of probability, mimetic desire leads to mimetic conflict. When two people are consistently attracted to the same object, at some point, conflict is bound to emerge. As long as the object is shareable—the same book, the same music, the same wine—everything is fine for us. The object that serves to unite us can also be used as a way of keeping the 'not us' out. The implicit statement as we enjoy our fine Bordeaux is that 'they' do not appreciate wine the way we do. But when the object is nonshareable, another level of conflict can arise. Girard holds that though the general mimetic capacity of humans is well recognized in a number of different fields, from the humanities to the social sciences, the imitation of acquisitive desire is not understood. If a person wants to acquire something, his or her companion will also desire to acquire it. This is decisive.

Given that one of the two is the model for the other, the mimetic relationship often takes the form of model and disciple. The disciple learns through imitation what is desirable from the model. In effect, the model is saying, 'Imitate me in what I desire'. If disciples imitate too well, they threaten to displace the model. If they compete for the same significant other, the message changes to 'Do not imitate me in what I desire'. This is an example of Gregory Bateson's (1972) idea of the 'double bind' that puts everyone in an untenable situation. No one can fulfil the contradictory command: imitate and do not imitate. While I am presenting this example as an instance of model and disciple, it is clear that it functions in larger social contexts, such as companies and universities. It has somewhat different but not unrelated dynamisms when the genders or races of the people involved are different. In this way, feminist theory as well as postcolonial theory adds important dimensions to Girard's analysis.

The conflictive relationship can be negotiated successfully. Still, the mimetic capacities of human beings to which Aristotle pointed add further complexity. First of all, a particular object's value is primarily a relation, and in this theory, value is derived from the object being desired by the other. This point opens this analysis up to economic factors that drive human behaviour in ways that seem to counter their own self-interest. The existence of more than one object or another object just as good as the first one does not automatically solve the problem—the model desires *that object*, and so the subject imitates by desiring *the same one*.

More vexing, the object can drop out of picture: the model and the subject become rivals. What the disciple desires is not *anything* the model *has* but rather who the model *is*. The *being* of the model is desired. The disciple senses a personal lack and a corresponding superiority in the model. Ultimately, 'imitative desire is always a desire to be Another' (Girard 1965, 83). The subject desires not only to have what the model has but also to be the model, and he hates the model for this. The 'modern' emotion of ressentiment plays an ever larger role in social relation. 'As the role of the *metaphysical* grows greater in desire, that of the *physical* diminishes in importance' (Girard 1965, 85). The model is now a rival, and rivalry is marked by fascination, a kind of love/hate, with the addition of a constant fear or anxiety of 'losing' to the rival.

It is plausible that the defining characteristic of modern society is that anyone can be the rival of anyone else. The birth of modernity is marked by the growing rivalry within a feudal and hierarchical society and hence the growth of what Girard characterizes as 'modern' emotions: envy, jealousy and hatred. But there was period of stability in which hierarchy buffered people of different stations, classes or castes from being envious of one another. When cultural distinctions are really working, they are invisible. But the invisibility cannot last. As Butler has pointed out in the context of performances, there are always 'ruptures' that allow us to catch a glimpse of the discursive system that normally is presumed. In this case, the person's place in the culture is not questioned; it is given. In this kind of cultural setting, 'external mediation' was possible. The king or the nobles could serve as models without becoming rivals of their subjects. A distance between the model and the subject was established.

With a loosening of the cultural ties and a loss of such distance, it becomes possible to enter into rivalry with one's models. The mediation now becomes 'internal'. For Girard, this means that internal mediation and thus mimetic rivalry and conflict have increased substantially with the spread of modernity.

The Paths to Crisis

The spread of mimetic conflict in any society leads to a crisis in that mimetic conflict does away with the differences of hierarchy. Cultural order is built on differences that are the basis of that order; mimetic rivalry and conflict tend to do away with the differences between rivals. Each move on the part of one rival is parried by a move on the part of the other. To the rivals, their opposition to each other is evident, but to a third party, they begin to resemble each other. This kind of conflict produces 'enemy twins', people faced off against each other who, in being opposed to one another, begin to resemble one another. This erasure of difference leads to disorder.

Shakespeare (2005) uses the word 'degree' to denote differences and writes in *Troilus and Cressida*,

> O! when degree is shak'd,
> Which is the ladder to all high designs,
> The enterprise is sick. How could communities,
> Degrees in schools, and brotherhoods in cities,
> Peaceful commerce from dividable shores,
> The primogenitive and due of birth,
> Perogative of age, crowns, sceptres, laurels,
> But by degree, stand in authentic place? (act 1, scene III, ll. 101–8)

Shakespeare's play goes on to portray the consequences of degree being gone: one has complete disorder and violence. Girard (1977) terms this a 'crisis of distinctions' (49), which points to a more fundamental crisis—the sacrificial crisis. The sacrificial crisis is *the* crisis in any cultural order because the cultural order itself is ultimately based on sacrifice; that is, it is based on making and maintaining the fundamental distinction between 'a violence that is holy, legal, and legitimate . . . opposed to a violence that is unjust, illegal, and illegitimate' (23). Society uses its 'good violence' to punish the purveyors of 'bad violence' and in so doing helps to make the fundamental distinction between the two types of violence.

If desire is mimetic, violence is more so. As Girard (1977) writes, the *mimetic* attributes of violence are extraordinary—sometimes direct and positive, at other times indirect and negative. The more men strive to curb their violent impulses, the more these impulses seem to prosper. The very weapons used to combat violence are turned against their users. Violence is like a raging fire that feeds on the very objects intended to smother its flames (31). This violence must be stopped, and the only thing that seems to work against violence is more violence. Girard's conclusion is that in the face of a contagion of unstoppable violence that now threatens the existence of the human community itself, human beings stumbled on a solution. The community directs and focuses its violence on a single victim. This target becomes the object upon which the violence of the community is now unanimously vented. A victim is killed by the mob and peace restored. In other words, a 'difference' is introduced and grounded: the difference between community and victim, between the profane group and the sacred corpse, between legitimate violence and illegitimate violence.

Sacrifice accomplishes this: 'The function of sacrifice is to quell violence within the community and to prevent conflicts from erupting' (Girard 1977, 16). Violence and the sacred are linked in sacrifice. Religion becomes 'another term for the obscurity that surrounds man's efforts to defend himself by curative or preventative means against his own violence' (23).

Sacrifice and, by extension, religion, as well as the legal system, work because human beings are persuaded of the transcendental quality of this system. Indeed, the misrecognition is crucial to the working of the system, and this allows us to see how the dominant form of discourse reinforces a certain system. Thus, we allow this sanctified, legitimate form of violence. If the essential quality of transcendence is lost, if this form of violence is taken away, then there is no way to define 'the legitimate form of violence and to recognize it among the multitude of illicit forms. The definition of legitimate and illegitimate forms then becomes a matter of opinion' (Girard 1977, 24).

This does not change the fact that the fundamental difference is arbitrary. The victims were neither the cause of the violence that threatened the community nor the cause of the peace and order that emerged upon their death. Again, we can see this as an act of substitution and thus of translation. The single individual is substituted for the whole community. The victim dies in the place of the community. A different victim (or even an animal) can be substituted for the human victim. These are all forms of translation.

A demystification of the sacrificial system brings about its disintegration. The more we understand the way in which sacrifice forms the distinction between good and bad violence, the less the distinction holds. 'The *sacrificial crisis*, that is the disappearance of the sacrificial rites, coincides with the disappearance of the difference between impure violence and purifying violence' (Girard 1977, 49). With the disappearance of this foundational distinction, all other differences are obliterated as well. The cultural order disintegrates unless it can find a new foundation.

THE CENTER CANNOT HOLD: CHRISTIANITY'S ROLE IN THE DISINTEGRATION OF THE SACRIFICIAL SYSTEM

Murder is widely recognized as a foundation of societal order. In the Bible, Cain kills Abel, and then, it is recorded, Cain builds the first cities. Likewise, the story of Rome's foundation, according to Roman mythology, records a similar murder of Remus by Romulus. Machiavelli (1988), in *The Prince*, cautioned against probing too deeply into the foundation of the governing order. Freud (1939), in *Moses and Monotheism*, also posited the murder of Moses as the beginning of civilization. Moses, the Egyptian outsider, is adopted by the Jews and then murdered by his followers who, nevertheless, adopt his monotheistic message. To recapitulate, desire leads to rivalry, which leads to violence, which leads to the founding of religion in sacrifice and to the sacrificial order of society, an order that is doomed to collapse under its own weight.

But this is not the form that cultural memory usually takes. As indicated above, the usual form is mythical. The gods wanted this sacrifice. The sacrifice placated them and brought blessings. We owe who and what we are to the sacred acts of substitution carried out at the beginning of our history, and we remember them by reenacting them.

Girard's theory tells us about violence and also peace. It seems to articulate two different things. On the one hand, it is possible to establish peace by re-sacralizing the violence. If people can, once more, remember the transcendent quality of their violence, it will become legitimate, and order will reign. This approach is still in use in some quarters today. On the other, the theory itself leads to a renunciation of violence and an embrace of forgiveness. It leads to a different form of memory and thus to a different form of dialogue. When the way in which order is maintained becomes conscious, it becomes possible for human beings to choose whether to continue maintaining the order in that way. This is how discourse comes to dominate our thinking.

Girard found the source of the memory of the victim in the Judeo-Christian scriptures. He noticed the striking resemblance between the myths of many different cultures about a dying and rising god and the Christian story of the crucifixion and resurrection of Jesus of Nazareth. For some, the historical rootedness of the Gospels in a particular time and place with a historical fig-ure suffering the fate of so many mythic heroes seemed to make Christianity a kind of inferior religion when compared to the more mythological accounts. This, in turn, had the effect of leading many twentieth-century apologists for Christianity to try to find ways exaggerate its difference from other 'pagan' religions for fear that Christianity really was just another variation on a uni-versal theme.

What Girard noticed, however, was the significance of the similarity. The Gospels remembered the same story as the myths but told it from an alterna-tive viewpoint—that of the victim. The victim was not guilty of the crimes with which he was charged; he was not responsible for the unrest that af-flicted the community. This form of translation, translating the problems that beset the community into an accusation against the victim, was a false form of translation based on a distorted memory. The coming together of the com-munity against him was not a real reconciliation of enemies based on true dialogue but rather simply the usual union of people united against a common enemy and based on a lie. Thus, the death of the victim did not bring about real peace. Unlike myths, the Gospel outcome is different. This victim is not divinized through the benefits that his sacrificial death bestowed; rather, he is already divine. The hard truth is that the sacrifice was desired not by God but by the people who killed him. The unity formed is a unity of a new com-munity of those who persecuted the victim and are now gathered together by this forgiving victim. As Girard (1987) writes, something unprecedented has occurred here, and it is this occurrence that I think may serve as a basis for 'rethinking' peace studies:

> Jesus is not there in order to stress once again in his own person the unified violence of the sacred; he is not there to ordain and govern like Moses; he is not there to unite a people around him, to forge its unity in the crucible of rites and prohibitions, but on the contrary, to turn this long page of human history once and for all. (204)

This revelation and undoing of the sacrificial mechanism suggests that Chris-tianity has a role to play in replacing or reordering the mechanism. Some scholars of peace studies have used Girard's mimetic theory, and some have dedicated great efforts to exploring its ramifications in this field.[1] Pertinent here is a comment made by Rowan Williams (2011) in his study of Dosto-evsky: 'The divine image establishes itself not by universally compelling attraction but by its endurance through disruption and defilement' (208). For our purposes, we can construe the divine image as an image of peace. Yet, is it still an image that has a 'universally compelling attraction' for us in our present state? The image is not divine because it represents an *absent* good, that is, something that neither exists in nor belongs to this world of history and choice. If it represents something that belongs to this world of history and choice, then it represents something that has limitations. It would seem that everything real is not divine because it is attractive only in a limited way; it has both an upside and a downside. But then nothing could represent the divine image, nothing could represent true peace. Thus, to establish a divine image can be done only by establishing not an image with only an upside but rather one that possesses a capacity to keep its goodness, its attractiveness, through disruption and defilement. This maintenance of beauty through defacement translates a truth that can lead to peaceful reconciliation through that endurance. This reconciliation happens in the same historical space as the defilement: the historical space of translation, memory, dialogue and discourse. This space is present in the world wherever violence occurs. Rather than the image of absence, we have the representation of what comes out of an abundance presence present in our reality.

FOLLOWING A POSITIVE PATH TOWARDS PEACE

When we understand how mimetic humans are, the usual reaction is a mixture of optimism and pessimism. The pessimism is fed by the clear understanding that wanting what other people want leads to a kind of rivalry that leads to conflict that leads to violence and eventually to sacrifice as a way of solving the violence. It also leads to a remembering of this sequence of events in a systematically distorted way. There is a certain mechanical necessity to it all that is depressing. Texts of persecution share certain stereotypes that are invariant in time and space. This kind of cultural formation of desire that leads to rivalry plays a role in discourse even as the discourse tries to overcome it.

The optimism is rooted in the acknowledgement that there are good models of behaviour, and these are as susceptible to imitation as the bad ones. There is a feeling that it is as easy as holding up the good models for imitation and that soon things will get better more or less automatically. Translation would not be difficult, memories would not be distorted and dialogue would be transparent. The mechanistic bent of both pessimism and optimism helps us to see that both are misplaced. Pessimism because the sacrificial mechanism is no longer so mechanical. People are too aware of its functioning for it to function very well. Optimism because good models do not appear as simply 'good'; they must be translated, remembered and discussed. All too often, the positive models are the undoing of the mimetic knots into which we have tied ourselves. They involve the patient work of accurate translation, working through traumatic memories and dialoguing with those we do not trust.

While it is certainly possible to imitate these models, few would argue that they appear attractive. Yet discovering an attractiveness that sustains itself in defilement is the heart of the mystery to which I have been pointing. It makes present a world in which peaceful possibilities emerge in violent situations and that does call forth hope.

NOTE

1. All the works by Roel Kapstein deserve a reading. Further, the two volumes edited by Vern Redekop and Thomas Ryba, respectively, *René Girard and Creative Mimesis* and *René Girard and Creative Reconciliation* (New York: Lexington Books, 2013 and 2014), are excellent introductions to the way in which mimetic theory has been used to support research in peace studies.

REFERENCES

Aristotle. 1984. *The Complete Works of Aristotle: The Revised Oxford Translation.* Edited by Jonathan Barnes. Princeton, NJ: Princeton University Press.

Bateson, Gregory. 1972. *Steps to an Ecology of Mind: Collected Essays in Anthropology, Psychiatry, Evolution, and Epistemology.* San Francisco: Chandler.

Freud, Sigmund. 1939. *Moses and Monotheism.* London: Hogarth Press and the Institute of Psycho-Analysis.

Girard, René. 1965. *Deceit, Desire and the Novel.* Baltimore: Johns Hopkins University Press.

———. 1977. *Violence and the Sacred.* Baltimore: Johns Hopkins University Press..

———. 1987. *Things Hidden since the Foundation of the World.* Stanford, CA: Stanford University Press.

Machiavelli, Niccolò. 1988. *The Prince.* Edited by Quentin Skinner and Russell Price. Cambridge: Cambridge University Press.

Shakespeare, William. 2005. *The Complete Works.* 2nd ed. Edited by John Jowett, William Montgomery, Gary Taylor, and Stanley Wells. Oxford: Oxford University Press.

Williams, Rowan. 2011. *Dostoevsky: Language, Faith, and Fiction.* Waco, TX: Baylor University Press.

Chapter Eleven

The Crisis of Japan's Constitutional Pacifism

The Abe Administration's Belated Counter-Revolution

Shin Chiba

The postwar Constitution of Japan, often referred to as the 'Peace Constitution', was promulgated on November 3, 1946, and went into effect the following year, on May 3, 1947, during the Allied occupation. The three basic principles of the Constitution are (1) popular sovereignty, (2) fundamental human rights and (3) pacifism. The pacifist principle is expressed particularly in the Preamble and Article 9. Portions from the first and second paragraphs of the Preamble and Article 9 are quoted below. They attest to both the tenor and the content of the Constitution's pacifist principle:

> We, the Japanese people . . . resolved that never again shall we be visited with the horrors of war through the action of the government. . . . We, the Japanese people, desire peace for all time and are deeply conscious of the high ideals controlling human relationship, and we have determined to preserve our security and existence, trusting in the justice and faith of the peace-loving people of the world. We desire to occupy an honored place in international society striving for the preservation of peace, and the banishment of tyranny and slavery, oppression and intolerance for all time from the earth. We recognize that all peoples of the world have the right to live in peace, free from fear and want. (Preamble)

> 1. Aspiring sincerely to an international peace based on justice and order, the Japanese people forever renounce war as a sovereign right of the nation and the threat or use of force as a means of settling international disputes.
> 2. In order to accomplish the aim of the preceding paragraph, land, sea, and air force, as well as other war potential, will never be maintained. The right of belligerency of the state will not be recognized. (first and second clauses of Article 9)

In later years, a significant number of scholars of constitutional law and politics agreed on the following thesis presented by Toshiyoshi Miyazawa, a prominent constitutional law scholar at that time. He then argued that the defeat of Japan on August 15, 1945, should be regarded as the 'August Revolution',[1] even though it may seem strange calling the defeat a revolution. Miyazawa argued that the defeat of Japan gave birth to the new Constitution, which delivered a radical change within the Japanese political regime. The oddity of calling it a revolution, however, was suggested by the fact that the pacifist clause was first given to Japan by the Allied forces, although later the overwhelming majority of the Japanese people enthusiastically welcomed this new Constitution. The oddity of referring to the defeat as a revolution can also be traced back to other factors. For example, one may rightly question the absence not merely of the so-called revolutionary people but also of the 'seizure of the ruling power' by the people. This was a peculiar revolution brought by Japan's defeat in the war and the subsequent series and concatenation of interactive political phenomena inside and outside the country. However, this defeat as we understand it can still be called the August Revolution. As Hannah Arendt ([1963] 1976) argues in *On Revolution*, the combination of both the constitution of liberty (*constitutio libertatis*) and the beginning of something new is considered to be the quintessence of modern revolution (29).

I have argued elsewhere for a theory of the two-step constitutional revolution, which took place immediately after the World War II period of Japan (cf. Chiba 2009, 122–29). The first moment was the great transformation of the political regime (i.e., constitution as the *body politic*). In mid-August 1945, the principle of divine right of kingship (absolute emperor system) was turned over to the principle of popular sovereignty (democracy). Miyazawa's August Revolution hypothesis directly spoke to this first moment. The second moment of the revolution was a social and political revolution that would be anticipated and followed in the future by the establishment of the constitutional document, that is, the Constitution of Japan (1946). The second moment of the revolution was a necessary outcome of the August Revolution, which was supposed to initiate a not-yet-realized substantial political and social transformation. The latter was postulated by and consonant with the three fundamental principles of the new Constitution mentioned above: popular sovereignty, fundamental human rights and pacifism. Therefore, the establishment of the Japanese Constitution was by nature not merely the result of the August Revolution but also an 'unfinished revolution'. In effect, the Japanese Constitution was furnished with the urgent task of initiating the anticipated and promised wholesale reform in every sphere of politics and society. The reform included but not was limited to the following: a system of representation, a party system, election, citizens' political participation, local autonomy, diplomacy, education, economy, social welfare and social security and agriculture. These interrelated dimensions of social and political reform were supposed to be guided and implemented by the new norms and criteria specified in the Constitution.

From the perspective of this August Revolution hypothesis of postwar history, the Abe administration that returned to power in 2012 appears to be a belated 'reactionary politics' as well as a 'counter-revolution' against the August Revolution. This reactionary politics, in my judgement, jeopardizes some of the accomplishments—however incomplete and insufficient—of postwar Japan, constitutionalism, democracy and pacifism in particular.

In which direction is the Abe administration heading? We are not absolutely certain, but there are many good reasons for becoming apprehensive about the administration's future. The administration and particularly Prime Minister Shinzo Abe are motivated and driven by the triangle engine: (1) more or less neoliberal globalized financial capitalism in the name of 'Abenomics', which induces the cleavage between the wealthy and the poor within the country; (2) deterrence-based military expansionism; and (3) narrow-minded *State-Shinto* based *Yasukuni* nationalism.[2] This parochial nationalist ideology and the problematic revisionism on 'history issues' go hand in hand. In the latter, Prime Minister Abe and some of his colleagues are reluctant to acknowledge imperial Japan's responsibility concerning aggressive war activities against the victimized nations in the Asia-Pacific region during World War II. Despite its nationalist ideology and historical revisionism, the Abe administration nonetheless pursue the pro-U.S. diplomatic, economic and security policies more earnestly than any previous postwar administrations and thus behaving as a kind of 'vassal state' to the United States.[3] The top agenda of the Abe administration has been to alter the Peace Constitution because they are eager to 'break away from the postwar regime'. There is an irony that at this very point of 'constitutional politics', the current emperor, Akihito, and empress, Michiko, as well as the majority of the Japanese people, are fully committed to Japan's postwar peace diplomacy and world peace as envisaged in the current Peace Constitution.

THE ABE ADMINISTRATION AND ITS *'SEKKYOKUTEKI HEIWASHUGI'*

'Lying in Politics'

Prime Minister Abe and the members of his administration began using the expression '*sekkyokuteki heiwashugi*' in 2013 as their basic diplomatic and security policy. The Japanese wording of '*sekkyokuteki heiwashugi*' literally means 'positive (or proactive) pacifism'. However, the Abe administration adopted the English translation 'proactive contributor to peace'. This Japanese expression first appeared in the document called '*kokka anzenho-sho senryaku nitsuite*' (About the strategy on national security) (December 17, 2013). This important document was adopted and issued by the newly established National Security Council (NSC) in Japan, but the council never explained the meaning of the phrase *sekkyokuteki heiwashugi*. In the later unfolding of the Abe administration's policymaking, arguments and behaviours, the meaning behind the ambiguous phrase has become apparent. *Sekkyokuteki heiwashugi* concretely aims to justify the strengthening of the deterrence-based military power by deploying the government's collective self-defence right as a national security policy. Thus, this Japanese phrase has proved to be both inaccurate and deceptive because this misnomer has nothing to do with a 'positive pacifist stance'. In other words, the contentious phrase is nothing but a deterrence-based positive military expansionism. Furthermore, the language of *sekkyokuteki heiwashugi* can be regarded as a clear example of Abe administration's deceptive politics, or what Hannah Arendt ([1966] 1972) once called 'lying in politics' (6–7). For this reason, the Japanese government is now allowed to send, when few criteria are met, the Self-Defense Force to every corner of the world, where, for instance, the United States and its allied forces are actively engaging in 'counter-terrorism wars'.

On July 1, 2014, the Abe cabinet went forward with adopting the notorious document on the legal framework for national security, which endorses the government's right of collective self-defence, without deliberating over the issues in the Diet. This move, which was regarded as anti-constitutional by almost all specialists of constitutional law, implied the incapacitation of Article 9. Therefore, the controversial document silenced the clauses that speak about the renunciation of war as well as the right of belligerency. The new measures also implied the denial of the long-standing interpretation of the postwar government forbidding the government's entitlement to the right of collective self-defence. Before then, the government had been interpreted by the Cabinet Legislation Bureau to be entitled only to the right of individual self-defence.

During the past two years, the Abe administration opened the way for exporting arms and their components to foreign countries by repealing the so-called Three Principles on Arms Export. They were also busy managing the selling and exporting of nuclear power plants despite the Fukushima Daiichi disaster in March 2011. Also, the government has been eager to cooperate with the United States and other allies under idea of 'support from behind' (*koho shien*), which lends support for frontline fighting from the rear. The government now explains the various needs for these policies and measures under the guise of *sekkyokuteki heiwashugi*. The intent is obvious: this euphemistic phrase is able to easily attract the blind support of a majority of voters who have very little interest in politics.

These well-crafted moves initiated by the Abe administration imply an infringement upon Japan's constitutional pacifism. And as a result, Prime Minister Abe's tactics triggered a series of critical events during the summer of 2015. Our recollection of that summer remains fresh and vivid. One witnessed a strong opposition by multiple citizens' groups against the security-related bills. The opposition was expressed on the streets, in public squares, in the halls, and at press conferences in manifold ways. Scholars and journalists published their opposition to these bills by writing books and articles. Furthermore, the opposition was made vocally both in demonstrations and in assemblies by a number of grassroots citizens' groups; in many cases, more than 10,000 people attended these protest events, and on August 30, 2015, more than 100,000 people participated in demonstration activities around the Diet. According to public opinion polls of various kinds, the majority of people expressed their opposition concerning the bills, and about 80 percent of the people opposed the passing of the bills during that on-going particular session of the Diet. However, the Abe administration forced the Diet to resolve the bills on September 17, 2015.

Sekkyokuteki Heiwashugi

The expression *sekkyokuteki heiwashugi* (positive or proactive pacifism) is clearly nothing but a problematic use of words. This seemingly pacifist but actually militaristic expression and stance is supposed to allow the government to engage in military activities freely. This proactive militarism directly contradicts the renunciation of war, the nonpossession of military forces and the denial of the right of belligerency that Article 9 upholds. The emphasis on *sekkyokuteki heiwashugi* is a sheer anticonstitutional move and incompatible with the substantial content of meanings that Johan Galtung and others long elaborated with regard to the notion of 'positive peace'. This well-known phrase within peace research first and foremost means social cooperation, social justice, equity, *kyosei* (living together or conviviality), harmony, overcoming of both structural and cultural violence and elimination of extreme poverty. This misused expression of *sekkyokuteki heiwashugi* coined by the Abe administration resembles the very 'doublethink' or 'doublespeak' that George Orwell uses in his well-read dystopian novel *Nineteen Eighty-Four*. This ideological phraseology of *sekkyokuteki heiwashugi* surely belongs to such deceptive wording as 'war is peace' and 'enslavement is freedom' that Orwell critically dealt with in his novel.

As was indicated earlier, the Abe administration translates *sekkyokuteki heiwashugi* in English as 'proactive contributor to peace'. When Prime Minister Abe was invited to the Hudson Research Institute, a conservative think tank, to deliver a lecture on September 25, 2013, he referred to China as a 'hypothetical enemy' and declared boldly, 'Call me a right-wing militarist, if you want'. In this lecture, he also used the expression 'proactive contributor to peace' as a translation of *sekkyokuteki heiwashugi*. Furthermore, the same expression appeared twice in his well-known speech titled 'Toward an Alliance of Hope' presented in the U.S. Congress on April 29, 2015.

THE CONSTITUTION OF JAPAN AS THE RESERVOIR OF PEACE IN MODERN JAPAN

The Imposition Hypothesis of the Constitution

Both the Abe administration and nationalistic political groups (especially the 'Japan Conference') have long argued for the imposition hypothesis regarding the Constitution of Japan. This one-sided hypothesis assumes that the Constitution was imposed on the people by the General Headquarters (GHQ), led by Douglas MacArthur, the Supreme Commander for the Allied Powers. The imposition hypothesis is obviously untenable when one thinks about the several key factors of contemporary history surrounding the draft of the new national charter. First, the GHQ asked Joji Matsumoto and his group to come up with an appropriate draft. However, the two versions that Matsumoto and his group presented proved to be not compatible with the democratization and demilitarization postulates of the Potsdam Declaration. The GHQ then found much better drafts among more than 100 drafts that had been penned by Japanese groups and individuals, such as Yasuzo Suzuki, a constitutional scholar. Some of the ideas found in Suzuki's draft had considerable influence on both the content and the expression of the new national charter. Second, a further analysis of the occupation period later showed that the pacifist principle among the so-called MacArthur's Three Principles was first hinted at by Kijuro Shidehara, then the prime minister of the postwar government. Reports reveal that MacArthur and Shidehara in their series of conversations concurred that the pacifist clause would secure Japan to become no longer a military power. They also believed that the special clause could become a beacon of hope to the world at large, which had suffered the two horrible world wars in the first half of the twentieth century. MacArthur also thought that, given the overall opposition by the international society to the emperor system, the introduction of the pacifist clause might help to persuade the

Allied nations to accept the maintenance of the emperor system not as an absolute divine-kingship type, as in the prewar era, but as a new symbolic emperor system. The imposition hypothesis is also difficult to endorse when one reflects on the fact that the overwhelming majority of Japanese people welcomed this GHQ-initiated draft of the national charter with Article 9 at the time its draft became known to the public in March 1946.[4] Also at the level of the Diet, a four-month process of earnest discussion surrounding the draft of national charter took place. The Diet then partly amended and added to the charter, and as a result, the new Constitution was finally approved on November 3, 1946.

Prewar and Midwar Pacifist Heritages in Japan

Some scholars and specialists argue that one of the main reasons for the widespread willingness to accept the postwar Constitution consisted in the fact that during the prewar and midwar eras, a number of peace-oriented strains of thought and opinions existed within the society. These multiple streams of 'small-power' (small country) pacifism left an indelible mark on the collective memory of the Japanese people. The Preamble and Article 9 came to be the reservoir of peace. Multiple 'pacifist veins of water', that is, pacifist heritages of the prewar and midwar Japan, had been poured into the words of the Constitution. Similarly, Shinobu Tabata (1993) stated the following: 'Diverse and multiple strains of peace ideas in modern Japan together poured into the Peace Constitution that was enacted right after the defeat of war. And out of this reservoir of peace there have issued forth a number of peace movements' (1).

Various pacifist streams existed in the background of the postwar ideas of peace. Heritages of peaceful ideas and their influences were buried like groundwater flowing down as the operative ethos inside the culture and tradition of Japanese society. These pacifistic ideas at times would rise to the surface of history to influence the entire ethos of society. Such examples can be found in the Buddhist ideas of 'mercy' (*jihi*) and '*nirvana* or inner peace' (*nehan jakujo*), 'deliverance of the soul' (*gedatsu*) and Prince Shotoku's idea of 'peace or harmony' (*wa*). Also running alongside these peaceful currents are the cultural embeddedness of certain religious and philosophical ethics, such as the classical Confucian (namely, Confucius and Mencius) ideas of 'benevolence' (*jin*), 'commiseration' (*jo*) and 'courtesy' (*rei*); Mozi's ideas of 'non-attack' [or non-war] (*hiko*) and 'universal love' (*ken-ai*); and Laozi's idea of 'non-strife' (*fuso*).[5]

The importance of conspicuous strains of Western influence on modern Japan should also be noted. They include the ideas and influences of Immanuel Kant, Leo Tolstoy, pacifist Christian churches (the Quakers, the Brethren, and the Mennonites) and some lineages that can be traced back to socialism, communism and anarchism. Since the beginning of the Meiji Restoration, pacifist strains have exerted influence on religions, academic circles, literature, journalism and other sectors of the society. These multiple streams of peace in the prewar and midwar periods have poured into the reservoir of peace, namely, the Peace Constitution. After World War II, the Peace Constitution has become the main institutional backdrop for various strains and movements of peace, human rights and democracy. This postwar Constitution has become the driving force for citizens' groups and movements that took up and carried on the issues and lawsuits against pollution and environmental degradation (e.g., Minamata disease in the 1960s and 1970s). What follows is a tentative list that suggests these prewar and midwar influences on individual leaders and peace movements:

1. Kant's influence: Amane Nishi, Emori Ueki, Sanjuro Tomonaga, Shigeru Nanbara and others
2. Tolstoy's influence: Kanzo Uchimura, Gien Kashiwagi, Tokoku Kitamura, Isoo Abe, Naoe Kinoshita and others
3. Christian influence (especially the impact of such pacifist churches as the Quakers, the Brethren, and the Mennonites): Inazo Nitobe, Kiyoshi Yabe, Toyohiko Kagawa, Tadao Yanaihara, Megumu Masaike, Sukeyoshi Suzuki and others
4. The pacifist lineage of socialism, communism, and anarchism: Sen Katayama, Toshihiko (Kasen) Sakai, Shusui Kotoku, Hitoshi Yamakawa, Kanson Arahata, Sanshiro Ishikawa and others
5. The pacifist lineage of *Jiyu-Minken Undo* (liberty and people's rights movement): Chomin Nakae, Emori Ueki, Shozo Tanaka and others
6. Taisho democracy: Sakuzo Yoshino, Ikuo Oyama, Nyozekan Hasegawa, Yukio Ozaki and others
7. Women's peace associations: Hide Inoue, Tsuneko Gauntlett, Fujiko Nomiyama, Michi Kawai and others
8. Literature: Soseki Natsume, Roka Tokutomi, Akiko Yosano, Raicho Hiratsuka, Kenji Miyazawa and others
9. Confucianism: Shonan Yokoi, Masanao (Keiu) Nakamura and others
10. Buddhism: Giro Senoo and members of New Buddhist Youth Alliance
11. Other religions: Onisaburo Deguchi and *Oomoto Religion* and Junzo Akashi of *Todaisha* (Jehovah's Witnesses)
12. Journalism: Kanji Maruyama, Tetsutaro Miura, Tanzan Ishibashi, Kiyoshi Kiyosawa and others

What is noteworthy about this list is, first, the influence of Kant and Tolstoy; their influence was a defining factor for establishing the early pacifist orientation in the Meiji era. Also, by the Taisho era, the ideas and practices of Mahatma Gandhi were introduced to modern Japan. Thus, the pacifism of modern Japan developed under the influence of pacifist ideas and movements of the world at large. Second, nonconformist and minority lineages, such as Christianity, socialism and communism, in Japan played an important role in contributing to the cause of pacifism and anti-war sentiment during the pre-war and midwar periods. Some of these groups have both countered—albeit insufficiently and poorly—and been persecuted by the *tennosei* (imperial) fascism furnished with ultra-nationalism and militarism.

Third, the non-political realm, such as literature, raised important voices for the cause of peace and non-war by criticizing—indirectly in most cases—the imperialistic nationalist policy and militaristic expansionism. For example, Soseki Natsume argues for the significance of individualism based upon the attitude of respecting the liberty for one's own as well as others. Another example can be found in Akiko Yosano's act of composing poems, such as 'I wish you would not die'. Furthermore, the war-experienced generations made important contributions to the anti-war and non-war cause. Their experiences of the miseries of war and their shared sense of contrition and remorse became the foundation for aspiring towards world peace in the years to come.

THE JAPANESE CONSTITUTION
AND ITS HISTORICAL MEANING

Constitutional Pacifism as an Expression of War Apology and Responsibility

The postwar years have been a time of gradual and steady evolvement. The general public have become more clearly aware than before of the extremely aggressive and plunderous nature of the imperial Japan's Fifteen Year War waged between 1931 and 1945. The public were informed by the works of several postwar Japanese and non-Japanese historians who had begun to investigate the country's past activities of warfare. The statistics showing the number of deceased victims from the period between 1931 and 1945 have become extremely important in unveiling the devastation of the war. The number of estimated causalities: 3.1 million Japanese as well as 15 million to 20 million non-Japanese soldiers and civilians as a whole in the Asia-Pacific region (the number of the latter has not yet been established). Thus, the pacifist Article 9 was also understood by a great segment of the Japanese populace as an act of contrition, war apology and acceptance of war responsibility. The pacifist Article 9 promised the peoples in the Asia-Pacific region and the international society that Japan would never again become a military power. However, the war-apology and war-responsibility acts—in the sense of actual deeds and compensation—on the part of the postwar Japanese government and civil society have remained utterly insufficient until today (Chiba 2008b, 178–85).

Thus, the Constitution alongside other documents and practices entail the nation's war apologies for the past colonialism and aggressive war as well as the symbolic act of bearing responsibility for the war. We can safely say that the majority of the Japanese people until today, regardless of the postwar government's intention and policymaking, strongly wanted that 'never again shall we be visited with the horrors of war through the action of the government' (Preamble).

In juxtaposition with the nation's extensive sufferings and later findings about the atrocious nature of imperial Japan's aggressive war activities, it may be understandable that a heavy emphasis should be given to *heiwashugi* (pacifism).[6] Thus, what can be called a positive attitude towards peace became both a public philosophy and a kind of spiritual existence, namely, a way of life for the general public in postwar Japan. That attitude has become, as it were, the soul's basic stance towards life for a majority of the Japanese. A kind of pacifism has gone beyond a cultural, social and political ethos and has transformed into a kind of spirituality and personal *Existenz* to many. But I must hasten to add that this pacifism basically has remained a rather negative 'war-weary' (or abhorrent) pacifism, not a courageous 'nonviolent' resistance type of Mahatma Gandhi's or Martin Luther King Jr.'s persuasion.

The Culture of Peace in the Postwar Era

The Preamble of the Constitution can be correctly said as having the content and character as that of the Peace Declaration. The Preamble and Article 9 together are nothing but the treasure of the August Revolution in our understanding. These pacifistic documents were perhaps a misfortunate fortune, brought out by imperial Japan's total defeat in the war and its consequent absolute surrender. It was *misfortune* because it invited the 'horrors of war', including atomic bombings in Hiroshima and Nagasaki. But it was *fortunate* in the sense that postwar Japan was furnished with the Peace Constitution, which has been regarded in some circles as the 'treasure' for the world of tomorrow. The Japanese surely 'embraced the defeat', as John W. Dower (1999) intimated in his excellent work: 'What matters is what the Japanese themselves made of their experience of defeat, then and thereafter; and a half century now, most of them have consistently made it the touchstone for affirming a commitment to "peace and democracy"'. This is the great mantra of postwar Japan. These are the talismanic words that individuals filled with their own often disparate meanings and continue to debate today' (30). In addition, we have observed the various streams of peaceful orientations of the past flowing into postwar Japan's constitutional pacifism. And overflowing from this reservoir, namely, the Peace Constitution, engendered multiple types of citizens' movements, such as those that worked towards peace, human rights protection, anti-pollution, environmental protection and anti-nuclear power plant protest in the postwar years.

In other words, the Constitution became the institutional backdrop for facilitating these movements. Without this constitutional support, perhaps all these postwar citizens' movements would have remained weaker and more restrained. Yet already in the beginning of postwar history, the Self-Defense Forces were established, and the U.S.-Japan Security Treaty was concluded. The expansion of the American military base in Okinawa was neither stopped nor controlled. While having some contradictions and setbacks, the form and substance of the 'peace nation' was somehow—albeit insufficiently—maintained. The sense of evading war and the liking for peace became deeply embedded in the political culture of postwar Japan.

However, when it comes to the social reality of present-day Japan, one is bound to notice some grievous and negative trends in our society. During the past 20 years or so, Japanese society has clearly and undeniably become somewhat unhappy, stressful and unpleasant. Japan is among the countries with the highest suicide rates; there have been more than 30,000 suicides per year for about 10 consecutive years until recently. Furthermore, Japan is counted as the sixth worst country among 35 Organization for Economic Co-operation and Development (OECD) member states in the so-called poverty ratio; according to data from February 2016, the gap between the wealthy and the poor has rapidly widened in the past two decades. Social phenomena, such as isolation, loneliness and the loss of meaning in life, have all been observed more clearly than before in Japanese society. People increasingly have begun to feel repressed and alienated, tension-filled and apprehensive about their present and future lives. These depressing facts and features indelibly mark Japanese society today.

No matter how insufficient and far from being perfect, democracy, respect for human rights and peace culture are rooted in Japanese society. Comparing statistics concerning peace and the rate of murdered victims internationally will further cement my argument. For the past 15 years, in the case of Japan, the murder rate has been around 0.60 person per 100,000 people. This is the second-lowest rate in the world, after only Iceland. Moreover, according to the Global Peace Index issued by the Institute for Economics and Peace, whose headquarters have been located in Sydney, Australia, for the past eight years or so, Japan was ranked as a 'peace nation', one that meets the conditions for peace, between third and ninth among the approximately 160 nations of the world. The 2018 index shows that Japan's level of enjoying peace is ninth from the top, following Iceland, New Zealand, Portugal, Denmark, Canada and others. One may rightly see the influence of the Peace Constitution in these international statistics. Moreover, since the establishment of the Self-Defence Forces in 1954, they have zero kills, and none of their members have lost their lives in the combat situation.

Despite these ambiguous and complex trends, the role of postwar constitutional pacifism was effective enough to prevent the forming of a 'military class' in the society as in prewar and midwar times. This constitutionally grounded peace also prevented prewar and midwar ultra-nationalism and militarism from being resurrected out of the foregone past. Since the 1990s, a number of nongovernmental and nonprofit organizations sprang up in every sector of society to promote various causes: civic and religious education, global peace, nonviolence, a natural environment, safety, the protection of human rights, the deepening of democracy, social welfare and social security. The formation of these groups served to revitalize the civil society of the country and contributed to forming the vital core of the sociocultural capital of peace in the postwar context.

FINAL REMARKS

We have entered the threshold of the twenty-first century, where we cannot but think that the world of today somehow appears more chaotic and anarchic. Beginning with the September 11 terrorist attacks, the international terrorism of al-Qaeda, ISIS and other groups is threatening the peace and stability of the world with their terrorist acts in Europe and elsewhere. The United States and other allied nations began engaging in the so-called counter-terrorism war, conducted mainly with aerial bombardments against these terrorist groups, especially in Afghanistan, Iraq and Syria.

In today's turbulent world, we are faced with several disturbing and pressing questions. Consistent with the stance that the Abe administration has maintained, should the Japanese people disregard constitutional pacifism as an irrelevant relic of the foregone past so as to be adjusted towards and cope with this increasingly violent world? Or rather, because the world has become increasingly hawkish and violence-ridden, does the Peace Constitution glow ever more brightly in this anarchic world? Today, the Japanese people are directly faced with these two contrasting narratives. The current Japanese government seems to have garnered strong support and welcome in the world for its positive steps towards deterrence-based militarism and proactive policy change for anti-terrorist warfare. Thus, unsurprisingly and with good reason, in view of the rapid change of today's international environment, certain specialists in the field of international politics and international relations have begun to look favourably at Japan's changing policy towards state security issues. Not only that, due to the generational shift, Japanese people and the young generation in particular feel insecure about the pacifist stance of postwar Japan. Both the nuclear threat of North Korea and the rapid military expansion of China have influenced the general perception of the Japanese people regarding the recent international plight, especially in East Asia. But in 2018, we have witnessed a possibility of surprising change in North Korea's attitude towards the denuclearization of its military and missile policies. A little sign of hope for engendering peace in East Asia suddenly has occurred.

'Common Security' and 'Cooperative Security'

Another crucial question is being raised today: will Japan be able to draw out and articulate a viable nonmilitary type of security mechanism compatible with the vision of the peaceable world as depicted in the Constitution of Japan?

In recent years, I have become more aware than before of the significance of nonmilitary types of security measures, such as 'common security' and, more recently, 'cooperative security', that evolved out of the former. During the Cold War era, the idea of 'common security' was invented and applied in Europe under the initiative of Scandinavian governments such as Norway, Sweden and Denmark. In 1975, the Conference on Security and Co-operation in Europe (CSCE) was established to overcome the excessive dependence on the North Atlantic Treaty Organization (NATO). This pan-European, nonmilitary security mechanism proposed by the 'small powers' of Europe opened the way for creating the task of confidence building and dialogical diplomacy aimed at building international friendship and cooperation between western European countries and their eastern European counterparts. The CSCE became the locale where the minister and ambassador class of political leaders of European nations gathered frequently and regularly in Vienna, Geneva and other European cities.

The CSCE adopted the so-called common security measure by which the European countries sought for the appropriate path for putting an end to the Cold War. They sought to formulate an agreement on issues surrounding the non-invasion of other countries, the exchange of information on military operations, disarmament and arms control, diplomacy based on open dialogue and confidence building and economic cooperation. With the presentation of the Palme Commission Report (1982), the pipe of the dialogue between the two camps widened further to accelerate the confidence-building effort. In the present-day scholarship exists a semi-consensus that the Cold War would never have ended by the militaristic measures of NATO alone. The CSCE made an inescapable and non-negligible role by supplementing the NATO operation in putting an end to the Cold War.

After the end of the Cold War, in 1994, the CSCE changed its name to the Organization for Security and Co-operation in Europe (OSCE). The OSCE played a vital role for reconciliation and peace-related activities particularly through the following three dimensions: (1) the politico-military dimension, (2) the economic and environmental dimension and (3) the human dimension (democratization, human rights, cultural exchange, and so forth). Today, 57 countries from Europe, central Asia and North America are active members—becoming the greatest regional security organization. Japan participates as an Asian partner country (semi-membership country).

Thus, operations of the CSCE/OSCE were later cojoined with UN-initiated peace-building activities. CSCE/OSCE then could be seen as a precursor for peace-building operations under the UN initiative (Chiba 2015, 179–82; Galbreath 2007, 6, 43, 65–91; Sandole 2007, xiii–xv, 45–64, 95–127). Today, the 'common security' measure under the CSCE/OSCE has evolved and developed into a more comprehensive 'cooperative security'. This non-war type of cooperative security has become the pivotal security mechanism among Scandinavian countries, Canada, New Zealand, Australia, Latin American countries and the Association of Southeast Asian Nations. They seek to develop security policies based on the fundamental principle of nonmilitary cooperation.

The scheme of cooperative security is rooted in the fundamental principle of nonmilitary measures and 'non-war-ism', which at the most basic level coincides with the pacifist principle of the Japanese Constitution. As a matter of fact, the Japanese government from time to time has shown interest in the idea of applying this security option in the context of East Asia. An attempt was made in recent years for a trilateral security cooperation among the three East Asian countries: the People's Republic of China, the Republic of Korea and Japan. This organization, officially established in 2011, is called the Trilateral Cooperative Secretariat. Some quarters hold high expectations for the future of the secretariat, that this organization will amend the situation of 'hot economics and cold politics' in this region. On May 9, 2018, these three countries held the seventh Trilateral Summit in Tokyo and made a 'Joint Declaration' (https://www.mofa.go.jp/a_o/rp/page4e_000817.html).

Kantian Features of Peace and Japanese Pacifism

Distinctively Kantian features reside in the current Japanese pacifism, which emphasizes constitutionalism and a culture of peace. This type of pacifism is unique in the history of ideas on peace and peace studies. First, the essential core of Kant's idea of peace is fully displayed in his classic *To Perpetual Peace: A Philosophical Sketch* ([1795] 1983), which implies that perpetual peace is nothing but 'the end of all hostilities' (*das Ende aller Hostilitäten*) (2). This is the Kantian version of 'positive peace', or, perhaps more accurately, 'unqualified peace', which means not simply the absence of war but also the annihilation of all wars and enmities. The word 'hostility' means both an external militant fight and an internal enmity or strong hatred. Second, among the six Preliminary Articles that Kant ([1795] 1983) wrote, the third is well known: 'Standing armies (*miles perpetuus*) shall be gradually abolished' (3). Herein certainly one finds Kant's idealism, but at the same time, the reason that he devises this proposition is sufficiently realistic. Kant explains that standing armies constantly threaten other nations with war by giving the appearance that they are prepared for battle. Thus, the internal mechanism of enmity and hatred, anxiety and insecurity cannot but help induce nations to ceaselessly seek to increase a boundless extension of military power. This is perhaps one of the earliest formulations of what present-day theorists of international politics call 'the dilemma of state (military) security'. Third, Kant's ideas on perpetual peace are derived from and integrated with his entire critical philosophy and philosophy of freedom. His fundamental claim can be identified with the following sentence as found in the last section of *The Metaphysics of Morals* ([1797] 1996): 'Now, as a matter of fact, the morally practical reason utters within us its irresistible Veto: "There shall be no war"' (264).[7]

These Kantian features specified above resonate strongly with the basic tenor of postwar Japan's pacifist Constitution. The Kantian posture and Japan's constitutional pacifism share a kind of normative idealism tinged with realistic insights. Without normative ideals with realistic insights, such as aspiring for 'the banishment of tyranny and slavery, oppression and intolerance for all time from earth' (Preamble), neither a single peaceful nation nor even a relatively peaceable world shall ever be able to be born, stand up, and begin to walk.

As a matter of fact, postwar Japanese constitutional pacifism has gone farther than the Kantian pacifism in some respects. For instance, a kind of hermeneutics of suspicion is directed towards the modern idea of state sovereignty in the case of constitutional pacifism. Observed here is a kind of self-limiting of the sovereign power of the state. For the right of belligerency (*jus belli*) constitutes the central category of state sovereignty in the modern Westphalian paradigm of international politics. Thus, the Peace Constitution is *anathema* to the modern notion of sovereignty. The first clause of Article 9 proclaims to 'forever renounce war as a sovereign right of the nation and the threat or use of force as a means of settling international dispute'. The second clause then insists, 'In order to accomplish the aim of the preceding paragraph, land, sea, and air force, as well as other war potential, will never be maintained. The central and overarching category of state sovereignty is the very foundation for the mainstream of the so-called realistic political science and international relations. In this volume, I acknowledge, there exists a shared understanding that peace studies should break away from the *very* common aporia seen both in big powers' current statecraft and in mainstream political science and international relations, that is, the modern *hegemonic* presence of the central paradigm of state sovereignty (see the chapters by Nandy, Bronner, Richmond and Shani in this volume).

The Unsuccessful Task of Translating Japanese Experiences

As is made clear in the introduction, it is our understanding and the premise of this volume that translation, no less than memory and dialogue, remains equally central to peace and peace studies. As is also indicated in the introduction, the English word 'translate' is derived from Latin word 'transferre', meaning 'to bear across', 'to carry' and 'to transplant'. The postwar pacifism in Japan lacks the strong effort and ingeniousness to engage in the translation (in the sense of communication, bearing across and transplantation) of Japanese experiences of war's calamities to the rest of the world. Also, Japan should more earnestly practice the spirit and principles of constitutional pacifism and highlight—in the sense of making known to the world—the significance of its postwar transition to a peace nation. Costa Rica, for example, is more devoted to and hence more successful in its mission of spreading its own 'peace constitution'. In the case of Japan, there are only a few effective and eloquent storytellers in academia and literature. One might hope that there can appear more peace-oriented comics, such as like Kenji Nakagawa's manga *Hadashi no Gen*, in popular culture (see Curran, in this volume).

I would like to conclude by returning to the pressing issue that the Japanese people are faced with. Will the Japanese pursue the increase of military deterrence, or will they promote a non-militaristic type of cooperative security? At this important crossroad for determining the future orientation of this country, it is needless to say that what is most required of the people is their careful deliberation, open discussion and astute judgement at the grassroots level and their decisive political will to choose a better alternative.

NOTES

1. Miyazawa (1946) argued as follows: 'With the war being ended a revolution took place. While the hitherto accepted doctrine of divine right of kingship was

thrown away, the new doctrine of popular sovereignty was adopted. . . . Here the fundamental tenet of the country underwent what can be called a Copernican turn' (68).

2. Yasukuni Shrine is the main State Shinto–based place where the state mourns, commemorates and honours the Japanese soldiers who sacrificed their lives to the country in various war activities.

3. The contradictory behaviour of Prime Minister Shinzo Abe of being a narrow-minded nationalist who has nostalgia for the prewar and midwar Japan and at the same time consistently maintaining a submissive attitude towards the United States resembles his grandfather Nobusuke Kishi, an A-class war criminal who later became prime minister from 1957 to 1960. Kishi was rescued from the imprisonment (due to his war responsibility) by the GHQ of the occupation forces, and later in the postwar period, Kishi received a great amount of funds from the Central Intelligence Agency due to his pro-American attitude and political astuteness. Although he seems to have kept this belief to himself and to his close comrades, his ideal era of Japan appeared to be the Fifteen Year War period from 1931 to 1945, when the nation became one and united in spirit as a like-minded community of shared destiny both in war victories and in defeats. But at the same time, Kishi in the postwar period determined to become obedient to the United States by his painful experiences at Sugamo Prison. His very DNA was somewhat inherited by his grandson, Prime Minister Abe. Therefore, in both figures, Yasukuni nationalism and a submissive attitude towards the United States can go together in a seamless unity.

4. The joint authorship of the Japanese Constitution is the majority view for Japanese constitutional law scholars. They emphasize the important role played by Shidehara in his consultation with MacArthur.

5. See Chiba, (2008b, 2011, 2014a). These Buddhist and Confucian ideas still remain the foundation of a culture of peace.

6. I want to emphasize here that the Japanese word for "pacifism" is *heiwashhugi* and that this word is broader in its meaning than the English equivalent. "Pacifism" tends to mean mostly religious and sometimes secular attitudes of nonviolence or nonresistance in the Western tradition. But *heiwashugi* means and covers diverse peace-oriented attitudes, not merely Christian, Buddhist and Confucian but also humanist, secular, utilitarian types of peace orientation.

7. See Chiba (2014b), 72. I have argued that Kant's position of war abolition and non-war-ism belong to what I call 'radical (or thoroughgoing) pacifism."

8. Here, I acknowledge that there exists a shared understanding that peace studies should break away from a common aporia seen in the big powers' current statecraft and mainline political science and international relations as well: the modern hegemonic presence of the central paradigm of state sovereignty. See the chapters by Nandy, Bronner, Richmond and Shani (in this volume).

REFERENCES

Arendt, Hannah. [1966] 1972. 'Lying in Politics'. In *Crises of the Republic*. New York: Harcourt Brace Jovanovich.

———. [1963] 1976. *On Revolution.* New York: Penguin.

Chiba, Shin. 2008a. 'On Constitutional Pacifism in Post-War Japan: Its Theoretical Meanings'. In *Peace Movements and Pacifism after September 11,* edited by Shin Chiba and Thomas J. Schoenbaum, 128–51. Cheltenham: Edward Elgar.

———. 2008b. 'For Realizing *Wa* and *Kyosei* in East Asia'. In *A Grand Design for Peace and Reconciliation in East Asia,* edited by Yoichiro Murakami and Thomas J. Schoenbaum, 176–97. Cheltenham: Edward Elgar.

———. 2009. *'Mikan no kakumei' toshiteno heiwa kenpo* [The Peace Constitution as an 'Unfinished Revolution']. Tokyo: Iwanami Shoten Publishers.

———. 2011. 'On Perspectives on Peace: The Hebraic Idea of *Shalom* and Prince Shotoku's Idea of *Wa*'. In *Building New Pathways to Peace,* edited by Noriko Kawamura, Yoichiro Murakami, and Shin Chiba, 48–64. Seattle: University of Washington Press.

———. 2014a. 'A Historical Reflection on Peace and Public Philosophy of Japanese Thought: Prince Shotoku, Ito Jinsai and Yokoi Shonan'. In *Visions of Peace: Asia and the West,* edited by Takashi Shogimen and Vicki A. Spencer, 85–102. Surrey: Ashgate.

———. 2014b. *Renposhugi to kosumoporitanizumu* [Federalism and Cosmopolitanism]. Tokyo: Fukosha Publishers.

———. 2015. 'Heiwa kochikuron no genzai' [The Presence of Theories of Peace-building]. In *Nijuichi seiki no seiji to boryoku* [Politics and Violence in the Twenty-First Century], edited by Kazuo Ogushi. Kyoto: Koyo Shobo Publishers.

Dower, John W. 1999. *Embracing Defeat: Japan in the Wake of World War II.* New York: Norton.

Galbreath, David J. 2007. *The Organization for Security and Co-operation in Europe.* London: Routledge.

Kant, Immanuel.[1795] 1983. *To Perpetual Peace: A Philosophical Sketch.* Translated Ted Humphrey. Indianapolis, IN: Hackett.

———. [1797] 1996. *The Metaphysics of Morals.* Translated by Mary Gregor. Cambridge: Cambridge University Press.

Miyazawa, Toshiyoshi. 1946. 'Hachigatsu kakumei to kokumin shukenshugi' [August Revolution and the Principle of Popular Sovereignty]. *Sekai Bunka* [World Culture]. May. Tokyo: Sekai Bunka Publishing.

Sandole, Dennis J. D. 2007. *Peace and Security in the Postmodern World: The OSCE and Conflict Resolution.* London: Routledge.

Tabata, Shinobu. 1993. 'Maegaki' [Preface]. In *Kindai nihon no heiwa shiso: Heiwa kenpo no shiso teki genryu to hatten* [Ideas of Peace in Modern Japan: The Stream Source and Development of the Ideas of the Peace Constitution], edited by Shinobu Tabata, 1–6. Kyoto: Minerva Publishing.

Part IV

Rethinking Peace

Dialogue (Fetish)

Alexander Laban Hinton

Dialogue is fetish, an ordering disorder, or at least it often is in peace studies and related fields like transitional justice and human rights. If a fetish suggests something alluring and invested with power (from the Portuguese *feitico*, suggesting 'charm' or 'sorcery'), dialogue fetish refers to the widespread assumption that dialogue has powers that provide a path to peace, overcoming silence and repression, founts of conflict.

This volume seeks to rethink such dialogue fetish. By doing so, we are not simply dismissing dialogue. But we warn against dialogue fetish, which often leads to the peace studies quaternity discussed in the introduction: hypostasis, teleology, normativity and enterprise. Like a psychological or capitalist fetish, dialogue fetish may lead to dysfunction that subverts its supposed ends.

The examples are legion. Indeed, we offer a warning. Dialogue fetish is epidemic. Do a search on the internet. Open the dictionary. Observe a training. Listen to diplomats. Look at related websites. Start with UNESCO's 'Dialogue for Peace'.

Over and over, we find the symptoms: dialogue as dyadic conversation leading to conflict resolution. We are overstating the case, of course, to make a point. There are exceptions. We point to Lederach's (2005) work as an example. But the exceptions are not the rule.

And, indeed, dialogue fetish may be a modality of rule and governmentality. What comes to mind when dialogue is mentioned? Consider the *Oxford English Dictionary*'s definition, which defines dialogue as 'conversation between two or more people as a feature of a book, play, or film' often aimed at the 'resolution of a problem'. In the peace enterprise, such dialogue is directed towards conflict resolution.

Both share a staging. Dialogue doesn't exist in a vacuum. It takes place in a structured setting in which positions, roles, conventions and speech acts are enabled and constrained. Discourse takes place in an arena of power, one linked to genealogy. Feminist peace researchers have provided one line of critique in this regard, highlighting the ways in which dialogue is mediated by gendered assumptions and prioritizations of voice.[1] Similar critiques have been made about (neo)colonial legacies and the disempowerment of the Global South's voice (see Nandy and Shani, in this volume).

What are we to do? Seek treatment, a dialogue fetish cure. Rethink peace. Denaturalize dialogue fetish. Focus on process, reflexivity, multidirectionality and relationality. Pay attention to domination and resistance, and the said and the unsaid—to return to the staging metaphor, the asides, nonverbal cures, pauses, silences, secondary actors and extras and 'hidden transcripts' (Scott 1992). In other words, examine who sets the stage (and who doesn't) and look for the 'black holes' to again invoke Nandy's metaphor.

If many of the chapters in this volume are suggestive in this regard, the chapters in this part, as well as the afterword, underscore the point. For example, Morgan Brigg's chapter, 'From Substantialist to Relational Difference in Peace and Conflict Studies', takes up issues of domination and hypostasis that are, in part, related to genealogies dating back to European colonialism and as well as contemporary Global North scholarship. Peace and conflict studies have often been informed by substantialist and identarian assumptions that hypostasize social difference, erasing relationality in preference for dichotomous categories of being.

In response, Brigg argues for rethinking peace studies in terms of relationality, including indigenous, Global South and feminist scholarship that show alternatives to the hypostasizing tendencies of substantialism. Here, then, is his cure to dialogue fetish: unpacking genealogies underpinning domination and other taken-for-granted assumptions, focusing on relationality as opposed to substantialist and identarian categories and drawing on voices and scholarship outside the dominant peace studies traditions.

Hartmut Behr's chapter, 'Peace through Dialogue about and across Difference(s): A Phenomenological Approach to Rethinking Peace', proceeds along similar lines, arguing for unpacking ontological assumptions and focusing analytical attention on relationality and nonessentializing approaches to difference. While Brigg highlights colonial legacies and related scholarly literatures, Behr starts with a genealogy of Western binaries of self and other that date back to antiquity and also inform relations of domination that structure the peace-building enterprise, including what I am here calling dialogue fetish. Behr seeks to rethink peace through a critical phenomenological approach—drawing on scholars ranging from Husserl to Derrida—in which binaries like self/other and individual/society (as well as global/local) are undercut by lived experience, interdependence, temporality, contingency and relationality.

By refocusing attention on 'momentary and transient "here and nows"', Behr argues that dialogue focuses on fluidity and difference as opposed to hypostasis of essentialized identities and related ontological categories. Referencing Galtung's peace diagram that is discussed in this volume's introduction, Behr argues for an empathetic positive peace that acknowledges and appreciates difference as opposed to colonizing it through preexisting assimilative categories linked to power. Behr's arguments for a 'peace-in-difference' phenomenological approach provide a means of escaping dialogue fetish in peace studies and related fields (on phenomenological transitional justice, see Hinton 2016, 2018).

If Behr's argument for a more phenomenological approach to peace and dialogue is more philosophical, Nitin Sawhney's chapter, '*Zona Intervenida*: Performance as Memory, Transforming Contested Spaces', is directly grounded in the lived experience of Guatemalan artists who grapple with the violent legacies of the past, including some who perform in a former military complex. Sawhney warns against the hypostasis, teleology and what I here call dialogue fetish that often mediate the work of peace activists and conflict mediators.

In the context of his field site in Guatemala, Sawhney argues, simple categories—the essentializations against which Brigg and Behr inveigh—break down. Distinctions between perpetrators and victims provide one example, a binary complicated by individual and community histories. Artists are able to underscore such complexities and question hegemonic memory discourses even as they are performatively contingent, part of the 'here-and-now' to use Behr's term. And, like Behr, Sawhney's regards lived experience and performance as a way to rethink and move beyond the quaternity of peace studies tendencies discussed in this volume's introduction.

Like Sawhney's chapter, my afterword, 'Look Again—Aleppo: The Last Lesson on Prevention', seeks to rethink peace through artistic (in this case literary) strategies. My poetic erasures freeze a period of time—the fall of 2016 as Aleppo was besieged and the controversial U.S. presidential election was drawing to a close. I use juxtaposition and erasure to undercut narrative, destabilize hypostasis and question teleology and enterprise.

At this moment in time, a battle between good and evil appeared to be being waged on multiple fronts, manifest in a set of images ranging from a crying child in Aleppo to political claims about the legitimacy of violence and war. As opposed to dialogue fetish, with the allure and charm of teleological narrative, the erasures are disjunctive, foregrounding interspersed lines of text with redactions. The erasure has no straightforward beginning or end: the first verse is the last lesson: look again, a call for revision and attending to what has been silence and obscured. On another level, the erasures also raise questions about memory, temporality, spectacle and (in) action since they focus on a recent moment of violence that has already been largely forgotten but was a dominant story at the time. By highlighting this moment, the erasure raises further questions about how our dialogues and narratives are fashioned, including prevention discourses that appear more rhetorical than imperative, another dimension of the dialogue fetish. By ending with this piece, *Rethinking Peace* strives to avoid peace studies fetish by underscoring the point that the process of rethinking is never finished.

NOTE

1. See, for example, the various contributions to the special issue 'Building Peace: Feminist Perspectives', *Peacebuilding* 4, no. 2 (2016): 121–229.

REFERENCES

Hinton, Alexander Laban. 2016. *Man or Monster: Trial of a Khmer Rouge Torturer.* Durham, NC: Duke University Press.
———. 2018. *The Justice Facade: Trials of Transition in Cambodia.* New York: Oxford University Press.
Lederach, John Paul. 2005. *The Moral Imagination: The Art and Soul of Building Peace.* New York: Oxford University Press.
Scott, James C. 1992. *Domination and the Arts of Resistance.* New Haven, CT: Yale University Press.

Chapter Twelve

Peace-in-Difference

Peace through Dialogue about and across Difference(s): A Phenomenological Approach to Rethinking Peace

Hartmut Behr

Whether we as individuals, citizens, political activists, politicians or, most importantly, as conflict parties act in a peaceful way or less so depends on our relation to our fellow humans. Thus, peace always articulates (as) a relation to the 'other'. Yet the question of the 'other' that underpins the conceptualization of peace includes another question, namely, that of difference. Consequently, issues around peace are to be thought of as questions of difference. Whether or not we act in a peaceful way is therefore a question of how we approach, think and negotiate difference. The first argument developed in this chapter is that nonessentialist ways of thinking and acting upon difference(s) are more conducive to peaceful relations than essentialized versions of difference. The second, subsequent argument holds that in practical terms, a nonessentialist way of dealing with difference surmounts in the maxim of political dialogue, a dialogue that is empathetic for differences and steadily moves to and provokes the edges of its own rationality. Such dialogue instils—and the approach to rethinking peace pursued in this chapter suggests—the creation of new meanings through nonessentialized perceptions of difference rather than relying on handed-down (and traditional) ontologies and their binaries in the legacy of (the discipline) of international relations and respective discourses of 'the state', 'the West', 'the other', or 'the local' (see Nandy, Richmond, and Shani, in this volume). Essentializing normativities, more or less explicit or implicit in these imaginaries, are to be replaced by the open-ended, generative norm of embracing differences through and in dialogue.

THE PROBLEM AND THE ARGUMENT

Peace as a question of difference sounds initially banal, as peace articulates always as a relation to 'the' 'other'[1] (as does 'violence', the antonym of 'peace'). The discussion of this relation leads us, however, to very complex issues.

The question of 'the' 'other' that underpins the conceptualization of peace thus bears another question, namely, that of difference why issues around peace are to be thought of as questions of difference. We can state that whether or not we act in a peaceful way and how conducive our action is towards or promoting peace is in the first place a question of how we approach, think and negotiate difference. The relation to 'the' 'other' articulates thus as a problem of difference and of how we act towards difference(s). Ultimately, peace is violated and violence breaks out because our perceptions of difference(s) are obstructing nonviolent social relations, trumping dialogue.

When framing the question of peace as a question of difference, we have to deal with two main problems: the first problem relates to the legacy of thinking difference in Western philosophy and political theory, and the second problem relates to how difference is usually seen and dealt with in peace studies and peace practices. The following discussions of these two problems include alternative thinking to respective legacies in Western philosophy and in peace studies (maybe non-Western traditions suggest and offer different legacies, but that is not addressed here). Such alternative thinking results in the paradigm of *dialogue across differences* for rethinking peace.

THINKING DIFFERENCE

When looking into modes of thinking difference as they have become handed down to us by Western philosophy, we learn that until recently, that is, until the beginning of the twentieth century, difference has been conceptualized as hierarchical relation between the (very) 'Self' and an 'other'. From Greek antiquity to the beginning of the twentieth century, we find *cum grano salis* no philosophical or political conception of difference that would not assume or directly posit the relation to 'the' 'other' as a top-down relation and as subordination of 'the' 'other'.[2] This has immediate consequences for how we think peace, namely, according to hierarchical thinking, 'the' 'other' always has to submit to the imaginations and practices of the 'self', be that one of the conflict parties or an outside peace builder. This kind of peace can be called 'imperial peace'. The big challenge then lies in the question, how can we conceptualize difference in a nonhierarchical way? A nonhierarchical approach to difference seems the only way that is conducive to peace, as it does not demand the subordination of one actor to another actor's political imaginations and practices (as probably the reason for the outbreak of violence in the first place).

Exploring Western philosophy for approaches of how to think difference alternatively to orthodoxies, we strike a movement that we can summarize as phenomenology and that comprises as its main authors Edmund Husserl (1965), Georg Simmel (mainly 1908, 1980, 1992), Alfred Schütz (1962, 1972), Martin Heidegger ([1929] 1962), Emmanuel Lévinas (1985, 1998, 1996a), and Jacques Derrida (1982, 1989). What is characteristic of this movement (why I group these authors together; see also Lévinas 1996b; Heidegger 2006, 2007) and what helps us thinking difference in a nonhierarchical way are the following two observations. First, phenomenologists emphasize that both 'self' and 'other' are interdependent and mutually constitutive constructions that are embedded in specific historic, political, economic and cultural circumstances and thus are subject to change, are not fixed entities and have no constant identities. (Early twentieth-century phenomenologists, mainly sociologists, are therefore the inventors of what has become mainstream in the discipline of international relations only some 60 years later, namely, 'constructivism'.) Second, underpinning such a constructivist outlook is a specific notion of the temporal fabric of all political and social 'things', that is, in shorthand, that the meanings that we give to these 'things' and that these 'things' have for us are permanently transforming, are transient and can be grasped and understood only in their passing articulations.

Motion and transformation are fundamental concepts in Simmel that he applies to theorizing about both the individual and society. This conviction is clearly communicated by the title of one his main writings—*Soziologie: Untersuchungen über die Formen der Vergesellschaftung* (1908).[3] Referring to his *Formen der Vergesellschaftung*, we recognize from the German 'Vergesellschaft*ung*' Simmel's emphasis on the processes of becoming that is expressed in the grammatical declination of '-*ung*'. We see here that society is always the product of a process of motion, fluctuation, change and transience. Society is essentially a historic formation ('*ein historisches Gebilde*') in that there were not just one presence; rather, the past and certain cultural, political and economic legacies become fundamental conditions of *each* presence, inherent in the process of becoming.[4] The same notion of becoming, however, applies not only to social formations but also, as Simmel (1918) argues in 'Vom Wesen des historischen Verstehens' (see also Simmel 1908), to the human being as an individual. He here argues decisively against the idea of the person as a fixed substance that would—and could—be characterized by something called 'identity'. Instead, the individual always traverses an unending lively development ('*eine lebendige Entwicklung*'). And in this context, we find Simmel's strongest argument against the dominant form of historiography in the nineteenth century, that is, against historicism and especially Leopold von Ranke's dictum about the purpose of historiography being to demonstrate how history actually was and how single events would have truly been ('*wie es eigentlich gewesen sei*'). Simmel argues against this vision of historical objectivity and criticizes this notion as a chimera.[5]

But Simmel goes further. He declares the notion of becoming to be the epistemic condition for our understanding of history per se. This is a logical consequence of his criticism of historicism, and it is remarkable that he has asserted this point some nine years before the publication of Heidegger's *Being and Time*. Simmel develops his argument not only by accentuating how understanding has to be *aware of* processes of becoming but also by arguing that understanding itself *is sustained and carried* by processes and movements. Only because of these sustaining and carrying processes and movements, history and life in general would be tangible *to* our understanding and become tangible only *by* methods of understanding, that is, by interpretation and hermeneutics.[6] Understanding is thus possible only because it is itself a process of becoming, not just because it is aware of historical processes of motion and transformation. At the same time, this means, however, that understanding is never terminated and finished but is itself an endless exegetic process of unveiling, unmasking and interpreting as well as of creating meaning.

However, this implies that understanding is never fully possible. If understanding is a process itself and engaged in grasping the meaning of phenomena that are themselves in motion, the human mind can accomplish only fractional and partial understandings of those phenomena. The phenomena are always fluctuating and thereby transforming their appearances and articulations as they present themselves to the human experience, like a flip book: a partiality and sectionality which, however, are the constituents of our understanding. To sum up, there are two reasons for the partiality of understanding and cognition: society and the individual are essentially historical and transformative, *and* the nature of understanding itself, focusing on such transformativities, is itself conditioned, limited and shaped by them.[7]

We find the same argument about temporality in Schütz. Schütz sees that the social and political world is 'not a world of being, but a world that is at every moment one of becoming and passing away—or better, an emerging world' (1972, 36). In his *Phenomenology of the Social World*, Schütz refers to Simmel, identifying two main problems of the social sciences: first, what he calls the problem of '*Verstehen*' (or understanding and hermeneutics) in general, and, secondly and more specifically, 'the way in which the other self is *meaningfully* given to us' (1972, 19, emphasis added).

In order to develop the question of how meaning is constituted, Schütz stresses the idea of the intentionality of action. Just as Simmel and, later, Heidegger, Schütz is influenced by and thinks in the legacies of Husserl's notion of intentionality. Thus, for Schütz meaning is being constituted by social and political action and interaction. He notes that '(meaning) is thus constituted as an intersubjective phenomenon' (1972, 32–33) and, on the part of each actor involved, indicates the actor's attitude towards as well as awareness and appreciation of his or her own duration, experienced in and through action. In other words, we find temporality at the very basis of an ontology of 'a world that is being constituted, never completed, but always in the process of formation' (36). The experience of the emergence, historicity and transience of all being—social, political and individual—has the same epistemic condition for understanding and knowledge as in Simmel. In short, *meaning is constituted by action, and acting is itself pervaded and interspersed with temporality; thus, our understanding of meaning is bound to and resting upon temporality*. It is rooted in 'internal time-conscious-ness' (36). Before discussing the temporality of acting in some greater detail, another quote which highlights the transience and transformation of being helps our understanding:

> What we, in fact, experience in duration is not a being that is discrete and well-defined but a constant transition from a now-thus to a new now-thus. (45)

The way in which Schütz develops the relation between temporality, action and meaning is through the figure of *modo future exacti.* Most basically, *modo future exacti* points to an ambiguity of 'action'. This ambiguity consists of the circumstance of multiple dimensions of temporality and temporal imagination inherent in the concept of action itself. This multidimensionality speaks out against imaginations of teleological and linear time underlying and characterizing action and human agency. Rather action implies two very different meanings, both of which must be understood as crucial for the constitution of meaning in the social and political world. This is why understanding and meaning are fundamentally bound to temporality. They are themselves modes of being-in-time. Schütz (1972) argues that, first, action can refer to an act as a 'completed unit' (39), a finished product (he describes this in German as '*Handlung*'), and, second, action refers to the course of an action during which it is constituted and comes into being. As such, action, as Schütz says, would be 'a flow, an ongoing sequence of events' (39) and always something 'enacted' (in the German original version ein '*Gehandelt-worden-sein*').

In this second dimension, action constitutively involves anticipation of the future. It is future-directed and planned into a future *with* and *in* every step and moment that it evolves. This directedness into the future and the very circumstance of being anticipated is, in the words of Schütz (1972), 'transformation of this Now into a Has-Been . . . action bears the temporal character of pastness' (61). Therefore, every action has the character of a draft, or project or plan,[8] anticipating the course of action and thereby turning each present moment into anticipated pasts prior to when the action becomes manifest at some point. There is, however, another consequence of these two temporal dimensions of action that is important for thinking and speaking of difference. What are implications and consequences of these temporalities for the perspectivity, complexity and heterogeneity of the social and political world? Schütz writes that the social world 'is given to us in a complex system of perspectives' (8). These perspectives emerge not only for every individual with regard to his or her own action but also, much more, in all intersubjective social actions. A multitude of projects, anticipations and articulations of actions emerge, unfold temporarily and vanish in complex interactivities.

The nexus of temporality, perspectivity, meaning and social and political action implies a critique of traditional Western ontology. Even more, this nexus in the subsequent problematizations of difference and 'otherness' and their normative potentials (one of which is, as here, to be enabled to a reconceptualization of peace) has become possible only *under the conditions of* such critique. Within the twentieth-century phenomenological discourse, we can follow this critique back into the article 'Vom Wesen des historischen Verstehens' by Simmel (1918). In this article, Simmel criticizes and dismisses what he calls the Greek style of thought. Its firm substantialism would be unified in the belief that only identical substances could recognize and identify each other. He terms this a 'naïve mechanistic dogma', as if the imagination and 'its' object were two units that could be and needed to be brought in full swing. As it becomes obvious, this is diametrical to the nexus of temporality, perspectivity, meaning and social and political action. And Simmel, as a phenomenological thinker, perceives of this kind of firm substantialism as an irrational traditionalism against the ontology of temporality and transformation. In his metaphorically rich language, Simmel describes this kind of traditional epistemic naïveté as the illusion of things real becoming constituted in our brain and their projection by some esoteric procedure in an empty space completely reserved for this projection—comparable to moving furniture in an empty flat.

Within this movement of phenomenological social and political theory, we observe a fundamental radicalization of the temporal thinking from early phenomenologists to the work of Lévinas and Derrida. Both argue (breaking with the philosophical notion of intentionality that is characteristic of all Western philosophy) that the temporal and temporalized nature of 'things' leads to a situation in which we cannot grasp and hold on to things, thus our claim to *understand* something would be misleading; what can at most be accomplished is partial apprehension and empathy. Opposite to more orthodox discourses on 'otherness', such as by Munasu Duala M'bedy (1977), which are, too, critical with Western philosophical history, Lévinas is not interested in and does not deem possible any kind of restoration of and reconnection to sources of Western philosophy. Rather, he focuses his thoughts on the development of an original and basic philosophy of openness—or of infinity and exteriority (*'infinité'* and *'extériorité'*; see Lévinas [1961] 1979). According to Lévinas, the main problem of Western philosophy would be symbolized in Socrates' dictum about the primacy of the 'self'/'Self', which delivers the intellectual, emotional, spiritual and physical framework for the understanding all other individuals. Thereby, 'the' 'other' would inevitably become reduced to the 'self'/'Self' and his or her experiences. This is a reduction which would itself be the result of Western essentialist ontology which Lévinas calls 'ontological imperialism' and 'egology', that is, an explanation, exploration, interpretation ('logos') and action upon the world from the vantage point of the 'self'/'Self'/the 'ego'.[9]

At the basis of ontological imperialism and egology, as Lévinas argues, is finally the idea of intentionality which pervades Western thinking and would, too, be key to Husserl's philosophy in his *Méditations Cartésiennes* ([1931] 1965) as well as in Heidegger's *Being and Time*. Lévinas identifies intentionality as exactly the very figure of thought which is responsible for ontological imperialism and egology. Hence, his criticism of the idea of intentionality is a decisive disassociation of phenomenological thinking in Husserl and Heidegger (but also from Simmel and Schütz). Intentionality, for Lévinas, would assume the existence of a correlation between *noesis* and *noema*, that is, between subject and object, between recognizing consciousness and the 'thing' recognized, and thus would presuppose a temporal simultaneity and synchronism between the 'self'/the 'ego' and everything exterior. Lévinas's fundamental criticism of the idea and assumption of intentionality appears as nothing but a consequence of an ontology of temporality and historicality. It dissolves and renders impossible synchrony and simultaneity because of the genuine openness, transformativity, transience and processurality of being. Lévinas appears as having followed the idea of temporality through and as having brought the consequence of temporality to a fundamental and forceful end. In an early article from 1964, 'Meaning and Sense', Lévinas notes that '[the] intelligible is not conceivable outside of the becoming' and that 'the world [is to be conceived] in its fundamental historicity' (Lévinas 1996a, 42, 43). This picture of being as permanent fluctuation, change, and transformation forbids him to speak of *manifestations* of Being. Accordingly, it would be much more appropriate to speak of a 'temporal series of articulations and expressions of being-in-time' (66).

In declining intentionality, Lévinas creates the basis for seeing the possibility of an unprecedented thinking of openness (or of *infinity*). Setting the 'thing observed' free from assumptions about its Being and delivering the categories *of* its cognition—through breaking with the transcendental correlation between observer and thing—Lévinas develops this liberation and the related idea of a dialogical 'towards' 'the' 'other' rather than the idea and claim of possessing (knowledge of) 'the' 'other. But what is the *'object' of this towards* if at all we can even speak of an 'object' under conditions of nonintentionality? This question might be put better as, what appears as the relational (as noun) of the towards (as noun)? Or, with Lévinas, what (or better *how*) is the relational of the 'rapport sans rapport', of this relationless relation? Here the argument developed can receive important support through Derrida's notions of 'advent'.

Derrida's notion of 'advent' provides more specific ideas with regards to *what is to come* in the processes of becoming. His notion of 'advent' is most explicit in his writings about democracy and Europe (the latter especially in *The Other Heading* [1992]). In both cases, the event—that is, democracy and/ or Europe—is not yet there/here as he says but rather is something 'that remains to be thought and to come' (Derrida 1993, 19). Derrida uses the French '*à venir*' and '*survenir*' to describe this situation of 'yet to be'. While both are derived from the Latin verb '*venire*' ('to come'), the French '*survenir*' contains a meaning which seems important and links with Derrida's emphasis on the temporality and transformativity of being. This nuance, however, seems lost in the English translation 'to come about' (as in *Psyche: Inventions of the Other* [2007, 24]): the special meaning of '*survenir*' is that something, an e-vent (from Latin '*ex*', i.e., 'out of something' [ex-], and '*venire*', 'to come'), comes about *suddenly*, *unexpectedly* and *unpredictably*. The 'ex-' as the realm, terrain, space or source from where the event is coming is unknown, undefined and undefinable. Otherwise, it would not come about suddenly and unpredictably.[10]

To keep this terrain unknown or undefined and thus to preserve the suddenness of the coming about of the e-vent (of democracy, of Europe and of 'the' 'other') is purposeful since it will preserve its transformativity to the highest possible degree. To do otherwise, that is, to foreclose the openness and namelessness of the terrain from where the e-vent is coming from, would mean 'to totalize, to gather, *versammeln*' (Derrida 1997, 13), would be a form of 'monogenealogy' (Derrida, 1992, 10) and depend upon and reproduce the 'contagious or contaminating powers of a reappropriating language, . . . the language of the Same that is foreign or allergic to the Other' (Derrida 2007,

155). To preserve openness, namelessness and dialogue and thereby the (chance of) transformativity of the e-vent (i.e., also of 'the' 'other') is crucial since it means to 'prevent totalitarianism, nationalism, egocentrism' (Derrida 1997, 14).

When democracy, Europe or 'the' 'other' are called events to come which remain to be thought, this does not mean that there would not be democratic and/or European institutions or experienced differences among individuals. Rather, it suggests that preserving a critical space of openness for their free, unpredicted and nonforestalled development and discursive articulation is a very deliberate and normative choice. This choice is convinced that it is the normative value of democracy/Europe/'the' 'other'/difference(s) to remain open *towards* the future. Their value is exactly (in) their openness. Their option to be and to let be is precisely their *provision of* and their *demand for* opened-up spaces for different modes of being where those modes are not becoming predefined, predetermined and/or anticipated but are being expected to approach, to emerge and to come about and to transform, suddenly and unexpectedly. The demands and value of democracy, the demands and value of Europe and the demands of 'the' 'other' 'consist in opening and destabilizing closed structures to allow for the passage toward the multiplicity and diversity of e-vents to come. This openness is enabled to come *through* them', that is, with regard to 'the' 'other'; that is, 'one does not make the other come, one lets it come by preparing for its coming' (Derrida 2007, 45), for its ad-vent.[11]

This normative choice for preserving a critical and dialogical space is, according to Derrida (1993), grounded in the 'aporetic experience of the impossible' (15). It proposes a reading of the question of 'otherness' and difference as *Dasein*, that is, as not an entity or essence but rather as a being-possible and becoming-possible (*'das Möglichsein'* according to Heidegger and *'das Möglichwerden'*), as a being which 'trembles in [from and *towards*] an unstable multiplicity'(9), and that therefore demands the *making*-possible of Being/being as *Dasein*.[12] The 'aporetic experience of the impossible' assumes the intrinsic dis-unity of and differences within all things (histories, id-entities, cultures, institutions groups and individual psyches) as well as the proactive elaboration on and widening of respective dis-unities and their mutual tensions as critical practice. What Derrida calls deconstruction and *'différance'* is important here inasmuch as the latter refers to deferrals, dislocations and disruptions of cultures, identities, groups, political and legal systems due to their intrinsic dis-unities and tensions. Derrida (1992) notes, for example, 'There is no culture or cultural identity without this difference *within itself* (9–10), or '[The] identity of a culture is a way of being different from itself; a culture is different from itself; language is different from itself; the person is different from itself (1997, 13). In *Margins of Philosophy*

(1982), Derrida describes *différance* also an activity of 'temporization' (9) and 'spacing' (9).

The question asked above about what is the *'object' of the towards* the 'other' and difference(s) receives a phenomenological answer here. The aporia of unity and essence as both an ontological and a normative demand longs for the opening up of intellectual and dialogical spaces that make possible the impossible (as the unknown/intangible/unintentional/un-definable/unpredictable). The impossible is here understood as unknown *what* 'the' 'other' may be and as the terra incognita *from where* 'the' 'other' may come from and suddenly appear ('advent'). This out of the sudden and complete masking of 'the' 'other' is of course not always the case, but it may be a possibility (and indeed seems to be the case very often). Thus, the ontological and normative demand is neither to work within the framework of totalities nor to work against them and to 'move out of the impasse' (Derrida 1993, 13), that is, to either accept their rationalities *or* to oppose and destroy them from outside. Instead, it demands the disruption of totalities by elaborating on and widening their *inherent* tensions and dis-unities. Such disruptions open up spaces for alternatives; shall prevent totalitarianisms, nationalism and egocentrisms; and finally articulate the condition for the relation *towards* 'the' 'other'. *And it is here, in a critical perception of difference(s) and 'otherness' as transformative becoming, as endless beginnings towards the unknown and the impossible-to-grasp, as discursively produced meanings and openings of alternative spaces for the articulation and embrace of difference(s) and for the 'advent' of the 'other', where we find both the limits of and conditions for the deconstruction of Western traditions of peace-building practice as well as for a positive rearticulation of a dialogical understanding of peace.*

To summarize, why do temporality, transformation and nonintentionality help us thinking difference in a nonhierarchical way?

Temporality liberates difference(s) from proclamations about what they *are* or would *be*; they also set them free from declarations why they are. Both temporality and nonintentionality therefore strongly suggest antiessentialist views and advise us to listen to 'the' 'other' and his or her articulations before claiming knowledge *about* them. A *dialogical structure* is inherent here that does not make statements about difference(s) and 'the' 'other' prior to having paid attention and having learned about 'the' 'other' through listening and attending. What characterized hierarchical ways of thinking and acting upon differences, namely, to subordinate differences(s) and 'the' 'other' under imaginations and categories of the 'self', becomes anathematic to a temporal and constructivist understanding.

As there are only momentary and transient 'here and nows' (Shapiro 1992) but no structure, essence or identity, all we have are continually transforming appearances ('transformativity' rather than 'identity'), exploring their emergence and developments via genealogies and acting towards them in dialogical empathy. When we take this seriously—and we should because this is, in terms of peace, the only way by which we can approach differences without violence—then we have to further ask what is practically implied in an emphatic approach to difference(s).

DIFFERENCE AND PEACE STUDIES AND PRACTICES

The most important practical implication of empathy—which Galtung (1967) considers a key variable in the equation presented in his keynote address (see introduction; see also figure 1)—that takes us straight to (rethinking) peace is the appreciation of differences as *positive*. If we cannot—and should not—define 'the' 'other' and/or his or her interests or identity as someone or something definite or finite and can get only glimpses and momentary impressions of 'the' 'other' whose nature, however, is hidden from us (and maybe, in a psychological perspective, also from him or her him- or herself), yet difference(s) is (are) something undeniable in society and politics as an irreducible and existential experience of human life (finally they are the reason for conflict in the first place) we are advised to develop a way to appreciate them as positive; we should then embrace, promote and cultivate them. From the acknowledgement of difference(s) to the nonsuppression of differences to their appreciation and cultivation is subsequently a *core trajectory for rethinking peace*.

The practical value of a temporal (and temporalized) notion of 'otherness' and difference for rethinking peace becomes thus immediately visible. As the vast majority of peace thinking in Western philosophy, peace studies, and international relations and of peace practice by international organizations· such as the United Nations and the European Union have been based on the dictum of assimilating differences ('*E Pluribus Unum*' is the famous motto here; see Behr 2014) in order to create and accomplish peace, the concept of 'peace-in-difference' presented here is suggesting precisely the opposite. Not the assimilation or nullification of difference(s) but rather their emphatic cultivation and dialogical negotiation are to be seen as the way to peace, based upon an antiessentialist approach to difference(s). In this vein, the avoidance and abolishment of a language of 'otherness' would therefore be a necessary step on the journey to set the other or difference(s), respectively, free.[13]

Consequently, 'peace-in-difference' is critical with conceptualizations of what is called 'liberal peace', its institutions and its Kantian (in theoretical terms; see Kant [1784] 1970, [1795] 1891) and Wilsonian (in more practical terms; see Wilson 1966, 2006) legacies, that become epitomized in the contemporary 'democratic peace hypothesis' and its strategies of international democratization in the Western image (as in Russett 2001). 'Liberal peace' is indeed the representative of a universal script—by and large composed of Western democracy, rule of law, Western human rights and free market economies—that is imposed in global conflict settings in order to conquer and overcome differences, promoting the perception and stigmatization of all actors, cultures, people and peoples outside the 'self' as different and as 'the' 'other'. Respective thought and practices become most visible in politics of the U.S. administrations under George H. W. Bush and Bill Clinton, under the U.K. governments of Tony Blair and Gordon Brown and in UN and EU peace-building politics over the past 25 years. This legacy has also come under severe attack from a postliberal peace approach suggested by Oliver Richmond and others over the past 10 years (see, inter alia, Richmond 2008) with which the concept of 'peace-in-difference' shares its criticism. However, a 'peace-in-difference' perspective suggests a novel epistemology and ontology of peace thinking and peace practice that a postliberal perspective does not include in its yet very important critique and suggestions to overcome 'liberal peace'. Postliberal peace is thus concentrating mainly on new practices as a hybrid blend of Western and local peace-building instruments that is theoretically based on a Foucauldian and postcolonial critique of Western, statist politics and its discursive and institutional power apparatus (Mac Ginty 2010; Richmond 2009, 2010; see also Richmond, in this volume) without, however, an own theoretical (i.e., ontological and/or epistemological) foundation that would go beyond critique (see Brigg, in this volume, and Shani, in this volume).

This 'going-beyond' is, however, hoped to be part of a 'peace-in-difference' approach according to which peace, just as 'otherness' or difference(s), cannot be fixed, cannot be defined and cannot be accomplished. Rather, peace is to be seen as a permanent process of and dialogue about the articulation and meaning(s) as well as a critical reflection upon difference(s) as they become expressed in political, social and cultural conflicts. This process consists primarily of *neutralizing essentialist thinking and action* that are based upon defining, stereotyping and pigeonholing political perceptions and worldviews. This includes the exploration of processes of identity formation and, if necessary, their active reorientation towards antiessentialist 'self' and 'other' perceptions.

Such exploration and engagement would further focus on forms of local, culturally situated knowledge, that is, local ontologies and epistemologies of communities as they underlie visions and practices of peace and political and social order to transform conflict. Those forms of knowledge and everyday practices of local communities that are directly involved in conflict and reconciliation are deemed much more conducive and legitimate than Western, universalized peace-building policies implanted into and imported from outside. The following kind of questions would populate a 'peace-in-difference' agenda: Is there in actual peace formation, peace negotiation and conflict reconciliation processes an awareness of the problem of difference(s) and 'otherness' and of how related perceptions are discursively framed? Are difference(s) and 'the' 'other' seen and thematized as natural enemies, are their characteristics essentialized (according to ethnic, national, religious, political, etc. criteria) and are they stigmatized a priori? What patterns follow the 'self'–'other' relations and definitions? Can distinct features of the 'self'–'other' relation be learned from successful peace formation, peace negotiation and conflict reconciliation processes? And, vice versa, can failed peace negotiation, peace formation and conflict reconciliation processes be traced back to distinct perceptions and framings of the 'self'–'other' relation? How are the relation and the actors' perception of the relation between peace, security and stability: are they equated and interchangeably used or distinguished? How and through what channels can a phenomenological epistemology of peace be communicated with and successfully introduced to conflict and warring parties? And, finally, how can local peace agencies coexist with international peace frameworks?

'Peace-in-difference' thus pursues the interrogation and interlocution of different ontologies and epistemologies in local conflict contexts. This does *not* include an uncritical reception of local identities, visions and practices, many of them ultimately involved in violent conflicts and faced with the demand to reconcile and rebuild society and politics. Thus, there is no dichotomy between 'Western' and 'local' politics. 'Peace-in-difference' offers guidance on how international and local actors may cooperate to create a more sustainable peace. In this regard, we can formulate a hypothesis for further research and agency in conflict settings: *The lesser the degree of essentialist attributions to difference(s) and the lesser essentialist perceptions and definitions of 'otherness', the less likely the outbreak of conflict and the more conducive this is for peace, conflict solution and reconciliation.* Put differently, *the less actors perceive of their difference(s) as constructed and transformative and the more unifying, essentializing and defining such perceptions and processes are, the more likely conflict and violence will break out, if they are not even caused or propelled.* Thus, 'peace-in-difference' focuses on the creative and positive capacities of differences for local and international peace formation.

NOTES

1. 'The' 'other'/'otherness': the single quotation marks indicate that 'otherness' is, just like the 'self'/'Self', a constructed attribute of something and/or someone and not an entity or id-entity which could be fixed, defined and presumed and which likewise depends upon, relates to, emerges from and is constituted by the relations to another person/other persons. The single quotation mark around 'the' indicates that there is never one general and/or a generalizable form of 'otherness' but only and always pluralities. In short, there is no 'otherness', nor is there a generalizable 'other' beyond discourse.

2. In the legacies of Western political philosophy before the intellectual tradition that is called 'phenomenology', we can identify five historic patterns of thinking difference. We find these in Greek mythology, especially in the narratives around Dionysus; in Greek political philosophy, notably in the work of Aristotle; in Christian theological thinking, notably in Aurelius Augustine; and in nationalist political thought. While all these patterns conceive of the figure of 'the' 'other' in one or the other form in hierarchical and subordinated terms, they are all informed by (different) imaginations of transmigration; that is, 'the' constructed 'other' can peel off his or her 'otherness' and become part of the respective collective 'Self' of the Pantheon, of the polis, of Christianity or of the liberal society, respectively. This is substantially different in national political thought, where the construction of 'otherness' is based on essentialized visions of belonging (namely, by birth and birthplace) that cannot be overcome or changed and thus are fixed and exclusionist as in none of the other cases. For a deeper and more detailed discussion, see Behr (2014, chap. II.2).

3. This book has not yet been translated into English. The title would be something like *Inquiries into Forms of Sociation*; see further two articles: 'Beiträge zur Philosophie der Geschichte' (Simmel 1909) and 'Vom Wesen des historischen Verstehens' (Simmel 1918).

4. This important and early argument may be quoted in full in its German version: 'Dies macht die Gesellschaft zu einem, seinem inneren Wesen nach, historischen Gebilde, d.h. sie ist nicht nur ein Gegenstand der Geschichte, sondern die Vergangenheit hat in ihr noch wirksame Realität . . . in der Form der gesellschaftlichen Überlieferung wird das Geschehen zum Bestimmungsgrunde des Gegenwärtigen' (Simmel 1909).

5. Very instructive here is also Rudolf Vierhaus (1977).

6. 'Die stetige Bewegtheit des Lebens ist der formale Träger des Verständnisses . . . von Sachgehalten, die ihrerseits das lebendig konkrete Vorkommen dieser Sachgehalte erst verständlich machen' (Simmel 1918; see also Simmel 1980, 1977).

7. As stated above, Simmel does not seem to be aware of this epistemic limitation, seemingly arguing in the legacies of Husserlian intentionality, which also appears to influence Schütz and Heidegger. Lévinas, however, is going beyond this by giving up the idea of intentionality. This abolishment emphasizes the limits of our understanding, while this limitation is nothing but a radical consequence of the primal notion of temporality and as such only consequent. Thus, Lévinas has taken the notion of temporality to its logic consequence; more on this below in this chapter.

8. In the German original version of *Phenomenology of the Social World* (1972), which is *Der sinnhafte Aufbau der sozialen Welt* (1932), Schütz uses the precise Heideggerian term of action as '*Entwurf*'. '*Entwurf*'—translated in Lévinas as 'project-in-draft' (see 1996b, 25)—is for Heidegger a key term of his ontology of Being as temporality, encompassing its fundamental conditions. According to Heidegger, the temporality and historicity of Being have to be understood in order to understand Being and in order for Being to (to be able) to be. Thus, understanding ('*Verstehen*') becomes temporal (temporalized or processuralized) and conditioned by temporality itself. This is discussed above in Schütz, and Heidegger writes, 'Understanding is the existential Being of Dasein's own potentiality-for-Being' (Heidegger [1929] 1962, 184). Herein we find the reason why Being and acting (as a mode of Being) are, cannot be more than and will always be as long as Being ('*Dasein*') is. However, they come into being only as drafts, plans or project/projections—as '*Entwurf*'. The latter condition is reflected in Schütz's *modo future exacti*. We read in Heidegger ([1929] 1962): Dasein has, as Dasein, already projected itself; and as long as it is, it is projecting. As long as it is, Dasein always has understood itself and always will understand itself in terms of possibilities. . . . As projecting, understanding is the kind of Being of Dasein in which it is its possibilities as possibilities' (185; translation by the author), emphasizing the ontology of Being as open, temporal, processural and transformative, that is, *not* ontically fixed as substance or essence.

9. For a discussion of his criticism of Western philosophy, see also 'Is Ontology Fundamental?', here in Lévinas (1996a).

10. Derrida's notions of 'event' and 'advent' are reminiscent of Heidegger's concepts of '*Ereignis*' and '*Sorge*', the latter best translated as 'care', but see the comprehensive comments on how to translate this German term into English in the English edition of *Time and Being* ([1929] 1962), for example, on p. 83. In this 1962 edition, '*Sorge*' is translated as 'concern', which, I would argue, is slightly misleading because 'concern' ignores or downplays the normative dimension implicit in '*Sorge*', which entails the desire that what is '*be-sorgt*' (i.e., what one is concerned with) shall be able to potentially unfold its being in a certain way. This normative implication is much stronger than in Heidegger developed in Derrida, as we will see below in the next paragraph. Here, however, a key sentence from Heidegger, 'Prolegomena zur Geschichte des Zeitbegriffs', on his concept of '*Sorge*': 'Das Sein [des] Seienden ist Sorge: Sorge besagt unter anderem: Aussein auf etwas, was es noch nicht ist. Als Sorge ist dieses Dasein wesensmaessig unterwegs zu etwas . . . was es noch nicht ist. Sein eigener Seinssinn ist es gerade, immer noch etwas vor sich zu haben, was es noch nicht ist, was noch aussteht' (Heidegger 1923–1944, 425). In English, this important passage would be, 'The Being of being is care. Care means, amongst others: to be oriented towards what itself not yet is. As care, being-in-time is en route towards what not yet is. Indeed, its own meaning of being is to always find something ahead of itself what not yet is, but remains to become' (translation by the author). Because of this reminiscence between Heidegger and Derrida, due to the much stronger developed normative character of Derrida's thinking, however, we can conclude that Derrida provides an ethical reading of Heidegger. This reading appears finally enabled through Derrida following Lévinas and critiquing Heidegger in this point.

The abolishment of the idea of intentionality opens the door to an ethical reading, leaving ontology behind. The dismissal of intentionality does likewise refuse each relation between Being and being ('Sein' and 'Seiendem'). Therefore, Lévinas (and Derrida follows in this point) can say that ethics is first philosophy and that ethics is before ontology.

11. In *The Other Heading*, Derrida (1992) writes, 'This *duty* also dictates opening Europe . . . opening it onto that which is not [and] never was. . . . The *same duty* also dictates welcoming foreigners in order not only to integrate them but to recognize and accept their alterity. . . . *The same duty* dictates cultivating the virtue of such *critique*, *of the critical idea, the critical tradition*, but also submitting it, beyond critique and questioning, to a deconstructive genealogy that thinks and exceeds it without yet compromising it' (Derrida (77).

12. A *making*-possible of being in multiplicity links back to democracy and (Derrida's vision of) Europe as space for this making-possible.

13. This step points to some necessary critique of Lévinas and Derrida (and beyond of much of the poststructural discourse by the way) insofar as they use a language of 'otherness' without the awareness of own stereotyping and of inherent power relations through the use of such language. It is thus surprising that both Lévinas and Derrida, who are otherwise authors with great reflectivity and linguistic awareness, use the language of 'otherness'. Both speak of '*l'Autre*', and although the notion of 'nonintentionality' in Lévinas and of '*inconnu*' and 'the impossible' in Derrida clarify their normative standpoint very clearly, a language of 'otherness' conceives and communicates differences always already in a preconceived way.

REFERENCES

Behr, Hartmut. 2014. *Politics of Difference—Epistemologies of Peace*. London: Routledge ('Global Horizons' series, edited by R. B. J. Walker and Richard Falk; 2015 paperback).

Derrida, Jacques. 1982. *Margins of Philosophy*. Chicago: University of Chicago Press.

———. 1989. *On Spirit: Heidegger and the Question*. Chicago: University of Chicago Press.

———. 1992. *The Other Heading: Reflection on Today's Europe*. Translated by Pascale-Anne Brault and Michael B. Naas, introduction by Michael B. Naas. Bloomington: Indiana State University Press.

———. 1993. *Aporias*. Stanford, CA: Stanford University Press.

———. 1997. *Deconstruction in a Nutshell: A Conversation with Jacques Derrida*. Edited with a commentary by John D. Caputo. New York: Fordham University Press.

———. 2007. *Psyche: Inventions of the Other*. Vol. 1. Stanford, CA: Stanford University Press.

Duala-M'bedy, Munasu. 1977. *Xenologie: Die Wissenschaft vom Fremden und die Verdrängung der Humanitaet aus der Anthropologie*. Freiburg: Karl Alber.

Heidegger, Martin. [1929] 1962. *Being and Time*. Translated by John Macquire and Edward Robinson. New York: HarperCollins (German edition: 'Sein und Zeit', *Gesamtausgabe*, I. Abteilung: Frühe Schriften, Bd. 2. Frankfurt am Main: Vittorio Klostermann).

———. 2006. 'Identität und Differenz'. *Gesamtausgabe*, I. Abteilung: Veröffentlichte Schriften, Bd. 11. Frankfurt am Main: Vittorio Klostermann.

———. 2007. 'Zur Sache des Denkens'. *Gesamtausgabe*, I. Abteilung: Frühe Schriften, Bd. 14. Frankfurt am Main: Vittorio Klostermann.

Husserl, Edmund. 1965. *Cartesian Meditations*. The Hague: Martinus Nijhoff.

Kant, Immanuel. [1795] 1891. *Perpetual Peace: A Philosophical Essay* (Facsimile). Edited by W. Hastie. Edinburgh: T&T Clark. http://oll.libertyfund.org/Home3/Book.php?recordID=0426.

———. [1784] 1970. *Idea for a Universal History of Mankind from a Cosmopolitan Point of View*. Edited with an introduction and notes by Hans Reiss, translated by H. B. Nisbet. Cambridge: Cambridge University Press (German version: 'Idee zu einer allgemeinen Geschichte in weltbürgerlicher Absicht', *Berlinische Monatsschrift*, November 1784, pp. 385–411).

Lévinas, Emmanuel. [1961] 1979. *Totality and Infinity: An Essay on Exteriority*. The Hague: Martinus Nijhoff.

———. 1985. *Ethics and Infinity*. Pittsburgh, PA: Duquesne University Press.

———. 1996a. *Basic Philosophical Writings*, Edited by Adriaan T. Peperzak, Simon Critchley, and Robert Barnasconi. Bloomington: Indiana University Press.

———. 1996b. 'Martin Heidegger and Ontology'. *Diacritics* 26, no. 1: 11–32.

———. 1998. *Otherwise Than Being, or Beyond Essence*. Pittsburgh, PA: Duquesne University Press.

Mac Ginty, Roger. 2010. 'Hybrid Peace: The Interaction between Top-Down and Bottom-Up Peace'. *Security Dialogue* 41, no. 4: 391–412.

Richmond, Oliver. 2008. *Peace in International Relations*. London: Routledge.

———. 2009. 'A Post-Liberal Peace: Eirenism and the Everyday'. *Review of International Studies* 35: 557–80.

———. 2010. 'Resistance and the Post-Liberal Peace'. *Millennium: Journal of International Studies* 38, no. 3: 665–92.

Russett, Bruce. 2001. *Triangulating Peace: Democracy, Interdependence, and International Organization*. New York: Norton.

Schütz. Alfred. 1932. *Der sinnhafte Aufbau der sozialen Welt*. Vienna: J. Springer.

———. 1962. 'The Problem of Social Reality'. *Collected Papers I*, 207–59. The Hague: Martinus Nijhoff.

———. 1972. *The Phenomenology of the Social World*. Translated by George Walsh and Frederick Lehnert with an introduction by George Walsh. London: Heinemann.

Shapiro, Michael. 1992. *Reading the Post-Modern Polity: Political Theory as Textual Practice*. Minneapolis: University of Minnesota Press.

Simmel, Georg. 1908. 'Exkurs über den Fremden' ("Excursus on the Stranger")'. In *Soziologie: Untersuchungen ueber die Formen der Vergesellschaftung*, 509–12. Berlin: Duncker & Humblot.

————. 1909. 'Beiträge zur Philosophie der Geschichte'. In *International Review of Scientific Synthesis*, vol. 6, anno. 3, no. 3–4, edited by G. Bruni, A. Dionisi, F. Enriquez, A. Giardana, and E. Rignano. Bologna: N. Zanichelli.

————. 1918. 'Vom Wesen des historischen Verstehens'. In *Geschichtliche Abende im Zentralinstitut für Erziehung und Unterricht*. Heft 5. Berlin: Ernst Siegfried Mittler und Sohn.

————. 1980. *Essays on Interpretation in Social Science*. Translated and edited with an introduction by Guy Oakes, Manchester: Manchester University Press.

————. 1992. *Soziologie: Untersuchungen über die Formen der Vergesellschaftung*. Frankfurt am Main: Suhrkamp.

Vierhaus, Rudolf. 1977. 'Rankes Begriff der historischen Objektivität'. In *Objektivität und Parteilichkeit in der Geschichtswissenschaft*, edited by Reinhardt Koselleck, Wolfgang J. Mommsen, and Jörn Rüsen, 63–76. Munich: Deutscher Taschenbuch Verlag (Beiträge zur Historik, Bd. 1).

Wilson, Woodrow. 1966. *Letters on the League of Nations*. Edited by Raymond B. Fosdick. Princeton, NJ: Princeton University Press.

————. 2006. *Essential Writings and Speeches of the Scholar-President*. New York: New York University Press.

Chapter Thirteen

From Substantialist to Relational Difference in Peace and Conflict Studies

Morgan Brigg

How to conceptualize human difference is a fundamental challenge for peace and conflict studies, not least because differences of one sort or another are at the heart of many conflicts. Much dominant thinking within the field follows a long tradition in European-derived scholarship, building upon Greek heritage and particularly the influence of Aristotle, of conceiving of human differences in 'substantialist' terms—of seeing the social world in terms of 'things' or 'entities'. In this pattern, things are conceived as internally consistent and having the character of 'substance' that sets them apart from other things. Thinking in terms of entities is 'identitarian' as well as substantialist; it suggests that a thing converges wholly and exclusively with itself. Following Aristotle, 'denoting the substance of a thing means that the essence of the thing is nothing else' (Aristotle 1941, 740). This substantialist and identitarian logic has allowed scholarship and science powerful capacity to isolate objects and variables, to sharpen understandings, and to advance causal analyses. It is this heritage that leads peace and conflict scholarship and practice to conceive of individuals, social groupings, organizations and nation-states as discrete 'things'.

However, substantialist and identitarian logics tend to stifle thinking about difference in peace building and conflict resolution. To think of human difference in terms of cultures, religions and ethnic groups conceived of as a 'thing/s' and as something 'other' in relation to the figure of the international peace builder or conflict resolution practitioner may seem common sense but is too simplistic. Cultures, religions and groups are not internally consistent or mutually exclusive, for instance (see Avruch 1998, 12–16). But the problem is also bigger than this because dominant ways of thinking crowd out other approaches to human diversity and domesticate and suppress the differences of diverse peoples in the schemes of European-derived knowledge. It is this therefore necessary to reformulate the overall ways of thinking about difference in peace and conflict studies.

This chapter proposes a way of rethinking difference by conceptualizing difference not as substantialist but as simultaneously *relational* and *essential* (see Behr, in this volume). The first section outlines the problem of conceptualizing difference in the field by arguing that predominant substantialist and identitarian logics combine with European-derived colonial legacies in globalized political relations to either selectively valourise difference or make it submit to the dominant order, including to the liberal peace. It then identifies and introduces four sources of inspiration for sketching an alternative relational and essential approach to difference: burgeoning relationality scholarship, Indigenous traditions, foundational thinking in the conflict resolution field, and feminist scholarship. The third section argues that the current interest in pursuing relationships in peace and conflict practice is insufficient and that realizing a relational-essential approach requires demoting the sovereign knower in peace and conflict studies in order to return to the world and enter into exchange and relation with diverse peoples and their knowledges. The final section outlines how a relational-essential approach to difference can be implemented, including how it can recast and extend 'positive peace', by avoiding traps of substantialist scholarship and turning fulsomely to relations. This approach very much aligns with the processual rather than static approaches to peace discussed and advocated by the editors to this volume (see the introduction).

SUBSTANTIALIST DISAVOWAL OF DIFFERENCE

In the age of colonial expansion, many European scholars arrogated to themselves the capacity to encompass and define all of humanity's peoples in the name of science. This occurred as part of what Bruno Latour (2002) terms the 'one nature/many cultures divide' (5). The modern scientific revolution revealed to Europeans the singularity of nature, which meant that all peoples 'shared a common make-up of genes, neurons, muscles, skeletons, ecosystems and evolution which allowed them to be classed in the same humanity' (6). Nonetheless, this same unity—and particularly access to it through the invariable laws of nature derived through science and reason—allowed human differences to be more strikingly revealed. These differences were initially often represented—and thus partially constructed and produced—through ideas such as race, ethnicity and tribe. Most of these terms have in time been replaced by the idea of culture. Those inhabiting European modernity (modernists) could more readily see multiple races/cultures against the backdrop of a single nature, remaining comfortable in the knowledge that a substrate, to which they had privileged access through science and reason, underpinned racial/cultural differences (Latour 2002).

One of the implications of the world-organizing one nature/many cultures divide is the iniquitous assertion of world unity on European terms. 'Passions may divide us, but we can rely on reason to reunite us' (Latour 2002, 7). In this schema, unity and peace are 'offered by science, technology, economics and democracy' (7). Peace studies participates in the comforts offered by science and reason in hypostasis, teleology, Eurocentric normativity and utopian enterprise as sketched out in the introduction to this volume. Of course, as Latour (2002) points out, there may be some misgivings and discomfort about the possible ethnocentrism of this schema, but these are readily and typically passed over as westerners point to the power of science and technology, economic progress and the democratic peace.

The most significant iniquity of the Eurocentric one nature/many cultures schema lies in the relative positioning of nonwesterners. Difference can be known as a thing, and this is a basis for judging it. Difference can be tolerated, even celebrated, through liberal multiculturalism, but nonscientific and non-Western knowledges are banned from participating in the serious business of providing ontological or other foundations for politics or knowledge (Latour 2002, 9). The 'academy's structures and discourses are built upon the assumption that there only is one episteme, one ontology, one intellectual tradition on which to rely and which to draw' (Kuokkanen 2007, 3). This is the world of nature and reason as defined and claimed by science. All else, all others, are 'cultures' and have no standing in serious matters. It is only European-derived knowledge that speaks to questions of progress, peace and the overall destiny of the species.

These dynamics are reflected in dominant peace-building practice that arose after the end of the Cold War. In this practice, local recipients of peace-building programs are likely to be recognized as different in line with the politics of recognition that informs liberal multiculturalism and recent inclusive moves in peace and conflict resolution practice. Yet if local people prepare to practice customary law or draw upon nonliberal political arrangements to organize their society and process conflict, they are likely to face the discomfort or resistance of their state or international donor partners who will point to the importance of modern rule of law and international human rights mobilized within a conventional political architecture. The all-encompassing remit of self-authorized European-derived knowledge and political architecture again comes to bear. Peace builders are bathed, as Latour (2002) points out, in the light of reason and peace 'offered by science, technology, economics and democracy' while simultaneously recognizing/celebrating and minimiz-ing/excluding difference (7, 9). In this way, mainstream knowledge and the practices that it licences serve as colonialism's counterpart in facilitating the submission of diverse peoples to the dominant order. Difference cannot find expression or grounding on its own terms. Instead, 'difference itself remains condemned and must atone or be redeemed under the auspices of reason which renders it liveable and thinkable' (Deleuze 1994, 262).

INSPIRATION FOR A RELATIONAL-ESSENTIAL APPROACH TO DIFFERENCE

How might difference be conceptualized differently in peace and conflict studies? In contrast to dominant substantialist and identitarian approaches to difference, a range of knowledge innovations and traditions treat differ-ence as simultaneously relational and essential. This section introduces four approaches that give greater conceptual importance—and in some cases priority—to relations over entities, thereby valuing difference without see-ing it as fixed, secondary or immutable.

Relationality Scholarship

Recent scholarship across the sciences and humanities is paying increased attention to the central importance of interactions and relations. This schol-arship is not entirely new in mainstream scholarly traditions—it may, for instance, resonate with and even draw directly upon the likes of the Greek philosopher Heraclitus through his famous dictum 'everything flows' or the English philosopher-mathematician Alfred North Whitehead—but it is be-coming more widely known. In this frame, phenomena that were previously thought of as things, such as organs, organisms and individuals, as well as natural phenomena and animal and human social systems, cannot be under-stood by focusing on discrete entities set in mechanistic relationship with each other. Instead, thinkers working in diverse fields—including complex adaptive systems, relational biology and complexity theory (e.g., Miller and Page 2007; Rosen 2000; Urry 2003)—are foregrounding the importance of interactions in ways that renders entities far more contingent and unstable than has conventionally been the case. In this approach, a wide variety of phenomena might be understood as continuous as much as discrete, with 'things' not as straightforwardly coherent or singular but instead arising from the ongoing and evolving effects of relations that cohere or fracture in more or less stable ways.

These relational approaches disrupt conventional approaches to difference because they eschew substantialist and identitarian thought. They do not—indeed cannot—recognize difference as fixed because they give priority to *processes and* process-relations (see Mesle 2008). This approach emphasizes the always-coming-into-being of 'things'. Brian Massumi (2002) describes the type of 'thing' that results as 'the being of the middle—the being of a relation' (70). In other words, what a relational approach introduces is the possibility of not only seeing relations between things but also seeing things as relations (Strathern 1995, 19).

Indigenous Traditions

The relatively recent interest in relationality in contemporary disciplines has some very old counterparts. There are antecedents and analogues for relationality in many knowledge, spiritual and religious traditions of the world, as well as in minor traditions of dominant scholarship. Many Indigenous peoples foreground relationality, as illustrated among Aboriginal Australian peoples, the world's oldest living culture (60,000 years on conservative estimates). While Indigenous peoples are remarkably diverse, it is possible to say that many Indigenous people emphasize unique links to particular places and that this in many cases is linked with relational philosophies.

Australian Aboriginal philosopher Mary Graham (1999) posits the maxim that the 'Land is the Law' (106). By this, she means that relations between people and land serve as a template for social and political order (106). Land participates in a reciprocal relation with human beings, serving as a poetic ordering principle for guiding relations among people. Places within the landscape bring humans and all of existence into being and provide the basis for the ordering of relations among them. Just as places in the landscape are related with each other, so it is with humans and other sentient beings. In this cosmology (see Shani, in this volume), beings, including human individuals, are not separate things that are positioned against others and the world. Instead, all beings, including humans, come into being in-relation, and this relational register is the basis for cosmological order.

Foundational Conflict Resolution Scholarship

Two remarkable women who are belatedly and increasingly recognized as key to the development of conflict resolution, Jane Addams and Mary Parker Follett, strongly advocate for a relational approach to peace. In a series of coincidences, both were active in the United States at around the same time—the late nineteenth to early twentieth century. Follett, who

focuses more explicitly on difference, is most well known in conflict resolution for her advocacy of 'integrative' and creative approaches to conflict
that seek to generate solutions to conflict in which the desires of all parties
'have found a place' (Follett, Metcalf, and Urwick 1941, 32). Follett (1918)
also developed sophisticated theorizing about human difference, including
by elaborating her claim that 'the essence of society is difference, related
difference' (33).

Integration and difference are not incompatible in Follett's work because in
a relational approach, phenomena can be continuous as well as discrete: 'we
can at the same moment be the self and the other, . . . we can be forever apart
and forever united' (Follett 1918, 33). Difference does not trouble Follett as
it does many Western political thinkers because, she argues, 'diversity is . .
. [life's] most essential feature'. In this frame, 'fear of difference is dread of
life itself' (Follett et al. 1941, 31).

Feminist Scholarship

Feminist thought is very diverse, including on the question of how to approach
difference. Nonetheless, these feminist differences are *relational* rather than
substantial. They resonate with each other to construct an overall feminist
stance that reaches out into the world. As Marilyn Strathern (2004) points
out, differences among feminists are thus 'neither opposed nor reconciled'
(33); there is no need to resolve contradictions into larger wholes. Rather,
apparently incompatible positions or stances get held together in a type of
working compatibility (35), and they are no less feminist for this. In this way,
feminism is a relational enterprise that reveals difference as essential.

Elizabeth Grosz offers a particularly bold and innovative feminism of relational difference by rereading Charles Darwin (see especially Grosz 2004).
She shows that difference—both sexed and cultural—is essential in the sense
that it arises as central to life in response to the 'problems that nature poses
to the living' (Grosz 2005, 51). In this frame, Darwin's natural selection is
'a theory of the becoming of life, and of the human, from earlier forms of
life, a becoming made possible only by reproduction, and primarily by sexual
reproduction' (Grosz 2013, 4).

Difference is the 'principle of identity' for all identities to the extent that
no entity is self-producing or self-identical, with each entity and relation a
product of the encounter of differences of different things and different orders (Grosz 2013, 4). In this encompassing view, the forces of nature 'have
enabled rather than inhibited cultural and political production' (Grosz 2008,
2). Darwin's natural selection is at bottom a relational (interactive) process
that both needs and produces difference.

For Grosz, as with Follett (1918, 33), it is difference that is life's most essential feature. 'According to Darwinian precepts, culture is not different in kind from nature' (Grosz 2004, 59). Darwin does not think of nature (or culture) in the ways that are usually attributed to him—natural selection is not a limited and knowable battleground that facilitates reductionist interpretations of human behaviour. Instead, evolution produces variety and change incessantly without any particular teleology, though it does so in ways that are wondrously creative and necessary for the survival of life itself (59). Culture is not the overcoming of nature or its logical end point. Rather, change and the future arise from the relational interplay of culture-biological-environmental factors such that 'each culture [is] a surprise to and a development of nature itself' (59). Differences of all types, including social and cultural, are the engine of life on earth.

These four knowledge traditions help to sketch the basics of a 'relational-essential' approach to difference. In each tradition, relationality is not only an interpretive frame. Rather, difference and relations among differences are cast as essential to the operation of the cosmos or of life itself. Paradoxically, relational differences are an essence that do not take substantialist or identitarian form. Relations are fluid, but differences that interact and arise from interactions are no less essential for having arisen in this way.

RELATIONALITY BEYOND EVERYDAY RELATIONSHIPS: DEMOTING THE SOVEREIGN KNOWER

Dominant peace-building practice has in recent decades been the subject of critique and reform proposals in the wake of practical failures and ethical shortcomings of the liberal peace. A large number of critics—key figures include Oliver Richmond (in this volume) and Roger Mac Ginty (2011)—have railed against the hubris, ethnocentrism and top-down arrogance of dominant approaches. They have also advocated for greater attention to local, everyday and diverse approaches to peace, including through notions of hybrid political orders, inclusivity and peace formation (e.g., see Boege et al. 2009; Richmond 2013). These approaches all imply greater exchange, interaction and relationship across human differences in peace and conflict resolution practice. This recent interest in relationships in peace building is promising, but a challenge arises because ideas of relationship are deployed in diverse ways that give differing weight to the idea of relation in conceptualizing and engaging the social and political world of peace and conflict. One way to represent the differing weight accorded to the idea of relation is by constructing a continuum from 'thin' to 'thicker' to 'thick' (Brigg 2016). Thin relationality calls attention to underappreciated relationships between entities or structures, thicker relationality points to the interactive and mutually conditioning ways in which entities come into existence, and thick relationality foregrounds relations in ways more akin to the four knowledge approaches sketched above, including by seeing things as relations.

Relations are both necessary and a prerequisite for much practice in peace building, so to draw attention to them in any form—thin, thicker or thick—is in many respects intrinsically worthwhile. However, celebrating or otherwise focusing upon thin relationality borne of an everyday approach to relationships comes with ethical, political and practice risks. The notion that peace and conflict interveners and diverse peoples can enter into a mutually appreciative relationship belies the asymmetrical power relationships that characterize most peacemaking and peace-building settings. Even more concerning than asymmetry itself is the fact that the language of partnership and relationship can prevail even as interveners maintain firm control of key knowledge, political, policy, bureaucratic, administrative and resourcing levers. In other words, the idiom of relationships can operate while changing very little about how diverse peoples and difference are approached in peace and conflict resolution efforts. Indeed, a progressive and warm-sounding language of relations that apparently celebrates and embraces difference can mask, as previously noted following Latour (2002, 7, 9), the continued subordination of difference. Local peace-building 'partners' can be partners in name only (see the critique of 'the local' by Shani, in this volume).

To generate meaningful changes in approaching difference in peace building requires the operationalization of relationality in an ontological sense that brings into play and acts upon the standing of knowledge and knowers in peace and conflict studies. Advancing this possibility requires that the apparently world-unifying powers of scientific knowledge that peace builders rely upon to authorize their practices return to the world and enter into exchange and relation with diverse peoples and their knowledges. A relational-essential approach offers a way of effecting this shift because it disavows an overarching a priori standing vis-à-vis the world and others, as occurs through substantialist and identitarian approaches to difference. Instead of knowing through and re-creating European-derived forms and meanings, a first move in a relational-essential approach is to acknowledge other registers and forms of knowing and, thereby, other ways of processing conflict and sustaining sociopolitical order. Doing so involves demoting the usually ascendant social science figure of the one who knows by placing him or her into relationship with others (see the introduction to this volume). This first step challenges dominant scholarship by placing knowing in the world of interaction rather than over and above the world and the peoples who inhabit it.

To invoke a relational-essential approach to difference is no doubt unsettling for some, as it renders knowing, including the very viability of the relational-essential approach itself, contingent upon interaction with the knowledge schemas and ways of being of peoples encountered in peace and conflict studies and practice. While dominant European-derived knowledge forms position the knowing subject as a sovereign knower—in an ascendant position vis-à-vis diverse others, in command of him- or herself and as the locus of knowing—a relational-essential approach suggests that knowing is always and necessarily emplaced and relational. Knowledge thus emerges through complex contingences that evince a relationally constituted knower rather than an autonomous and preexisting sovereign knower. In this frame, knowers are cast into relation and thus into exchange and negotiation with diverse peoples and traditions, including capacities and processes for conflict resolution and sustaining order. While perhaps unsettling, demoting the sovereign knower through a relational-essential approach does not necessarily invite the spectre of relativism. Relational knowing does not preclude the development of firm knowledge; it simply seeks to develop knowledge through relational processes rather than by asserting the authority of a sovereign knower or one knowledge tradition over others.

RELATIONALITY: RECONCEPTUALIZING POSITIVE PEACE

This final section spells out two moves that peace and conflict studies can make to conceptualize difference in ways that avoid reproducing structural or cultural violence identified through the notion of 'positive peace'. The idea of positive peace, most commonly associated with Johan Galtung, gained traction as a catalytic concept for grounding a normatively charged approach to peace in the late twentieth century. But, as the editors note, positive peace paradoxically facilitates both critique of ossified relations of domination and violence in prevailing social and political structures *and* the emergence of utopian, teleological and Eurocentric projects that generate or perpetuate such structures of domination in peace and conflict studies and their practice counterparts in peace building and conflict resolution. Relationality provides two useful ways of intervening in the problematic paradoxes of positive peace by turning attention away from projects, entities and categories to foreground interactions and exchanges alongside human difference.

First, a relational-essential approach suggests the need to avoid (or at least be highly circumspect about) commonly deployed and apparently common-sensical categories and concepts to describe or categorize difference. This includes continuing to question and move beyond long-standing notions such as tribe, culture and ethnicity. The problems with these concepts have been rehearsed in peace and conflict resolution debates, especially in discussions about culture in conflict resolution beginning from the late 1980s (e.g., see Avruch 1998; Avruch and Black 1993; Brigg 2010; Rubinstein and Foster 1986). Avruch (1998), for instance, many years ago, argued that culture is not a thing. Other disciplines and subfields have also challenged conventional conceptualizations of difference, sometimes in striking and sophisticated ways. Roy Wagner (1975) has famously argued that culture is more about the cosmology, ontology and epistemology of anthropologists/westerners than about the peoples they study, and Mahmood Mamdani (2012), among others (see Nandy, in this volume), has shown that categories of cultural/ethnic difference have in some cases been consolidated or produced through practices of colonial rule. Despite these discussions, long-standing categories and concepts continue to be applied to conceptualize human difference, so it is necessary to redouble efforts to move beyond them.

It is also necessary to avoid the proliferation of new concepts that, while appearing to address an urgent issue or need, actually reproduce, in whole or in part, the problems of dominant of the foregoing well-worn concepts. The most salient recent example is the burgeoning of the term the 'local' set against the 'international' (or the 'liberal') in recent peace and conflict studies debates. These terms are mobilized in efforts to deal with contemporary complexities and challenges of peace building and conflict resolution, including to recognize the necessary contributions of approaches and peoples that are very often excluded from dominant efforts to build peace. However, these terms unduly ossify very complex sets of relations into aggregations that falsely suggest that the 'local' and 'international' really exist (for similar criticism, see Paffenholz 2015; Shani, in this volume). A key difficulty here is the removal of empirical nuances and the creation of a sense of false oppositions that, in the pursuit of critique, paradoxically limit the possibilities of interaction and exchange across differences that practitioners and scholars are attempting to pursue and advance.

The related notion of 'hybridity' may be intended, in the hands of many of its purveyors, to evoke and support engagement with the interplay of intersecting orders in conflict-affected societies, but it suffers a similar problem to the concepts of the local and the international. Hybridity may go some way towards capturing dynamics that have not been able to be grasped through conventional social science analysis. However, serious problems arise here too. The hybrid cannot ultimately have standing other than as a derivative effect of already constituted entities; the hybrid is unable to stand without the underlying categories to which it refers (Brigg 2014). This undermines the ontological impact of hybridity: relations are minimized because without preexisting entities, the hybrid 'vaporize[s] into logical indeterminacy' (Massumi 2002, 69). Hybridity thus risks distracting analysts and practitioners from relations, including by inserting the 'hybrid' as a kind of quasi entity or reified category imbued in the minds of critics with transformative emancipatory power.

Second, a relational-essential approach suggests turning directly and fulsomely to relations (including more directly than is suggested by hybridity) to enable more direct analysis of diverse constellations of relations, including the power relations that inevitably circulate in efforts to resolve conflict and support peace and sociopolitical order. In a relational-essential approach, terms such as 'culture', 'tribe' or 'local' fade into the background in favour of attending to practiced relations and differences. This works against myriad wholesale substantialist claims, whether made by academics or identity entrepreneurs amidst conflict dynamics. It offers, instead, an ambidextrous approach to 'cultural' and other differences. In this frame, difference is the means through which humans both articulate their differences and interact together (see Behr, in this volume). Differences are simultaneously essential—central to life—and form dynamically through shared processes. This frame enables an inductive and relatively open approach to examining the interactive effects and sets of forces at play in any peace building or conflict resolution context. It does so, crucially, by acknowledging the essential place of difference without ossifying it: a relational essential approach suggests that the difference formed in-relation is no less significant for being relationally formed (Brigg 2014).

In this way, a relational-essential approach is an argument for extending upon a type of pragmatist 'muddling through' that many organizations and practitioners already undertake or are capable of mobilizing. Many peace and conflict organisations, especially relatively small and nimble nongovernmental organizations, are well versed in operating flexibly in fluid and contested environments. Larger organizations, including donors and multilaterals, have also recently begun to value such flexibility. Many individual peace-building and conflict resolution practitioners are also familiar with dealing with high levels of uncertainty and contingency in the field and are capable of negotiating these circumstances in order to forge and implement flexible programs and projects. These practitioners also often possess the necessary skills and experience to negotiate these types of exchanges. Because the skills and necessary self-reflexivity for engagement with diverse constituencies are already quite highly valued, the capacity for engaging with difference through a relational-essential approach already exists in somewhat latent form in the peace and conflict field.

No doubt, the extant peace and conflict capacity and willingness that is necessary for acknowledging the essential place of difference comes up against entrenched ways of conceptualizing difference critiqued earlier and against the accompanying entrenched systems, norms and structures for engaging across difference (including those for program design, contracting, reporting, financial accounting and monitoring and evaluation). A relational-essential approach does not seek to cut across these relations with new categories (such as the local/international). Rather, it suggests getting among relations, including the systems and structures that currently disavow and subordinate difference. To do so, a relational-essential approach does not suggest the pursuit of engagements and partnerships across difference in a mode that merely seeks to accommodate or negotiate diverse interests in a political economy or similar calculus. Instead, it suggests valuing difference as central to the endeavour of undertaking peace and conflict resolution work.

To put a relational-essential approach into practice is certainly difficult, not least because individuals and organizations working to respect diverse approaches to peace continue to have to contend with slow-changing structures and systems of contemporary peace-building and conflict resolution practice. Nonetheless, there are glimmers of possibility in contemporary practice. 'Partnering' is becoming a focus of review and critical analysis through mechanisms such as the Keystone Partner Survey (https://keystoneaccountability.org). And individual organizations are developing tools, such as two-way reporting (Morris 2016), that promise to take serious account of differences and support reflection and analysis for a strong approach to respecting and working across difference. These developments are consistent with core peace and conflict studies commitments to noncoercive, participatory and emancipatory modes of conflict processing. Extending these normative commitments into how the field engages with diversity and difference offers a way of reconceptualizing positive peace by tracking structural and cultural violence that is embedded in the peace and conflict studies field itself. To this extent, the possibilities of 'muddling through' seem to endorse Mary Parker Follett's bold claim that difference is not an obstacle but can be the vehicle for creating new social wholes. Because differences are always in-relation rather than standing apart as substantialist entities, working through differences can generate new social wholes that are about more than rearranging the balance of power and what already exists (Follett 1924, iv).

REFERENCES

Aristotle. 1941. *Basic Works*. Edited by Richard Peter McKeon. New York: Random House.

Avruch, Kevin. 1998. *Culture and Conflict Resolution*. Washington, DC: United States Institute of Peace Press.

Avruch, Kevin, and Peter W. Black. 1993. 'Conflict Resolution in Intercultural Settings: Problems and Prospects'. In *Conflict Resolution Theory and Practice: Integration and Application*, edited by Dennis J. D. Sandole and Hugo van der Merwe, 131–45. Manchester: Manchester University Press.

Boege, Volker, Anne Brown, Kevin Clements, and Anna Nolan. 2009. 'On Hybrid Political Orders and Emerging States: What Is Failing—States in the Global South or Research and Politics in the West?' In *Berghof Handbook Dialogue No. 8, Building Peace in the Absence of States: Challenging the Discourse on State Failure*, 15–35. Berlin: Berghof Research Center for Constructive Conflict Management.

Brigg, Morgan. 2010. 'Culture: Challenges and Possibilities'. In *Palgrave Advances in Peacebuilding: Critical Developments and Approaches*, edited by Oliver Richmond, 329–46. Houndmills: Palgrave Macmillan.

———. 2014. 'Culture, 'Relationality', and Global Cooperation'. In *Global Cooperation Research Papers*, 6. Duisburg: Centre for Global Cooperation Research.

———. 2016. 'Relational Peacebuilding: Promise beyond Crisis'. In *Peacebuilding in Crisis: Rethinking Paradigms and Practices of Transnational Cooperation*, edited by Tobias Debiel, Thomas Held, and Ulrich Schneckener, 56–69. London: Routledge.

Deleuze, Gilles. 1994. *Difference and Repetition*. London: Athlone Press.

Follett, Mary Parker. 1918. *The New State: Group Organization, the Solution of Popular Government* [ebook]. The Mary Parker Follett Network. http://api.ning.com/files/C17EiH1KfPbDjH3R-BuX6M7Vd7tuGpi1cUsij53b64HrvWvMr3MigDaC*r Rdl6C-n6Qh0gUdlSorO2PWFwD8QOIQRePiw6DC/TheNewState.doc. Accessed 16 April 2013.

———. 1924. *Creative Experience* [ebook]. The Mary Parker Follett Network. http://api.ning.com/files/rAA1QP8kOSQOpLSk7CEyTtfQ*KYcTMZ3B53Avjx5R0By QcgyY9Su3e9Tfk-N1eKmrw9neAnWYkj0BHWlSmgE6qDvjZh9qnm-/Creative-Experience.doc. Accessed 14 April 2013.

Follett, Mary Parker, Henry Clayton Metcalf, and Lyndall F. Urwick. 1941. *Dynamic Administration: The Collected Papers of Mary Parker Follett*. London: Pitman.

Graham, Mary. 1999. 'Some Thoughts about the Philosophical Underpinnings of Aboriginal Worldviews'. *Worldviews: Environment, Culture, Religion* 3, no. 2: 105–18.

Grosz, E. A. 2004. *The Nick of Time: Politics, Evolution and the Untimely*. Crows Nest: Allen & Unwin.

———. 2005. *Time Travels: Feminism, Nature, Power*. Crows Nest: Allen & Unwin.

———. 2008. *Chaos, Territory, Art: Deleuze and the Framing of the Earth*. New York: Columbia University Press.

———. 2013. 'Significant Differences: An Interview with Elizabeth Grosz'. *Interstitial Journal* (March), 1–5.

Kuokkanen, Rauna. 2007. *Reshaping The University: Responsibility, Indigenous Epistemes, and The Logic of the Gift*. Vancouver: University of British Columbia Press.

Latour, Bruno. 2002. *War of the Worlds: What about Peace?* Translated by Charlotte Bigg. Chicago: Prickly Paradigm Press.

Mac Ginty, Roger. 2011. *International Peacebuilding and Local Resistance: Hybrid Forms of Peace.* New York: Palgrave Macmillan.

Mamdani, Mahmood. 2012. *Define and Rule: Native as Political Identity.* Cambridge, MA: Harvard University Press.

Massumi, Brian. 2002. *Parables for the Virtual: Movement, Affect, Sensation.* Durham, NC: Duke University Press.

Mesle, C. Robert. 2008. *Process-Relational Philosophy: An introduction to Alfred North Whitehead.* West Conshohocken, PA: Templeton.

Miller, John H., and Scott E. Page. 2007. *Complex Adaptive Systems.* Princeton, NJ: Princeton University Press.

Morris, Lynn. 2016. *Peace Direct Introduces Two Way Reporting to Partners.* https://keystoneaccountability.org/2016/09/19/peace-direct-introduces-two-way-reporting-to-partners. Accessed 27 March 2018.

Paffenholz, Thania. 2015. 'Unpacking the Local Turn in Peacebuilding: A Critical Assessment towards an Agenda for Future Research'. *Third World Quarterly* 36, no. 5: 857–74.

Richmond, Oliver P. 2013. 'Failed Statebuilding versus Peace Formation'. *Cooperation and Conflict* 48, no. 3: 378–400.

Rosen, Robert. 2000. *Essays on Life Itself.* New York: Columbia University Press.

Rubinstein, Robert A., and Mary LeCron Foster, eds. 1986. *Peace and War: Cross-Cultural Perspectives.* New Brunswick, NJ: Transaction.

Strathern, Marilyn. 1995. *The Relation: Issues in Complexity and Scale.* Cambridge: Prickly Pear Press.

———. 2004. *Partial Connections*, updated ed. Walnut Creek, CA: AltaMira Press.

Urry, John. 2003. *Global Complexity.* Cambridge, MA: Polity Press.

Wagner, Roy. 1975. *The Invention of Culture.* Englewood Cliffs, NJ: Prentice Hall.

Chapter Fourteen

Zona Intervenida

Performance as Memory, Transforming Contested Spaces

Nitin Sawhney

Traces of war and injustice often disappear from physical sites of conflict, lingering only in the fragmented memories of witnesses and those who have lived through the atrocities committed and the indirect violence experienced despite the silence and repression imposed. These contested sites may not readily reveal the traumas and fractures hidden beneath their surface, while witness testimony and archival records of untold events that took place there may remain repressed, inaccessible or intentionally obfuscated. Under these conditions, how can the body reactivate and transform suppressed or disputed memories? What role do movement, music and poetry play to viscerally make sense of invisible histories in neglected sites of conflict? How does capturing these interventions through media reveal new meaning within the empty silence of these contested spaces?

In this introspective chapter, I explore such questions through a performance-based cinematic inquiry conducted over a three-year period at a contested urban site in Quetzaltenango, Guatemala, with a collective of local and international artists residing there. Decades of civil war, forced disappearances and military repression has induced many Guatemalans into a sense of fear and silence about atrocities committed in the past, while human rights investigations (when permitted by authorities) only deepen fissures in a divided society. Approaching such sites challenges the role of mediators (including peace activists, journalists and filmmakers) demanding greater ethical responsibility and sensitivity in the process of engaging diverse voices, intervening in undesignated sites of memory and seeking nonconfrontational, subversive or artistic modes of expression.

BRUTAL LEGACY OF CIVIL WAR
AND VIOLENCE IN GUATEMALA

Father, in this place there is nothing but silence. Time has left its traces, the same feeling as brutally awakening from a dream.

Father, 'war' should have been just another word, instead of that rabid dog that once bit our hands. Everybody stayed here. They stayed like goats, like soil, like seeds.

If we look for them, we will find the blacksmith, the barber, the cook. Ghosts don't leave, they stay forever.

I was born in 1982, I come from blood, I come from pain, I am a soldier's child. I have inherited silence.

These are excerpts from a spoken-word performance by Marvin García, a young poet whose father worked in a Guatemalan military base in Quetzaltenango in the 1980s. The performance captured on film took place in the same location, now partly converted into a cultural centre with little if any sign of its oppressive past lingering on the dilapidated site.

More than 200,000 people were killed or 'disappeared' over the course of a brutal 36-year-long civil war in Guatemala, the longest in Latin America, beginning in 1960 and ending with the signing of the peace accords in December 1996. Guatemala's civil war is grounded in its colonial legacy and historic oppression at the hands of an elite minority backed by U.S. and Western interests in the region, not unlike many Latin American countries at the time. Guatemala's democratically elected president, Jacobo Árbenz, was overthrown in 1954 by a U.S.-backed right-wing military dictator, Carlos Castillo Armas, in an 'anticommunist' military coup d'état. Árbenz attracted the attention of the U.S. Central Intelligence Agency thanks to his land reform policies designed to benefit displaced farmers at the expense of private interests, such as the U.S.-based United Fruit Company. Guatemala's economy relied on the exploitation of indigenous labour and land, while a democratic regime posed a direct threat to the political and economic elite as well as their main trading partner, the United States. An ensuing military rebellion by Marxist insurgency groups against the new regime and the counterinsurgency tactics and state-based violence against 'supporters' of the guerrilla forces in the early 1960s led to the protracted civil war in Guatemala. The conflict intensified in the late 1970s and early 1980s, during which the most brutal atrocities, civilian massacres and human rights violations were committed; many commentators today refer to it as a genocide.

According to a 1999 report written by the UN-backed Historical Clarification Commission titled 'Guatemala: Memory of Silence' (1999) and republished by Daniel Rothenberg (2012), nearly 83 percent of those killed were indigenous Mayans and 17 percent Ladino. The report also found that the vast majority of human rights violations, 93 percent, were perpetrated by U.S.-backed state forces and related paramilitary groups, while 3 percent of the violations were attributed to insurgency groups. Among the victims of arbitrary execution, forced disappearance, torture, rape and other violations of fundamental rights were children, priests, indigenous leaders and noncombatant women and men with no ties to insurgency groups. The inability of the state to deal with political instability during the armed conflict led to the creation of an intricate system of repression driven by military intelligence and an underground, illegal punitive system that has permeated Guatemala's political system to this day with little or no judicial accountability for the perpetrators of the human rights violations or justice for the vast majority of victims and their families. The commission was not allowed to include names of perpetrators or call for prosecution in its report; hence, there has been very limited success in prosecuting perpetrators, including former soldiers and military officials.

In July 2005, an explosion near an abandoned warehouse (a munitions depot) in Guatemala City prompted investigators to unexpectedly discover a vast trove of documents detailing the history of the defunct Guatemalan National Police and its role in the civil war. This archive contained approximately 80 million pages of information dating back as far as the late nineteenth century (1882) through 1997, the largest such collection of state secrets ever found in Latin America. A human rights investigator, Kate Doyle, a senior analyst of U.S. policy in Latin America at the National Security Archive, described her impressions:

> During a visit to the site in early August, I saw file cabinets marked 'assassinations', 'disappeared' and 'homicides', as well as folders labeled with the names of internationally-known victims of political murder, such as anthropologist Myrna Mack (killed by security forces in 1990). There were hundreds of rolls of still photography, which the PDH (*Procuraduría de Derechos Humanos—Guatemala's human rights office*) is developing now. There were pictures of bodies and of detainees, there were lists of police informants with names and photos, there were vehicle license plates, video tapes and computer disks. The installations themselves, which are in a terrible state of neglect—humid and exposed to the open air, infested with vermin and full of trash—contain what appear to be clandestine cells. The importance of the discovery cannot be overstated.

Over the years, international teams of forensic specialists, data analysts and archivists have been carefully identifying, classifying, preserving and digitizing this vast cache of historical documents (nearly a quarter of it to date) into a digital archive of the *Guatemalan National Police Historical*

Archive, currently hosted at the University of Texas, Austin, to facilitate scholarly and legal research. A publication based on these archives, *From Silence to Memory: Revelations of the AHPN* (Archivo Historico de la Policia Nactional 2013), elucidates the 115-year history of the National Police and the savage repression employed by the state to crush not only the armed opposition groups but political and social activists agitating for the country's future. Evidence from the archives has been successful in bringing many perpetrators to trial, including the former head of the national police, Hector Bol de la Cruz, who in 2013 was sentenced to 40 years in prison for his role in the kidnapping and death of a young student union leader in 1984. That same year, substantial evidence from the archives also supported the conviction of Efraín Ríos Montt, head of the Guatemalan army, who was formally indicted for genocide and crimes against humanity, in particular for his role in the killings of 1,771 Maya Ixil Indians, including children, in the early 1980s. Ríos Montt was sentenced to 80 years in prison, the first-ever former head of state to have been convicted of genocide by a court in his own country. However, the Constitutional Court of Guatemala overturned his conviction within days, and the trial, which resumed only in January 2015, did not lead to a jail sentence before his death in April 2018. The Guatemalan Justice Department continues pursuing prosecutions related to war crimes to help some Guatemalan families bring closure for their tragic loss; however, the archives can provide actionable evidence to bring only a relatively small number of perpetrators to trial, while the vast majority of victims and their families may never see justice served. The process of healing in Guatemala is not simply limited to judicial procedure but also, as many have argued, involves a collective reckoning with historical memory.

ARCHIVAL VERSUS EMBODIED PRACTICES
FOR ENGAGING HISTORICAL MEMORY

In *The Archive and the Repertoire*, performance studies scholar Diana Taylor (2003) asks us to reconsider the ways in which cultural expression and knowledge is understood or mediated distinctly by modes of archival versus embodied practices. *Archival* memory, comprising written narrative, physical materials, sound and image, is often captured, organized and transmitted through supposedly authentic and enduring forms of documents, literary texts and audiovisual media. While these are considered unmediated and resistant to change, any element of such an archive is also prone to corruptibility and political manipulation and can easily be erased. Taylor argues that the ephemeral *repertoire* of embodied performance practices, such as dance, ritualized movement and spoken word, offer an alternative system of learning, storing and transmitting social knowledge, memory and identity. The repertoire involves the presence of people participating in the production, interpretation and *live* transmission of such ephemeral knowledge; rather than documenting or reducing it to narrative description, the repertoire legitimizes or revalourises expressive, sacred and indigenous knowledge, enacting embodied memory as social 'acts of transfer' and generating new forms of meaning in the process. The archive and repertoire exist in a constant state of interaction and could work in tandem to offer a more affective rendering, multiplicity of understanding and analytic rethinking of complex human conditions, emotions and experiences that are not easily accessed or articulated in written form alone. When archival knowledge and witness testimony are unavailable or politically repressed, what role can embodied performance play in addressing ephemeral concerns dealing with people's fears and aspirations, contested memories and unimaginable sites of conflict? How are these embodied practices archived and transmitted by practicing artists (especially during periods of conflict) but also repressed and manipulated by the state seeking to control their message, aesthetic forms and influence on historical memory?

In *The Dance That Makes You Vanish*, Rachmi Diyah Larasati (2013) chronicles the potency of Indonesian dance forms (mainly of court traditions) and the lives of its female practitioners, many of whom were repressed and persecuted by the Indonesian state. Over one year (1965–1966), nearly a million Indonesians—including a large percentage of the country's left-leaning musicians, artists and dancers—were killed, arrested or disappeared as part of the 'New Order' led by the Indonesian military leader and president, Suharto, who ruled the country for the next 30 years. In her writing, Larasati explicates, from a personal and academic perspective, the highly complex relationships between the artistic traditions and bodies of female dancers and the aims of the Indonesian state. Her own memoir and poignant narrative, as an Indonesian national troupe dancer from a family of persecuted female dancers and activists, makes the case that 'the reconstruction of [national history and memory] serves to erase the extreme violence and chaos on which Suharto's New Order state itself was founded' (22).

The Suharto regime pursued a dual-edged strategy that vilified, persecuted and made to disappear female dancers perceived as communist or left leaning while simultaneously deploying and replacing them as 'replicas'—new idealized state-aligned bodies trained to standardize and unify the 'unruly' movements and voices of those vanished as cultural representatives of Indonesia's autocratic rule. Larasati states that 'dancing bodies seeking to challenge prevailing paradigms of historical memory must constantly navigate the paradox of speaking through the aestheticized, ideological language of the politically and economically dominant in order to mobilize the interests of the local or the suppressed' (https://cla.umn.edu/about/directory/profile/laras001). She demonstrates the conflict between local and state aesthetic values by discussing how mothers transmitted artistic practices to their daughters in villages and how certain non–court dance traditions, such as *Jejer* and *Tayub*, were popular among large male crowds. In contrast to the subdued, graceful court dance, these quick-moving dances included darting eyes and circular torso movements. Such village-based dance practices were considered unrefined, uncontrolled and dangerous by the Suharto regime and have been banned since 1965. The state recognized these aesthetic dance practices as both efficacious in communicating identity, memory and embodied experience while manipulating them to their own ends to project an image of harmony, national unity and civil obedience within and outside Indonesia.

RETHINKING PEACE THROUGH LOCALIZED AND RELATIONAL NARRATIVES

Archival memory in conjunction with embodied practices can work to communicate, transform and influence (or manipulate) public discourse at the level of the nation-state and global understandings of peace building and transitional justice. How can such mechanisms function on a localized scale with complex, relational and multidirectional narratives in conditions of conflict and injustice that defy linear and singular articulation, judicial solutions or temporally bound closure? In their introduction, the editors of this volume have challenged contributors to move beyond the hypostasis, teleology and normative tendency prevalent today while recognizing how these tendencies often manifest as monologic and utopian enterprises to justice and peace building. They have encouraged a generative and open-ended approach embracing cultural, humanistic and social science perspectives outside of the dominant discourses in international relations, security and peace studies while critically challenging the ways in which Enlightenment-based liberal thinking undergirds global peace-building and democratization efforts today without recognizing or responding to localized complexities.

One of the editors, Giorgio Shani, in his chapter, 'Saving Liberal Peace Building? From the "Local Turn" to a Post-Western Peace', discusses the challenges of moving beyond the Eurocentric gaze and colonial framing of peace, conflict and security studies, which tend to focus on the nation-state as the primary unit of analysis and Western institutions, including the United Nations, as agents for maintaining order (extending the critiques by Bronner, in this volume). Attempts to reorient towards a 'local turn' by empowering individuals and communities in an emancipatory approach to peace (as argued by Richmond, in this volume) often fail to meaningfully engage local populations on their own terms and end up instrumentalizing the 'local'. Rather than arguing for a 'postliberal' hybrid peace that seeks a local–global dialogic, Shani emphasizes a postsecular approach that embraces a multiplicity of claims grounded in a diversity of alternative traditions. Hartmut Behr also argues for this relational, dialogic approach to peace studies in his chapter, 'Peace-in-Difference: Peace through Dialogue about and across Difference(s)', noting how peace articulates in relation to the 'other' and how political dialogue must negotiate and empathize with differences in nonessentialist ways. Ashis Nandy shares crucial insights in his chapter, 'The Inner Battles of Peace Studies: The Limits and Possibilities', about the 'black holes' through which traces of everyday injustices, suffering, aspirations and values disappear from being subjects of research or become exiled from historical memory. Nandy suggests that these may survive in individual and collective memories as pluralistic narratives, emerging unexpectedly to subvert or challenge existing teleological articulations.

Natasha Zaretsky's chapter, 'Justice in the Land of Memory: Reflecting on the Temporality of Truth and Survival in Argentina', describes how civil society engages with cultural memory as a means to resist erasure and protest the political violence endured by families of the disappeared or forgotten victims of genocide in Argentina despite the continued impunity of its perpetrators. Her work also chronicles the aftermath of the most significant terrorist attack in Argentina—the 1994 AMIA bombing in Buenos Aires that killed 85 people and wounded hundreds, a decisive turning point in Jewish Argentine history. Zaretsky discusses how political protest movements, musical performance, literature and acts of commemoration in public sites have been organized by citizens to seek justice, belonging, healing and pluralism in Argentina. Yael Zerubavel's chapter, 'Negotiating Difference and Empathy: Cinematic Representations of Passing and Exchanged Identities in the Israeli–Palestinian Conflict', shows how contested narratives and identities remain caught up in singular histories of loss and victimhood anchored in a traumatic past. However, Zerubavel suggests that the arts (e.g., through cinematic portrayals of identity exchanges in films) offer an alternative venue for moving beyond a polarized public discourse and the potential for engaging in empathy for the other (as argued by Behr, in this volume). Finally, Leigh Payne's chapter, 'Silence: "Do Not Confuse It with Any Kind of Absence"', urges the reader to consider the expressive power of silence for remembrance, subversion and struggle against forgetting. In contrast to vocal protests and iterative expressions of condemnation, silence can be engaged in powerful forms of unspoken performances, embodied practices and sacred sites of memory.

Many of these themes are best embodied in the work of renowned Guatemalan performance artist Regina José Galindo. In one of her early works,

¿Quién puede borrar las huellas? (Who Can Erase the Traces?), a haunting performance in 2003, Galindo walked barefoot from the Constitutional Court to the National Palace of Guatemala, leaving traces on the ground by dipping her feet every few steps into a large white bowl of human blood she held as a vigorous protest against the presidential candidacy of Guatemala's former dictator Efraín Ríos Montt, as described in an article by Elena Shtromberg (2015). As the soldiers guarding the palace and surrounding passersby watched the artist defiantly insert her body into this contested public space, Galindo offered a powerful reminder of Guatemala's bloody past and the unresolved justice for the victims of its brutal 36-year-long civil war.

Galindo described her visceral experience in an interview with writer Francisco Goldman (2006):

Every performance requires a different energy, and in each of them I have experienced distinct sensations and thoughts. The process of this performance was a bit cold, clinical. I went out to buy the human blood in the morning, and then I began the walk. It probably lasted about 45 minutes: that walk on pavement that did not burn. I suppose my mind fell completely silent during that time. I was focused on the image of dipping my feet and leaving my footprints at every step along the way. But when I got to the Palacio Nacional and saw the line of police officers guarding it, I ignited. I walked more firmly, I reached the main doors, I saw the eyes looking back at me, and I left two final footprints side by side. I left the basin holding the blood there too. Nobody followed me, nobody said anything.

While this brief silent performance was witnessed by only a few people, the archival memory documented through video and photographs was circulated widely, being published in newspapers at the time and entering the public imagination as an iconic visual protest, leaving a far more significant ephemeral trace on the site.

In the second half of this chapter, I chronicle my own experience working with an artist collective in Guatemala engaged in a performance-based inquiry of a contested site. The inquiry, conducted through archival and embodied practices, reveals multilayered narratives of historical memory and attempts to transform public discourse about the site.

ENCOUNTERING A CONTESTED SITE IN QUETZALTENANGO, GUATEMALA

Since mid-August 2012, I began visiting Quetzaltenango, a bustling historic city nestled in the highlands of Guatemala, where I met a young theatre artist and activist Bonifaz Díaz (or Boni), who took me to see a seemingly abandoned and enigmatic site at the heart of the city. The site, consisting of a vast complex of buildings and interconnected spaces, was formerly built as the main train station in Quetzaltenango and later converted into a strategic military training base in the heart of the Guatemalan highlands in 1945, where untold violence was perpetrated for decades. The site today, repurposed partially as a cultural and sports complex by the municipality, remains paralysed in the midst of a fragile peace imposed in Guatemala since the late 1990s. Local residents have variously called the site *Ferrocarril de Los Altos*, *Zona Militar* or *Centro Intercultural*, referring to its shifting identity and character through its transformation over the decades; even today, these names are used interchangeably. Any evidence of the site's tortured past has gradually been removed (and literally whitewashed) from its walls, while few if any public records of its historic significance exist. However, the powerful and deteriorating place reveals a haunting sense of its historic memory to anyone who walks through its vast and unusual architectural space.

PERFORMANCE AS INQUIRY
FOR SILENCED MEMORIES

Over the course of three years, I found myself regularly visiting this site with Boni, while he began drawing together an eclectic group of young artists, writers, dancers, poets, musicians and filmmakers to join us in investigating and intervening on this site. Our collaboration with this emerging collective (*Colectivo Andén*) evolved through an artistic exploration of the contested site, bearing witness to historic memories of civil war and intermittent moments of economic revival in Guatemala. The project was initiated through photography, film and interviews with local historians, writers and witnesses, while regular workshops were conducted with the artist collective to develop site-specific performances to investigate and temporarily intervene on the site. The overall process and performances conducted was captured in a documentary film, *Zona Intervenida*[1] (Zone of Intervention), currently under production. The film follows these young artists who use movement, music, seeds and spoken word to activate and transform the dark memories of the space while engaging public imagination and bringing light to Guatemala's silenced past. The film footage, shot over a two-year period, captures the process through which these performance-based investigations take shape across the site while revealing how they affect the participants' own perceptions of the place and its historical memory viscerally through their bodies.

The film begins with a first-person encounter of an abandoned space with the camera moving rapidly (on a bicycle) through a complex of dilapidated buildings. We hear a voice recounting the 'strange feeling' of being there, with the powerful energy of the place acting like 'a gust of wind moving below my feet'. The voice is that of Boni, and the place is the former train station and military base, which becomes the main architectural site and cinematic character central to the narrative of the film. During his childhood, Boni lived a mere two blocks away from the site and has only now begun to come to terms with the violent events and forced disappearances that were perpetuated here through the civil war in the 1980s. He also recounts the curious wonder of its time in the early 1930s, as told by former city residents, when it functioned as a train station for only three years before being taken over by the Guatemalan military.

The military repurposed the site as its central base of operations in the highlands of Guatemala until the late 1990s, when it was finally demilitarized after the peace accords were signed in 1996. This base, Military Zone Number 5, later called *Manuel Lizando Barillas*, was one of the few established in Guatemala located in the heart of a major city (the second largest in the country). Today, most of the place remains abandoned, while a small portion of it (less than a quarter) has been converted for use as an intercultural centre by the municipality. As the viewer continues to explore the space, one can visually sense the tragic stillness and historical significance of the site.

SUBVERSIVE PERFORMANCE INTERVENTIONS

In the film, we follow Boni and Carlos Lucas (a musician) as they set out to reimagine the space by re-creating its nearly forgotten past through a series of performance-based interventions. Along with a collective of artists, poets, dancers and musicians, they begin initiating their own creative and personal inquiry of the place. Their goal was to repurpose the site as a centre for artistic/cultural production and community engagement but also to aesthetically reclaim the memory of its silenced past. Boni and Lucas begin to conduct historical research, workshops and artistic experiments at the site, engaging dozens of local and international artists and practitioners living in Quetzaltenango. Over the course of a year and a half, these members of Colectivo Andén intervene regularly in the space using a series of improvised and orchestrated performances. Most performances were conducted subversively at the beginning to evade the municipal authorities that did not support any public acknowledgment of the past atrocities that were committed at the site. After their request to gain access to the site was denied in May 2013, the collective chooses to continue developing its ideas by performing discreetly there.

The film moves the viewer through these performances (usually depicted in black and white), evoking the timeless aesthetic of historical memory while intercutting between narratives of their personal motivations and inner struggles as they conceptualize and intervene on the site. Haunting melodies carry the viewer through the film and into the space as one hears a woman playing on her cello while accompanied by a young man on his guitar. Their music begins to reconstruct and retune the acoustic architecture of the space, while on-site sound recordings add layers of depth and texture.

A key character in the film is Marvin García, a young poet whose father worked in the military base as an auto mechanic in the 1980s. Marvin recalls his father's memories as he walks silently among one of the abandoned warehouses on the site, which he often visited with his father as a child. Marvin's farther mentions how this base in Quetzaltenango was strategically more important to the Guatemalan military than the main headquarters in Guatemala City because it functioned as a military school for their elite soldiers and remained an influential site of operations against the Guerrilla resistance in the highlands. These soldiers were known to be trained in the most brutal practices, witnessing or participating in the violent torture, rape and killings of many captured Guerrilla members and civilians suspected of supporting their movement. The military used to say, 'What you saw here, what you lived here, not even your wife should know about'. As Marvin remembers his father's words while walking through the abandoned warehouse, he shudders with the knowledge of undiscovered bodies that may lie buried under his feet

Figure 14.1. Marvin García reads a poem while reflecting on his father's memories of the place, with their shadows and reflections juxtaposed on its walls.

and the gruesome acts committed in the name of democracy throughout this dark period in Guatemala.

Marvin returns to the place late one evening, mustering his strength to read a poem he composed reflecting on his father's words. The action is rendered using a video-based performance with a projection of Marvin's father on the inner walls of the abandoned building. In one moment of the performance, Marvin reads, 'Now that I think about it, father . . . we are the cracks in the glass, the stained floor, the echo in the empty rooms'. He continues, 'So many things stayed with me, as tattoos on my skin, honoring our memory. Father, in this place there's nothing but silence. Time has left its traces, the same feeling as brutally awakening from a dream'. The poem later reveals, 'I was born in 1982, I come from blood, I come from pain, I am a soldier's child. I have inherited silence'. Marvin's solitary delivery, set against his illuminated shadow in the darkened walls and his father's moving image, creates a powerful poetic intervention that remains a haunting image one is unable to escape throughout the film even as other moments of collective performance and public theatre enliven the space later.

Members of Colectivo Andén develop several collective actions using their bodies to generate symbolic and poetic movement in the space. One such action involves more than a dozen bodies moving slowly and methodically in unison behind one another across one of the abandoned rooms of the warehouse space (with barbed wire along its roof and walls), enacting

Figure 14.2. Members of Colectivo Andén perform a coordinated movement symbolically cleansing the halls of the Zona Militar complex.

a ritualistic form of cleansing of the soul by splashing water in their faces after circumambulating through the space. Another involves a young woman intentionally running back and forth in a locked room, reliving the horror of panic and rape while trying to escape through its broken windows during a thunderstorm. The next action reveals more than a dozen bodies arranging themselves among the sunlit squares of light beaming down through the high ceilings while performing a coordinated series of bodily gestures and cleansing the space with their brooms. The synchronized rhythm of their movements creates a powerful cinematic spectacle.

Each action becomes visually stunning as the collective movement of bodies reshapes the vast proportions and intimidating structure of the space. After most actions, I film the performers reflecting on how their individual and collective interactions with the space reveal powerful feelings of the silenced and brutal memories contained within it. Julio Serrano, a poet-writer who agreed to join the performers moving in the space, feels as if they are 'acting like a big machine' while performing mechanical movements, possibly aligning themselves with the 'historic body' of the place. He remarks about the strange feeling of reclaiming the space by claiming his own body first while performing for the first time there.

Another group of women choreograph their own improvisational performances in the space using found objects, such as rope, chairs, wooden frames and books, to devise theatrical gestures and graceful movements. One of them, Blanca Carbonell, recalls how the experience leaves her with many more questions, leaving the place as enigmatic as ever. Another performer, Anne Marie, perceives the action more as an encounter of meeting someone and having her body penetrated and transformed by the past. Ana Valeria instead finds it a liberating experience as she dances in her bathing suit in an open space between buildings during heavy, pouring rain; her playful solo performance helps her escape the site's tortured past while reinserting her own reimagined narrative there.

ENGAGING PUBLIC DISCOURSE WITHIN GUATEMALAN SOCIETY

As Boni continues to coordinate the work of the collective, he believes that this very process of intervening in the space allows Guatemalan society to begin recovering its historic memory. Probing the past may provide a better perspective on the present, one that many young people in Guatemala are unable to grapple with given the unjust silence still being perpetuated today. He feels it may help people understand or perhaps avoid repeating the political actions of previous generations that led to the decades of sustained violence in Guatemala. Boni is determined to engage the wider public in Quetzaltenango with the site and makes another attempt to secure permission from the authorities to provide access. Boni and Colectivo Andén tactically reframe their proposal as one of commemorating the site as a former train station as part of a potential public event. Their subsequent presentation to the municipality and mayor of the city finally grants them approval for a commemorative event to be held there several months later.

Over the course of a year and a half, many young Guatemalans join the collective, stretching its creative actions along different directions, including the use of seed bombing across the fields enclosed within the complex site. Juan Pablo Echeverria is a young urban gardener who runs his own backyard urban farm in Quetzaltenango. His father was a member of the Guatemalan military stationed at the base, and he recalls coming there to attend military parades and festive events as a child. He grew up listening to one side of the story (the military's narrative) and only later learned about the other side. He understands that people in Guatemala remain divided about the war and feels that it is time for them to find common ground and seek reconciliation by engaging with silenced memories that are connected to the various sites of atrocities, such as the one in this former base. Juan Pablo decides to conduct a workshop on seed bombing at a former firing range on the site, teaching dozens of people to combine four different kinds of seeds tightly packed into a ball of dirt to help nurture the grounds. Juan Pablo says, 'We might still not have their approval to work here, but the idea is to start enriching the soil by natural means now'. As the seeds take root, he sees an opportunity to promote a physical transformation of the place but also to sensitize people into acknowledging the past and giving new meaning to that space.

Juan Pablo continues to work closely with Boni and Colectivo Andén to develop a shadow theatre performance as part of the commemorative public event to be held shortly. We witness the rehearsals for the playful performance planned as the artists use colored paper, stick figures, and paper cutouts with humorous voiceovers to construct a magical visual narrative about the historic adaptations of the site, from its beginning as a train station and its transformation during the war to a place where the public can reimagine and reengage culturally today. The shadow theatre play itself serves as a metaphor for the journey the collective has taken in their series of interventions in the space while moving from subversive actions to the public sphere. Boni feels that these public performances can help reactivate the space in new ways and reshape the indifference that locals have by making its creative potential more visible. As dancers rehearse their own performances in the space, posters around the city create a buzz about the first public event by the collective at the Centro Intercultural. On the opening day, hundreds of local residents come to attend the art exhibit and performances led by the collective after more than a year of tactical preparations unknown to the public. A resounding applause marks the night's impact on the audiences in a moment of brief exuberance for Colectivo Andén.

EPILOGUE: UNRESOLVED
MEMORIES AND CONTESTED NARRATIVES

A closing sequence filmed a year later brings together Juan Pablo and Marvin in a sombre tone as they walk together through the fields around the site looking for the seeds they planted, pondering the legacy of their fathers, whose lives and memories were shaped by this place. Their fathers hold on to very different narratives of the conflict, reflecting the silent divisions that remain within Guatemalan society. Yet this generation of young artists and activists continue their struggle to understand their past and nurture a new future. The film ends in a haunting sequence as we watch the scars of the place unchanged and dancers performing as dark angels from the past, circling musicians performing in the space in the present day. A visual montage of the site emerges with the many faces of everyday Guatemalans who were affected by the decades of violent conflict, repression and loss. The site remains one of just many that have witnessed the historical memory of repression in Guatemala, yet the work of Colectivo Andén may have begun to reactivate and transform it, reengaging the public to imagine a new form of reconciliation with the past.

Over the three-year period of the film's production, many members of Colectivo Andén helped shape the film's trajectory; emerging rough cuts screened among local audiences in Quetzaltenango and Guatemala City often led to vigorous and extended discussion. In some ways, the film remains incomplete as we struggled to resolve its narrative arc and aesthetic impact rather than treating it simply as documentation of the collective's interventions at the site. Editing the film required traversing a delicate balance between the artistic and political sensibilities of the collective and the film's intended audiences (within and outside Guatemala); it has also been challenging to resolve the embodied ephemeral experiences of participants at the site, with the complex threads of intersecting historical narratives unfolding across a much longer time span. The medium of a linear documentary film (the *archive*) and the on-site performances (the *repertoire*) can offer both aesthetic and affective opportunities. The process of producing the film, enacting performances and engaging audiences clearly had an effect among participants and generated new meanings about the place. Centro Intercultural, while transformed briefly in the public imagination through the film and performances, remains an unresolved site of contested memories and political tensions experienced through Guatemala's decades-long military repression, civil war and human rights injustices. In 2015, as thousands of Guatemalans participated in a series of mass protests to seek electoral reforms against corruption, many young student leaders and activists began engaging politically for the first time. Several members of Colectivo Andén began reframing their own artistic work by undertaking socially engaged projects, critical pedagogy, and traveling theatre performances around Quetzaltenango and the indigenous rural highlands in Guatemala.

NOTE

1. Website for the documentary film project: http://www.ZonaIntervenida.org.

REFERENCES

Archivo Historico de la Policia Nactional. 2013. *From Silence to Memory: Revelations of the AHPN.* Foreword by Carlos Aguirre. Preface to the English translation by Kate Doyle. Eugene: University of Oregon Libraries.

Goldman, Francisco. 2006. "Regina José Galindo." *Bomb* 94 (Winter 2006). http://bombmagazine.org/article/2780/regina-jos-galindo. Accessed 15 June 2018.

Historical Clarification Commission. 1999. *Guatemala: Memory of Silence.* Guatemala City: Historical Clarification Commission.

Larasati, Rachmi Diyah. 2013. *The Dance That Makes You Vanish: Cultural Reconstruction in Post-Genocide Indonesia.* Minneapolis: University of Minnesota Press.

Rothenberg, Daniel. 2012. *Memory of Silence: The Guatemalan Truth Commission Report.* New York: Palgrave Macmillan.

Shtromberg, Elena. 2015. "Amnesty and Justice for All: The Art of Regina José Galindo." *Los Angeles Review of Books.* https://lareviewofbooks.org/article/amnesty-justice-art-regina-jose-galindo. Accessed 15 June 2018.

Taylor, Diana. 2003. *The Archive and the Repertoire: Performing Cultural Memory in the Americas.* Durham, NC: Duke University Press.

Afterword

Look Again—Aleppo

The Last Lesson in Prevention

Alexander Laban Hinton

1.

The Last Lesson:
Look again --

2.

"Who's at Risk?" (United to End Genocide)

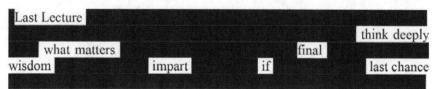

3.

4.

Critical ██████ Prevention ██████

An image of a bleeding and soot-covered Syrian boy rescued from the rubble after a devastating airstrike in Aleppo has gone viral. The image encapsulates the horrors inflicted on the war-ravaged northern city. The boy . . . was pulled from a damaged building after a Syrian government or Russian airstrike . . . He was one of 12 children under the age of 15 treated on Wednesday – not a particularly unusual figure.
—*The New York Times*, August 18, 2016

5.

The ██████

██████

████████████████████████████████ assumed ████ common knowledge████ definitive ██████

██████████████████ *unique*

the present ██████████

██████ point forward ██████████ defining ██████
██████████ generalized ██████████████
█ enough ██████████████████████
██████ stressing 'the' ██████████████ best known █
most important ██████ type ██
██████████████████████ indicate ██████████
██████ relation ██ other ██████████
Origin ██████ this that ██████████████

6.

'"We will not let Aleppo become another Rwanda": UN envoy likens Syrian civil war to genocide'.
—*South China Morning Post*, October 7, 2016

7.

Aporia

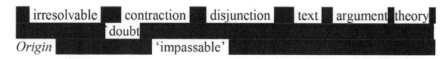

█ irresolvable █ contraction █ disjunction █ text █ argument█ theory█
█████ doubt ███
Origin ██████████ 'impassable' ████████████████████

8.

1st Aporia of Critical Genocide Prevention
Genocide prevention is a hope that founders at the impassible limit of the utopian dream it promises. Once glimpsed, it disappears in the sea of particularity. Genocide prevention always remains "to come," even as we look again—

9.

2016 Statement █*UN Special Adviser*█*Genocide Prevention* █ *Responsibility*
█ *Protect:* █ Sept ██████████ Aug ███████ Jul █████████ Jun
████████ Jun ████ Jun Syria ██████████████ Feb ████
Feb Syria ██████████████████████████████████████

10.

"If you had █ one █ to give, what █████████?"
—"Last Lecture," UCSC Student Life webpage

11.

█ Last █████

█
█ Coming after all others █ time █ order█ final█
    lowest in importance █ *rank*

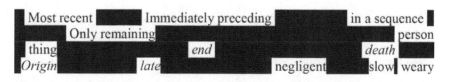

Most recent ████████ Immediately preceding ████████ in a sequence █
████ Only remaining ████████████████████████ person
█ thing ████████████ *end* ██████████ *death* █
█*Origin* ████████ *late* █████████ negligent█████slow█ weary

at last   *long last*   *last minute*   *last order*   *last thing*   *last moment*
last word *last hope*   *last hurrah*   *last of*   *the last*   *last person*

█ final ████████ pronouncement ████████████
████████████████████████████████████

12.

U.S. Presidential Debate, October 9, 2016

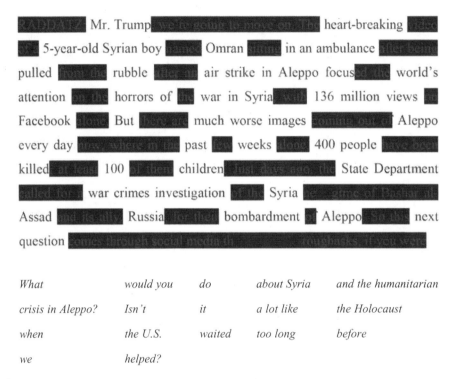

RADDATZ Mr. Trump ████████ heart-breaking ███ 5-year-old Syrian boy ████ Omran ████ in an ambulance ████████ pulled ████████ rubble ████ air strike in Aleppo focus██ ███ world's attention ████ horrors of ██ war in Syria ████ 136 million views ██ Facebook ████ But ████████ much worse images ████████ Aleppo every day ████████ past ██ weeks ████ 400 people ████████ killed ████ 100 ██ them children ████████ State Department ████████ war crimes investigation ████ Syria ████████ Assad ████████ Russia ████ bombardment ██ Aleppo ████ next question ████████████████

What	*would you*	*do*	*about Syria*	*and the humanitarian*
crisis in Aleppo?	*Isn't*	*it*	*a lot like*	*the Holocaust*
when	*the U.S.*	*waited*	*too long*	*before*
we	*helped?*			

13.

2nd Aporia ████████ *Genocide Prevention*

Genocide Prevention seeks to save *the* victim. The more it does so, the more people it fails to save.

14.

█ Lesson**: *the* critical difference

A lesson	a period	of learning or
teaching	a thing	learned
serving as	a warning	or encouragement.
A passage	from	the Bible
read aloud	during	a church
service	archaic	instruct
or rebuke	from Latin	*legere*
"to read"	lecture	legible

"an occurrence from which something can be learned"

Synonym: class, session, session, seminar, tutorial, lecture, period, period of instruction/reading

Antonym: none.

***Warning*. A lesson is a word without an opposite. A reading: to be unread, reread. A learning: to be unlearned, relearning. An instruction: to be illegible, discerning. A lecture: to be silent, then look again, searching for the critical difference.

15.

█ What would you do █ about █
Aleppo █

16.

'What is Aleppo?'

—U.S. Libertarian Presidential Candidate,
Gary Johnson, September 8, 2016

17.

Allepo

 Arabic *Halab* French *Alep* city north Syria

Aleppo gall
 hard nut-like gall forms on oak response
  larva of gall wasp acid
  for dyeing inks

gall¹ Bold behavior
 Bitter cruelty denoting bile
annoyance resentment chafing
  sore on a horse abnormal growth
response to insect larvae mites

Aleppo rue
   bitter regret event
wish it undone perennial shrub bitter scent

Aleppo pepper
 hot spice ground

Pepper v.

Scatter liberally over
Hit repeatedly missiles gunshot
 inflict severe punishment suffering

Allepine
 Aleppo its inhabitants fine fabric
woven wool silk cotton

18.

'Powerful images of wounded Syrian girl go viral' ('Injured girl in hospital calls desperately for her father after a Syrian airstrike')
    —CNN, October 11, 2016

19.

Aleppo ▮▮▮ Guide

▮▮▮ حلب ▮▮▮ largest city ▮ Syria ▮ pop▮▮ 2.1 million▮▮▮

WARNING**

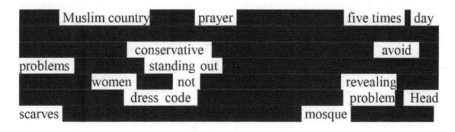

Travel ▮▮▮ not recommended ▮▮▮ civil war Since 2011 thousands ▮▮▮ injured ▮ killed ▮ opposition paramilitary ▮▮▮ government security forces Aleppo ▮▮▮ center ▮▮▮ intense fighting ▮▮▮ not safe for any ▮▮▮ tourists ▮▮▮ mixed control ▮▮▮ rebel groups ▮ government forces ▮ aerial bombardment ▮▮▮ hourly on rebel districts ▮▮▮ incredibly dangerous ▮▮▮ not ▮▮▮ safe target ▮▮▮ chemical attack ▮▮▮ forces

UNDERSTAND

▮▮ Muslim country ▮▮▮ prayer ▮▮▮ five times day ▮▮▮ conservative ▮▮▮ avoid problems ▮▮▮ standing out ▮▮▮ women ▮▮ not ▮▮▮ revealing ▮▮▮ dress code ▮▮▮ problem Head scarves ▮▮▮ mosque ▮▮▮

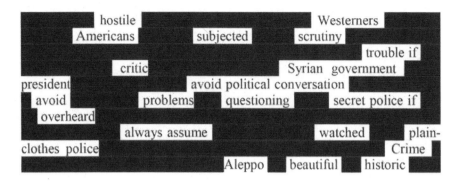

hostile   Westerners
Americans   subjected   scrutiny
                                                    trouble if
            critic   Syrian government
president   avoid political conversation
    avoid   problems   questioning   secret police if
    overheard
            always assume   watched   plain-
clothes police   Crime
                        Aleppo   beautiful   historic

Note   2014 Aleppo   under siege
battleground   Syrian civil war Part   controlled by
Assad   human rights violations   war crimes
        civilian   part   by   Islamic
Front   al-Qaeda   funded   Qatar Most
        population   fled   Unless   reporter
                    no reason   to go

GET IN

GET AROUND

                    more taxis than people However   most civilians
fled   movements   threatened   snipers   conflict
    no drivers   be incredibly suspicious   any   offer
ride

Minibuses   "serveece"   small white vans   drive around
    hop on   off   signaling   driver   not currently operating

Rental cars   not available   conflict

SEE

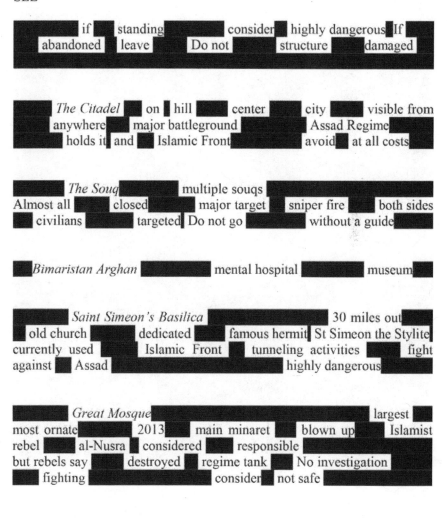

if standing consider highly dangerous If
abandoned leave Do not structure damaged

The Citadel on hill center city visible from
anywhere major battleground Assad Regime
holds it and Islamic Front avoid at all costs

The Souq multiple souqs
Almost all closed major target sniper fire both sides
civilians targeted Do not go without a guide

Bimaristan Arghan mental hospital museum

Saint Simeon's Basilica 30 miles out
old church dedicated famous hermit St Simeon the Stylite
currently used Islamic Front tunneling activities fight
against Assad highly dangerous

Great Mosque largest
most ornate 2013 main minaret blown up Islamist
rebel al-Nusra considered responsible
but rebels say destroyed regime tank No investigation
fighting consider not safe

DO

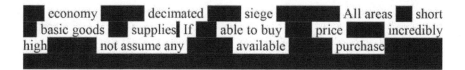

economy decimated siege All areas short
basic goods supplies If able to buy price incredibly
high not assume any available purchase

EAT

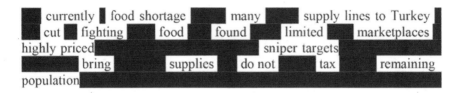

██ currently █ food shortage ████ many ████ supply lines to Turkey █
█ cut █ fighting ████ food ████ found ████ limited ██ marketplaces
highly priced ████████████████ sniper targets ██████
████████ bring ████ supplies ███ do not ████ tax ████ remaining
population ████████████████████████████████████

SLEEP

███ currently unknown ████ whether ████ hotels are operating ████
unstable situation ████████ websites ████████ no longer
work ████████ ongoing conflict █ Aleppo ████████████

CONTACT

Internet ███ electricity ████ intermittent ████████████████████
██

GET OUT

██████████████████████████

**This article* ████ *outline* ████ *needs more* ████ *a template* ████ *not enough*
████████ *Please* ████████████ *help* ████████████████

20.

Look

Direct one's gaze … appearance …
… impression … rely on … do something … make sure

Look at, into, for, to, down on, through, in the eye, sharp, after, back, forward, around, up, in, on, out, up to, over . . .

Synonyms: attention, beholding, contemplation, evil eye, gaze, glance, glimpse, introspection, keeping watch, leer, look-see, marking, noticing, observation, peek, regarding, scrutiny, sight, speculation, squint, start, surveillance, swivel, view.

Antonyms: disregard, ignorance.

21.

Genocide Risk Assessment … *Early Warning* …
[10-12%] Myanmar … [5-10%] Sudan … [>5%] South Sudan
… Iraq … Iran … Libya
… Syria …

22.

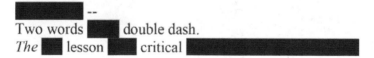
Two words … double dash.
The … lesson … critical …

23.

'I guess I'm having an Aleppo Moment'.
     —September 28, 2016, U.S. Libertarian Presidential Candidate, Gary Johnson

24.

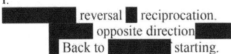 again

Adv.
I.
reversal █ reciprocation.
opposite direction
Back to █ starting.
2. a. Into a former contradiction, state, or situation; once more . . . anew; as before.
3. in return, in reply. in response.

II. Expressing repetition █ continuation █ time . . .

III expressing repetition in fact . . .

prep
expressing position or motion toward or facing something

Origin: from OE *ongean* 'toward, opposite, against, in exchange for'

25.

Aleppo (The New Dictionary of Genocide)

city of	ruins and rubble	suffering	war	lost dreams
fire	smoke	starvation	guns	snipers
bombed	buildings	blood, wounds	tears	airstrikes
friends	enemies	collapsed	humanitarian	corridors
little hope	mourning	homes lost	fled	city divided
incendiary	bunker	busting	bombs	perhaps
300,00	besieged	no promise	day	snipers
voices	silenced	thousands dead	comrades	blocked exits
trauma	geopolitical	pawn	bystanders	perpetrators
victims	foul water	mass murder	in plain	sight
genocide	alerts	no prevention	city	forgotten
in a million	Aleppo	moments	a city	at which
we	need	to	look	again

26.

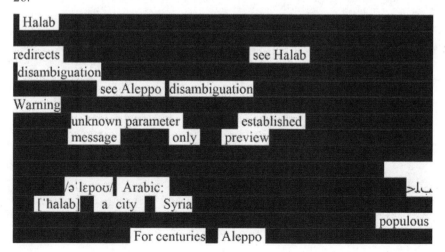

Halab

redirects see Halab
disambiguation
see Aleppo disambiguation
Warning
unknown parameter established
message only preview

/əˈlɛpoʊ/ Arabic:
[ˈhalab] a city Syria حلب
populous
For centuries Aleppo

region's

third-largest after Constantinople

Cairo population

2,132,100 2004 Syria's largest city

before Civil War

Aleppo

ancient metropolis one of

oldest

may have been since 6th millennium

Excavations

show

occupied since at least

3rd millennium BC

cuneiform tablets

Mesopotamia

noted commercial military proficiency

history strategic

trading center between

Mediterranean Sea modern

Iraq

significance history location

Silk Road passed

Suez

Canal 1869, trade diverted

Aleppo began slow decline the fall

Ottoman Empire World War I Aleppo

ceded hinterland to Turkey

important railway connecting to

Mosul 1940s lost access to sea

Turkey

isolation Syria past few decades

exacerbated decline

preserve old city

medieval architecture tradition heritage

"Islamic Capital of Culture"

historic landmarks

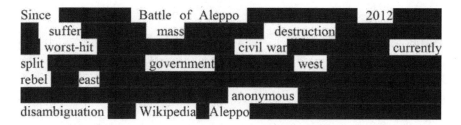

Since ▮▮ Battle of Aleppo ▮▮ 2012 ▮ suffer ▮ mass ▮ destruction ▮ worst-hit ▮ civil war ▮ currently split ▮ government ▮ west rebel ▮ east ▮ anonymous disambiguation ▮ Wikipedia ▮ Aleppo ▮

27.

Aleppo Moment (The New Dictionary of Genocide)

n.
a state of blankness; the condition of being unaware, rendered mute, lacking a response, devoid, lifeless.

v.
to blank; to be unaware, barren, vacant, empty, vacuous, absent, hollow, missing, desolate, scarce, void.

adj.
unseeing, in need of looking again.

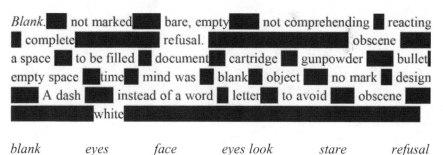

Blank. ▮ not marked ▮ bare, empty ▮ not comprehending ▮ reacting ▮ complete ▮ refusal. ▮ obscene ▮ a space ▮ to be filled ▮ document ▮ cartridge ▮ gunpowder ▮ bullet empty space ▮ time ▮ mind was ▮ blank ▮ object ▮ no mark ▮ design ▮ A dash ▮ instead of a word ▮ letter ▮ to avoid ▮ obscene ▮ ▮ white ▮

blank   eyes   face   eyes look   stare   refusal

28.

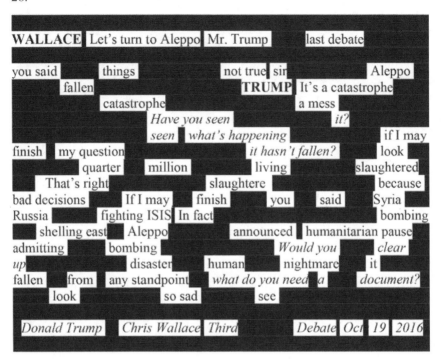

WALLACE Let's turn to Aleppo Mr. Trump last debate
you said things not true sir Aleppo
fallen TRUMP It's a catastrophe
catastrophe a mess
Have you seen *it?*
seen *what's happening* if I may
finish my question *it hasn't fallen?* look
quarter million living slaughtered
That's right slaughtere because
bad decisions If I may finish you said Syria
Russia fighting ISIS In fact bombing
shelling east Aleppo announced humanitarian pause
admitting bombing *Would you* clear
up disaster human nightmare it
fallen from any standpoint *what do you need* *a* *document?*
look so sad see

Donald Trump *Chris Wallace* *Third* *Debate* *Oct* *19* *2016*

29.

'Wary of Russian Guarantees, Residents Stay Put in War-Torn Aleppo'
(*Russian-designated 'Humanitarian Corridors' in Aleppo are lined with
bombed-out buildings*)
       —*The New York Times*, October 20, 2016

30.

That picture 4-year-old Aleppo blood his
face haunting

Hillary Clinton *Third* *Debate* *Oct* *19* *2016*

31.

3ʳᵈ Aporia ███████████ *Prevention*
Whenever you look, you disregard. To see is blinding.

32.

███████████████ 'The Darkness' ███████████████

lasting	scars	a haunted	life	harsh	tactics
secret	prison	a threat	face	changed	I forget
it	is always	there	The Darkness	comes	a life
interrupted	hanging	in chains	a ghost	walking	plagued
later	built	a cage	for pigeons	sells	sits with
breeds	them	away	from people	sits	a long time
alone					

33.

4ᵗʰ Aporia of ████████████
When genocide ends, it continues ██████

34.

'Anne Frank Today is a Syrian Girl'.
                —Nicolas Kristoff, *The New York Times*, August 25, 2016

35.

the last
        first
  all   lessons
Look

SOURCE MATERIAL (by stanza, as applicable)

2.
'Who's at Risk?', United to End Genocide, endgenocide.org (August 2016).

3.
"Last Lecture Series." University of California Santa Cruz Dean of Student Life http://deanofstudents.ucsc.edu/get-involved/dos-events/last-lecture-series/index .html (accessed October 17, 2016).

4.
Bernard, Anne. 2016. "How Omran Daqneesh, 5, Became a Symbol of Aleppo's Suffering." *The New York Times*, 18 August. https://www.nytimes.com/2016/08/19/ world/middleeast/omran-daqneesh-syria-aleppo.html.

5.
"The." 2016. *Concise Oxford English Dictionary*. Oxford: Oxford University Press.

6.
Staff. 2016. "'We Will Not Let Aleppo Become Another Rwanda': UN envoy likens Syrian Civil War to Genocide." *South China Morning Post*, 7 October http:// www.scmp.com/news/world/middle-east/article/2025957/we-will-not-let-aleppo -become-another-rwanda-un-envoy-likens.

7.
"Aporia." *The Oxford English Dictionary Online*. 2013.

8.
"Aporia." 2013. *The Oxford English Dictionary Online*. Derrida, Jacques. 1990. "The Force of Law: The 'Mystical Foundation of Authority.'" *Cardozo Law Review* 11: 920–1045.

9.
Office of the Special Adviser on the Prevention of Genocide. 2016. "Public Statements." New York: United Nations. http://www.un.org/en/preventgenocide/ad viser/statements.shtml (accessed October 11, 2016).

10.
"Last Lecture." University of California, San Francisco Student Life. https://student life.ucsf.edu/events-programs/last-lecture (accessed October 17, 2017).

11.
"Last." *The Oxford English Dictionary Online*. Oxford: Oxford University Press; "Last." *Online Etymological Dictionary*. www.etymonline.com; "Last." Thefree dictionary.com.

12.

The New York Times Staff. 2016. "Transcript of the Second Debate." *The New York Times*, 10 October https://www.nytimes.com/2016/10/10/us/politics/transcript -second-debate.html.

14.

"Lesson." *The Oxford English Dictionary Online*. Oxford: Oxford University Press; "Lesson." *Online Etymological Dictionary*, www.etymonline.com; Johnson, Barbara. 1978. "The Critical Difference." *Diacritics* 8(2): 2–9.

15.

Rappeport, Alan. 2016. "'What is Aleppo?' Gary Johnson Asks, in an Interview Stumble." *The New York Times*, 8 September https://www.nytimes.com/2016/09/09/ us/politics/gary-johnson-aleppo.html.

16.

Rappeport, Alan. 2016. "'What is Aleppo?' Gary Johnson Asks, in an Interview Stumble," *The New York Times*, 8 September https://www.nytimes.com/2016/09/09/us/ politics/gary-johnson-aleppo.html.

17.

"Aleppo." *Oxford English Dictionary Online*, 3rd ed. Oxford: Oxford University Press.

18.

Narayan, Chandrika, and Mohammed Tawfeeq. 2016. "Powerful images of wounded Syrian Girl Go Viral." *CNN*, 11 October. http://www.cnn.com/2016/10/11/world/ syria-wounded-girl/index.html.

19.

"Aleppo." Wikitravel http://wikitravel.org/en/Aleppo. (accessed October 15, 2016).

20.

"Look." 2016. *Oxford English Dictionary Online*. Oxford: Oxford University Press, 2016; "Look." Thefreedictionary.com.

21.

2015 Genocide Risk Assessment, United States Holocaust Memorial Museum Early Warning Project. https://www.ushmm.org/confront-genocide/how-to-prevent-geno cide/early-warning-project.

23.

Bromwich, Jonah Engel. 2016. "'I Guess I'm Having an Aleppo Moment': Gary Johnson Can't Name a Single Foreign Leader." *The New York Times*, 28 September https://www.nytimes.com/2016/09/29/us/politics/gary-johnson-aleppo-moment.html.

24.

"Again." 2016. *Oxford English Dictionary Online*. 3rd ed. Oxford: Oxford University Press.

26.

"Aleppo." Wikipedia. www.Wikipedia.com.

28.

Third 2016 Presidential Debate, October 16, 2016. In Blake, Aaron. 2019. "The Final Trump-Clinton Debate Transcript, Annotated." *The Washington Post*, October. https://www.washingtonpost.com/news/the-fix/wp/2016/10/19/the-final-trump -clinton-debate-transcript-annotated/?utm_term=.d22498c8928b.

29.

Barnard, Anne. 2016. "Wary of Russian Guarantees, Residents Stay Put in War-Torn Aleppo." *The New York Times*, 21 October, A10. http://www.nytimescom/ 2016/10/21/world/middleeast/aleppo-syria-russia-cease-fire.html?r=0.

30.

Hillary Clinton, Third 2016 Presidential Debate, October 16, 2016. In Blake, Aaron. 2016. "The Final Trump-Clinton Debate Transcript, Annotated." *The Washington Post*, 19 October. https://www.washingtonpost.com/news/the-fix/wp/2016/10/19/ the-final-trump-clinton-debate-transcript-annotated/?utm_term=.d22498c8928b.

32.

Risen, James. 2016. "An Ex-Detainee, but still a Captive of 'The Darkness.'" *The New York Times*, 12 October, A1. http://www.nytimes.com/2016/10/12/world/cia-torture-abuses-detainee.html.

34.

Kristoff, Nicolas. 2016. "Anne Frank Today Is a Syrian Girl." *The New York Times*, 24 August. https://www.nytimes.com/2016/08/25/opinion/anne-frank-today-is-a -syrian-girl.html.

Index

action: ambiguity of (mondo future
exacti), 177; inequality of, 177–178
advent, 180, 182; Heidegger, 187n10
aesthetics of juxtaposition, 132
agency, 35–36, 49; critical, 38; everyday, 35–36; local-scale, 49
Al-Qaeda, 11
American intervention, 23–24, 206;
Afghanistan, 23; Guatemala, 206;
Iraq, 23; Lebanon, 24; Libya, 23;
Syria, 23
An Agenda for Peace, 45–46
Arab Spring, 25–27
archival memory, 208, 210–212
archive, 208, 219
Argentina: ; 1976–1983 Dictatorship,
75,77, 88n3; coup, 114; crimes
against humanity trials, 80; ESMA
trial, 79, 80, 82, 87 88n3; genocide,
77, 88n4; Land of Memory, 75–76
August Revolution, 152–153, 160

becoming, process of, 176; individual
processes, 175; societal processes, 175
being-as-temporality, 187n8
Boutros-Ghali, B., 45–46

civilizing mission, 48
collective memory, 85

collective vulnerability, 70
comics, 129, 131
comix, 131
common security, 163
CONADEP. *See* National Commission
on the Disappeared
Conference on Security and
Cooperation, 163–164
confession, post conflict, 80
conflict resolution, 195–197; feminist,
196–197; integrative, 196; relational,
196
conflict transformation, xxxn2
cooperative security, 163
cosmology, 49,53; Aboriginal
Australian, 195
crisis of distinctions, 144
critical peace studies, xv–xvi
CSCE. *See* Conference on Security and
Cooperation
cultural memory, 60–61, 63–65, 72, 76,
77–78; morality, 68
cultural order, 144, 146

'Dasein' otherness, 181
democracy: ; India, 10; Islam, 16
developmental authoritarianism, 9
dialogic process, 86
dialogical space, 181

About the Contributors

Jeremiah Alberg is professor of philosophy and religion in the Humanities Department of International Christian University, Tokyo, Japan. He is also director of both the Center of Teaching and Learning and the University Library. He is president of the Colloquium on Violence and Religion, a group dedicated to the exploration of the thought of cultural theorist René Girard. His most recent work is focused on Kant and has been published in *The Kantian Review* and *Kant-Studium*.

Hartmut Behr is professor of international politics at Newcastle University (United Kingdom). He gained is doctoral degree at the University of Cologne (Germany, 1996) and his "Habilitation" at the University of Jena (Germany, 2003). He was a postdoctoral Humboldt Fellow at the University of Pittsburgh and a JSPS postdoctoral Fellow at the University of Tsukuba (Japan). Among is publications are "A History of International Political Theory: Ontologies of the International" (2010) and "Politics of Difference: Epistemologies of Peace" (2014) as well as book chapters and articles on international relations theory, peace studies and social and political theory.

Morgan Brigg is senior lecturer in peace and conflict studies at the University of Queensland, Australia, and a professional mediator and facilitator. He is a specialist in conflict resolution, peace building, governance and innovative approaches to cross-cultural relations and the politics of knowledge. His work facilitates exchange between Western and Indigenous political systems and philosophies as part of a wider exploration of the politics of cultural difference, governance and selfhood. His books include *The New Politics of Conflict Resolution: Responding to Difference* and *Mediating across Difference: Oceanic and Asian Approaches to Conflict Resolution* (coedited with

Roland Bleiker). He blends political and social theory with professional practice, including as an accredited practicing mediator and provider of policy and technical advice. For more information, see https://www.researchgate.net/profile/Morgan_Brigg/publications.

Stephen Eric Bronner is Board of Governors Distinguished Professor of Political Science at Rutgers University. His most recent books are *The Bigot: Why Prejudice Persists* (2014) and *The Bitter Taste of Hope: Ideals, Ideologies, and Interests in the Age of Obama* (2017).

Shin Chiba is a representative and well-known leading Japanese political scientist and philosopher. From 2002 to 2006, he was the dean of the Graduate School at International Christian University (ICU) in Tokyo and most recently held the position of chair of ICU's Department of Politics and International Studies and the director of the Peace Research Institute. His research interests include peace studies, religious studies, ecology, democracy and civil society and the genealogy of freedom. His research projects include Arendt studies and radical democracy studies as well. He served the United Board for Higher Education in Asia as trustee for several years until 2014 and has been playing a leading role in the field of Christian higher education.

Beverley Curran teaches linguistic, cultural and media translation in the Department of Society, Culture and Media at International Christian University in Tokyo, Japan. She is the author of *Theatre Translation Theory and Performance in Contemporary Japan* (2008, 2014) and coedited *Multiple Translation Communities in Contemporary Japan* (2015). She is the current editor of IASIL Japan's *Journal of Irish Studies*.

Paul Hastings is the executive director and chief executive officer of the Japan ICU Foundation in New York. He is a graduate of Bowdoin College and received his MA in international education from Teachers College, Columbia University. He is the recipient of the Aspen Institute's Nakasone Scholarship and is a member of the American Friends of Asian Rural Institute's board of trustees. He spent 11 formative years in Japan, living in Kanazawa, Kobe and Tokyo between the ages of 4 and 18. He lives with his wife and two sons in Maplewood, New Jersey.

Alexander Laban Hinton is Distinguished Professor of Anthropology, director of the Center for the Study of Genocide and Human Rights and UNESCO chair in Genocide Prevention at Rutgers University. He is the author or Editor of more than a dozen books, including, most recently, *Man or Monster?*

The Trial of a Khmer Rouge Torturer (2016) and *The Justice Facade: Trials of Transition in Cambodia* (2018). In recognition of his work on genocide, the American Anthropological Association selected him as the recipient of the 2009 Robert B. Textor and Family Prize for Excellence in Anticipatory Anthropology. He is also a past president of the International Association of Genocide Scholars (2011–2013) and was a member/visitor at the Institute for Advanced Study at Princeton (2011–2013). In 2016, he served as an expert witness at the Khmer Rouge Tribunal. For more information, see https://sasn.rutgers.edu/about-us/faculty-staff/alex-hinton.

Ashis Nandy is an Indian political psychologist, social theorist and critic. A trained clinical psychologist, he has provided theoretical critiques of European colonialism, development, modernity, secularism, Hindutva, science, technology, nuclearism, cosmopolitanism and utopia. He has also offered alternative conceptions relating to cosmopolitanism and critical traditionalism. In addition to the above, he has offered an original historical profile of India's commercial cinema as well as critiques of state and violence. He was senior fellow and former director of the Centre for the Study of Developing Societies for several years. Today, he is a senior honorary fellow at the institute apart from being the chairperson of the Committee for Cultural Choices and Global Futures, also in New Delhi. He received the Fukuoka Asian Culture Prize in 2007. In 2008, he appeared on the list of the Top 100 Public Intellectuals Poll of *Foreign Policy* magazine, published by the Carnegie Endowment for International Peace.

Leigh A. Payne is professor of sociology and Latin America at the University of Oxford (St Antony's College, United Kingdom). Her chapter on silence reconsiders her approach to talk as a political resource found in two of her books—*Unsettling Accounts: Neither Truth nor Reconciliation in Confessions of State Violence* (2008) on Argentina, Brazil, Chile and South Africa and *Revealing New Truths about Spain's Violent Past* (2016)—that analyze the confessional performances of perpetrators of state violence. She is currently working on confessional texts by the armed left in Latin America, tentatively titled *Left Unsettled*.

Oliver Richmond is a professor of international relations, peace and conflict studies in the Department of Politics, University of Manchester (United Kingdom). He is also international professor, College of International Studies, Kyung Hee University (Korea), and a visiting professor at the University of Tromso. His publications include *Peace Formation and Political Order in Conflict Affected Societies* (2016) and *Failed Statebuilding* (2014). He is editor of the Palgrave book series Rethinking Peace and Conflict Studies and coeditor of the journal *Peacebuilding*.

Nitin Sawhney is assistant professor of media studies at the New School in New York. His research, teaching and creative practice engage the critical role of technology, civic media and artistic interventions in contested spaces. He examines social movements and crisis contexts through forms of creative urban tactics, participatory research, performance and documentary film. He completed his PhD at the MIT Media Laboratory and taught at the MIT Program in Art, Culture and Technology. He has conducted digital storytelling initiatives with Palestinian youth in refugee camps and codirected the award-winning documentary *Flying Paper*, coproduced with children in Gaza with support from *National Geographic*.

Giorgio Shani (PhD, London) is chair of the Department of Politics and International Studies and director of the Rotary Peace Center at International Christian University, Tokyo. From 2016 to 2017, he was visiting senior fellow at the Centre of International Studies at the London School of Economics and Political Science. Author of *Sikh Nationalism and Identity in a Global Age* (2008) and *Religion, Identity and Human Security* (2014), he is a series editor of Critical Perspectives on Religion in International Politics (Rowman & Littlefield International). From 2014 to 2018, he served as president of the Asia-Pacific region of the International Studies Association. For more information, see https://icu.academia.edu/GiorgioShani.

Marita Sturken is professor in the Department of Media, Culture and Communication at New York University, where she teaches courses in visual culture, cultural memory and consumerism. She is the author of *Tangled Memories: The Vietnam War, the AIDS Epidemic, and the Politics of Remembering* (1997), *Practices of Looking: An Introduction to Visual Culture* (with Lisa Cartwright, 3rd ed., 2018), and *Tourists of History: Memory, Kitsch, and Consumerism From Oklahoma City to Ground Zero* (2007). She is currently writing a book on post-9/11 visual culture.

Natasha Zaretsky, is a cultural anthropologist focusing on human rights, genocide, migration and the politics of memory and truth in the Americas. A former Fulbright scholar, she holds her PhD in anthropology from Princeton University. Currently, she is a senior lecturer at New York University and visiting scholar at the Center for the Study of Genocide and Human Rights (Rutgers University), where she leads the Truth in the Americas project. Her recent book *Landscapes of Memory and Impunity* (coedited with A. H.

Levine) examines memory and survival in Argentina; additionally, her writing about human rights and diaspora communities in the Americas has appeared in *The Tablet*, *Global Americans*, and *Foreign Affairs*. She also serves as executive director of Sound Potential, an organization engaging music and the arts to address humanitarian issues. Currently, she is working on documentary films about Argentina and Cuba and finishing a manuscript about memory and transitional justice in Argentina, "The Liminality of Repair."

Yael Zerubavel is the founding director of the Allen and Joan Bildner Center for the Study of Jewish Life and professor of Jewish studies and history at Rutgers University. She has published extensively in the area of history and memory, Israeli collective memory and identity, national myths and war and trauma. She is the author of *Recovered Roots: Collective Memory and the Making of Israeli National Tradition* (1995) and *Desert in the Promised Land: Nationalism, Politics, and Symbolic Landscapes* (under review). Her current book project is *Biblical Reenactments and the Performance of Antiquity in Israeli Culture*.